Libya

Libya

History and Revolution

RICHARD A. LOBBAN, JR.
AND CHRISTOPHER H. DALTON

Foreword by
General Carlton W. Fulford, Jr., USMC (Ret.)

Praeger Security International

 PRAEGER

AN IMPRINT OF ABC-CLIO, LLC
Santa Barbara, California • Denver, Colorado • Oxford, England

10/13/14
GB
$52.00

Library of Congress Cataloging-in-Publication Data

Lobban, Richard Andrew, 1943–
    Libya : history and revolution / Richard A. Lobban, Jr. and Christopher H. Dalton ; foreword by General Carlton W. Fulford, Jr., USMC (Ret.).
        pages cm — (Praeger security international)
    Includes bibliographical references and index.
    ISBN 978–1–4408–2884–3 (hardback) — ISBN 978–1–4408–2885–0 (ebook)
    1. Libya—History—1969– 2. Libya—History—Civil War, 2011– 3. Qaddafi, Muammar.
I. Dalton, Christopher H. II. Title.
DT236.L63   2014
961.204′2—dc23   2013045792

ISBN: 978–1–4408–2884–3
EISBN: 978–1–4408–2885–0

18 17 16 15 14   1 2 3 4 5

This book is also available on the World Wide Web as an eBook.
Visit www.abc-clio.com for details.

Praeger
An Imprint of ABC-CLIO, LLC

ABC-CLIO, LLC
130 Cremona Drive, P.O. Box 1911
Santa Barbara, California 93116-1911

This book is printed on acid-free paper (∞)

Manufactured in the United States of America

The authors are only expressing their own views; these are not the views, or policies of the United States Government or any of its agencies.

We dedicate this writing to those courageous American and Libyan citizens and service members who have given their lives in the struggle to return Libya to a free and democratic nation. And for those who continue to risk their lives to build a brighter future for Libya.

(Cartography by Bookcomp, Inc.)

Contents

Foreword

Libya is strategically important to the security of the entire Mediterranean region as well as the North African Continent. Its wealth in natural resources; its geographical location; its relatively well-educated, capable workforce and the long history of the people all contribute to the importance of this nation. Yet, much like its neighbors in North Africa, Libya remains unsettled and its course uncertain. The same spark may have ignited the Arab Spring in Tunisia, Egypt and in Libya. To view the cause and effect of these three uprisings as mirror images to be resolved with similar policies would be a monumental foreign policy and security mistake, however.

Dr. Lobban and Lieutenant Colonel Dalton provide us with a superb book that helps us better understand Libya and why this nation behaves as She does. Policy makers would be wise to read and understand these issues before attempting to institute plans and programs in an effort to help stabilize Libya and promote long-lasting security, economic growth, and constructive relationships with its African neighbors.

The authors take us back to the archaeological and cultural beginning of the component tribes of Libya. They then describe the immense damage and physiological scars on the people of this region left by the North African Campaign of World War II. They detail the impact of post war decisions by the United Nations to unify three different geographical and cultural regions under one national banner.

Next, the authors do a very good job in describing the influence of oil on the region, and the advantages and disadvantages provided through oil wealth and/or the oil curse. This wealth holds great potential for this nation, for Europe, and for the Mediterranean region. Harnessing this wealth for good is crucial to any future scenario for the Libyan people.

The authors lead us through a detailed discussion of Muammar Gaddafi; what his leadership did to the people, for the nation and for the region. Their description of Gaddafi as a nationalistic yet egotistical leader who desperately wanted to be a force in the world, but lacked the capacity to make sound decisions, inspire the populace, or influence his contemporaries is very important in evaluating the impact of his leadership. All but ignored by the Arab League, he turned to the Africa Union as a place where he could influence his peers. More than a few leaders of African countries have told me that they knew Gaddafi to be a flawed individual, but that his generosity was something that they could not ignore. Thus, he travelled around the continent, spreading his wealth, but nurturing few real friends and fewer concrete examples of progress and stability. He wound up supporting pariah regimes and terrorist causes around the world, and in doing so, further isolated himself and his country.

Dr. Lobban and Lieutenant Colonel Dalton then describe, in detail, the events leading up to the Libyan "Arab Spring" and the subsequent journey taken to establish the New Libya. This story is far from complete. Like many of its neighbors in North Africa and the greater Middle East, events unfold every day that are complex but nonetheless important in determining direction and in attempting to put meaningful policy in place that will allow Libya to become the economic powerhouse it can be while providing its own citizens the region of stability, human security, and development they deserve.

Reading this book will certainly enhance understanding and hopefully, promote meaningful decisions that will support Libya and allow her to "stand tall" in the region.

Carlton W. Fulford, Jr.
General, U. S. Marine Corps (Ret.)

Preface

This book describes and analyzes the context of Libya's ancient, colonial, and monarchical history. The focal point is the Gaddafi era and what the "Arab Spring" revolution that eventually brought him down, opening a new and perilous future for this oil-rich nation, means to Libya and the world. Libya's history reflects their ancient and extremely convoluted roots, beginning well before Arabs arrived. It is comprised of Berber, Greek, and Roman occupations and includes a significant chapter from early American naval history. Such lineage is all the more impressive given the fact its three geographical components were rarely unified. In the face of recurring foreign aggression, the normally peaceful Sanusiya brotherhood moved religious retreat to steadfast anticolonial resistance and began consolidating the Libyan people. The brutality of Italian colonialism was faced collectively and stoically. In 1951, when the United Nations could not determine what to do with the lands of Tripolitania, Cyrenaica, and the Fezzan, a central monarchy was installed, though it never had one, and planted a flag that it had never seen, and called it Libya. This poor fit was kicked into the modern spirit of Arab nationalism in 1969 by Muammar Gaddafi, who grabbed power with an eclectic mixture of Arabism, Islamism, Socialism, and Nomadism. After four decades of generous yet tyrannical, liberating and frustrating, pioneering yet stubborn, revolutionary, confusing, and erratic and yet amazing changes, all swimming in oil wealth, this syncretic historical mixture tumbled down in 2011. Now, Libya is embarking on a new course, without known charts and an uncertain compass. This book records their remarkable past, traces the twists and turns of Gaddafi, and prepares the reader for some of the potential scenarios that lie ahead, based on the political tracks flowing in the Libya sands.

We settled on spelling Gaddafi in this way, even though we are aware of the many alternative spellings—Kaddafi, Qaddafi, Kadhafi and Gadhafi, for example. While only Arabic is technically "correct," we have arbitrarily chosen to use Gaddafi, since this book is in English.

We believe that our coauthor tag team of an anthropologist and Marine Corps officer has added a layer of depth to our meshed analysis of war and politics that has been the essence of much of Libyan history, especially in the last 40 years.

While our book is informed by the considerable body of historical literature on Libya, we have sought to make this current and projective, not only for Libya itself, but for Libya as a regional actor in Africa and within the African Union and Gaddafi's support of radical causes. Libya is also a major oil producer, which has proven to be a blessing and a curse; and here Libya offers another case study of the unfolding alternatives in the wake of the "Arab Spring." Not to mention the intersecting topics of security, foreign and military relations, rebuilding the greatness of old Libya, and forging a "new" Libya.

Thus, in the following chapters we have examined: Libya's historical context; Libya before Gaddafi; Libya under Gaddafi; Libya's strategic importance in oil production; Libya and the Arab Spring; and Libya after Gaddafi. The Libyan revolution is still underway, and the published, book-length works chronicling these events are few in number and stop at the beginning of the revolution. The preponderance of material is historical in nature; analysis of a "future" for Libya doesn't move beyond Gaddafi's reign. The speculation is what a potential post-Gaddafi Libya might be like. Our work seeks to fill the gap that exists along the spectrum of tying in the historical Libya of colonizers, to the twentieth-century Libya of Italy and then Gaddafi, and substantively moving into the post-Gaddafi era, discussing, analyzing, and providing thoroughly researched potentialities for the "new" Libya.

Some of the previous works on Libya have informed us. *Qaddafi's Alchemy: Transforming a Coup into a Revolution* by Mark Soane (1982) gave insights on the methods used to continue Gaddafi's regime in midterm. *Libya: The History of Gaddafi's Pariah State* by John Oakes (2012) is close to our end product; but events, of course, keep quickly moving on and we have dealt with the aftermath of Gaddafi's rule beyond his death and the challenges faced by the new nation. The classic work *A History of Modern Libya* by Dirk Vandewalle (2012) updated his 2006 book on the same topic, including details of what led to the revolution and what Gaddafi's legacy may be; but again, events keep moving quickly ahead. *Libya since Independence: Oil and State-building*, also by Dirk Vandewalle (1998), is one of the pioneering studies found that discussed the economic/military impact of being an oil-rich state in a strategic location of the world.

Libya: Continuity and Change (The Contemporary Middle East) by Ronald Bruce St. John (2011) took us into the historical, socioeconomic, and political study of the 40 years of Gaddafi's volatile reign and his efforts to legitimize his rule and increase the opportunities and influence of Libya. *Libya: Qadhafi's Revolution and the Modern State* by Lillian Craig Harris (1986) also offers an historical, political, and sociological profile of Libya of Gaddafi. It analyzes the man, his internal politics, foreign policy, and the economy of oil with its widespread disparities in distribution of the wealth. The book ends with contemplations on the future of his rule and a Libya after Gaddafi, but projections of 1987 and beyond are now passed. The moment a book is written, this tends to be its normal fate, to which our book will also suffer. As such, we have tried to make this current and to use our joint political and military perspectives to provide a distinct vantage point and add to the mix.

Acknowledgments

We would like to thank Steven Catalano at ABC-CLIO for his guidance and support.

Richard wants to thank the Naval War College for offering a forum to discuss Libya; for creating the opportunity to have student "Desk Officers" keeping us current; and for inviting the first senior naval officer and his family from Libya in 40 years who became his friend.

Chris would like to thank Richard for considering him for this project as this has been the penultimate opportunity to learn from a master, in their mutual love for the African Continent and peoples. Additionally, to his family for enduring many long nights and weekends as this project unfolded.

Introduction

Our book is couched in the study of the archaeology, politics, history, ethnography, and anthropology of Libya, but these disciplines are linked closely together by military and political science, as reflected by sections detailing Libya's past and recent history. As such, we survey Libya's long historical context geographically, her native populations, the arrival of Arabs and Islam, the centuries of Ottoman rule, and the brutal colonial ambitions of the Italians, who faced off against the heroic resistance of Mukhtar, the Lion of the Desert, and of Jebel Akhdar.

The physical geography of Libya traces a path from coastal Tripolitania to mountainous Cyrenaica; from its independence-minded city of Benghazi to the deserts of the Fezzan as we also seek, through multidisciplinary examination, to understand why it can be difficult to hold Libya together as a unitary state.

Recognizing the historical and emotional impact that World War II had upon the people and landscape of Libya, to include its once and future "Brother Leader," we delve a bit into the struggle by two world powers to control the longest coastline in North Africa, which also contained historically significant deepwater ports and provided the perfect jumping-off point for either protection from or invasion of southern Europe. While the internationally addicting substance of petroleum had yet to be discovered below the Tripolitanian, Cyrenaican, and Fezzan landscape, the vast open plains and throughways to Tunisia and Egypt, and thus a major avenue to the Suez Canal, were heavily in play. We look at the tactical brilliance of German and British commanders and logistical ignorance of the German high command, namely Adolf Hitler, which greatly hamstrung

Field Marshal Rommel's campaign to capture and occupy this northern stretch of territory.

All of this represents Libya before Gaddafi. He held no sway or influence over the previous generations of turbulence and sanguinity. He wasn't the architect of Libya's geography, culture, archaeology, scholarship, architecture, or religion. He had no influence over the imposition of a monarch for this nation, partially engineered by the British vanquishing Nazi rule under Field Marshal Rommel.

The young, inexperienced, yet exceptionally passionate Colonel Muammar Gaddafi truly loved his people and nation, in the only way he knew how. He was infuriated by the corrupt despots he saw as puppets for the European powers. His visceral sense of nationalism was tempered, or enriched, by his Islamic values that came from his desert Arab roots. He profoundly felt that Libya could be much more influential to the world order, fairer, better, and a leader to be emulated. His contemporary models for leadership were secular Arab nationalists, such as Gamal 'Abd al-Nasser of Egypt; some of the syncretic and militant Ba'athists, and sometimes even leftists such as Gaafar Nimieri of Sudan or Siad Barre of Somalia (for a while anyway). At least they spoke the words of resistance regarding the Zionist state of Israel, who was recurrently at war with all of its Arab neighbors and continued to grow bigger at Arab expense. Anti-Zionism, at the very least, was used as a justification and diversion for the military rule and repression in their home nations.

Although he was a devout Muslim, Muammar Gaddafi was also an opponent of Islamism, Salafism, and *al-Qa'eda* and all forms of Islamic extremism, especially those who used religion to resist the ideas of Gaddafi. As he found his ideological path through this field of contradictions, Gaddafi's Green Book emerged as his intellectual resolution. The book was read as doctrine and one could freely offer any thoughts about it, as long as they were supportive and idolizing. In order to hold his grandiose nation-building project intact, Gaddafi turned to his trusted kinsmen and increasingly centralized the instruments of repression and domestic security intelligence.

Gaddafi's state architecture gradually shut him off from the wider world as xenophobic regulations steadily isolated Libya. Well, isolated to some extent, but Gaddafi's ambitions for anticolonial and anti-imperial leadership sent him and his resources in other directions as well. African, Arab, and world ambitions and an apparent frustration in how quickly he achieved his vision resulted in ventures of support, monetarily and physically, with terrorist and insurgent groups from around the globe. He wasn't above direct engagement in terrorist activities, as two of his most notoriously reckless and murderous plots, the downing of civilian airliners over the skies of Scotland and Niger, resulted in his banishment from the international political and economic arena. He had self-induced pariah status. Ironically, for Libya, oil and water *did* mix in the case of the continent's most prodigious proven reserves of oil and gas that gave Gaddafi the funds for his ambitious projects such as the Great Man-Made River and a strong market for the global arms dealers to sell him weapons he really did not need.

Blessed with the largest known recoverable reserves of crude oil on the continent of Africa, ranging from 47 billion to 50 billion barrels, depending on the source, Libya fell into opportunity for becoming the penultimate "rags to riches" nation. Equally endowed with relatively untamed lands and superb port facilities, Libya had every advantage when it came to transitioning from an agrarian-based subsistence economy to a sophisticated, educated, cultured, and financially independent model of hard work and self-sufficiency.

Unfortunately, Gaddafi's tempestuous nature, which served to ignite the passions of advancement in Libya, also served to ignite sentiments that turned the largesse of oil revenues into funding streams for groups with designs on terrorizing and fomenting revolution. Within 10 years from taking over leadership of Libya, Gaddafi had initiated a worldwide oil panic and driven prices through the roof. Over the ensuing 24 years, he would be fighting to retain his hard-won economic gains and trying to figure out how to mend some of the fences he had torn down during the era sponsoring terrorism. How Libya came by such a mother lode of natural advantage, how they adeptly negotiated or coerced the international powers to bend to their will, and how they managed to economically shoot themselves in the foot due to Gaddafi's increasingly reckless behavior, mood swings, and poor judgment regarding international relations mark several of the main themes in discussing Libya's natural resources.

Increasingly, suffering from conspiracy paranoia at home, rebuffed in the Arab world for his unpredictable antics, and isolation on the world stage, Gaddafi turned inward, to Africa, to win over, or buy off, African "allies" with hotels, construction projects, and African Union dues-paying. He sought to become the "King of Africa" as well as power broker and peacemaker, but more often than not, he was also a troublemaker because of his erratic policies and practices, in Libya and in world forums.

Like so many other African dictators who ran out of options, allies, and years of life, Gaddafi's path was destined to collide with new and changing realities. In this case, the suicide of a humble Tunisian fruit-seller was the spark that ignited the fuse, which burned brightly across North Africa and became known as the Arab Spring. As 2011 started, it looked like just another year of the four decades of Gaddafi's rule. But the Libyan people had had enough, and the revolt in Benghazi rapidly became a world issue, thinly couched in the "responsibility-to-protect" that launched NATO and American air intervention to create a protective no-fly zone. This speedily became a motion for regime change. The second-to-last chapter details this life-and-death struggle day by day in 2011 as the shouting became shooting. It finally concluded with the ignoble death of Gaddafi, being pulled from a roadside culvert and killed, as well as the exile or capture of the leading members of his family and loyalist government. To put a final stamp on the end of the Gaddafi reign, his tent cantonment, the Bab al-Aziziya fortification in Tripoli, was ransacked as this icon of his power and fear fell into destruction.

Our last chapter mimics the recent history and as yet unfinished future of Libya. We try to document the issues and trends of the two years since the fall of Gaddafi's rule. Putting the pieces of Libya back together, in a unitary state, has been a difficult project. Resurrecting the dormant oil industry and returning oil production back to the glorious heights has not been easy and has a ways to go. Creating a democratic parliament and constitution as well as holding elections that are predominantly "fair and free" has been a huge problem; however, given the history and context of Libya, they have been more or less successful. Libya's biggest hurdle at present is reconstructing its national police and armed forces while concurrently trying to disarm and regroup the plural militias that had filled the gap in these transitional years. Some extremist groups of the Salafist and al-Qa'eda franchises remain factors as they are reluctant to give up their arms and authority to a centrally controlled body. The fact that they could organize a bold and bloody attack on the American mission in Benghazi, as well as other foreign and domestic targets of these Islamists, highlights just how precarious the central governments foothold on power in Libya is at the moment. The present cases of Tunisia, Egypt, Sudan, and Syria show that a compromising middle ground on this matter is a virtual impossibility, thus placing a lot of stock in this "Arab Spring" test tube. This is equally true for the (re)construction of Libya's systems of justice and prisons, as they seek to build both credibility and justice.

Libya's battle for post-Gaddafi transparency and accountability is also aimed at fulfilling its great strategic importance to the region, the African continent, and the world. Libya's roles as an oil producer, arms buyer, and case study of the Arab Spring are other gigantic features at stake. Its roles as a potentially stabilizing regional actor in Africa and within the African Union are no less important, but rounding up the stray small arms and less sophisticated, yet very much deadly rocket-propelled grenades and shoulder-fired surface-to-air missiles scattered throughout Libya is a crucial task if there is to be a calming down of insurgent revolts across the Sahel and reduction in arming antigovernmental forces in Syria. The final chapter of the Libyan revolution is still underway, and the few published, book-length works that chronicle these events stop at the outset of the revolution. We hope to take this analysis to the start of the new era. Our work desires to fill the existing gap along the spectrum of tying in the historical Libya of colonizers, to the twentieth-century Libya of Italy, transiting through Gaddafi's rule, and substantively moving into the post-Gaddafi era. Along the way, in-depth discussion, analysis, and thoroughly researched potentialities for the "new" Libya as a regional economic power and military player throughout North Africa and the Middle East are keen objectives of our work. This Libyan future is accelerating rapidly, but the question remains: will its road map just encounter some speed bumps and traffic lights as they navigate through the roadways of progress, or will they fail to heed the warning lights and signs and proceed on a collision course?

CHAPTER 1

Historical Overview

INTRODUCTION

Physically, Libya is a land of contrasts.

The gorgeous waters of the coastal Mediterranean Sea have been the routes of maritime occupiers, and the vast interior sand seas have provided routes for the trade that linked the coast to sub-Saharan Africa. The sea-desert dichotomy is one perspective on this ancient land, but these two domains are also deeply linked as areas of corridors for refuge, resistance, settlement, and commerce. Equally, Libya is a vast crossroads that links the great civilizations of the ancient Egyptian Nile to the east, the Savanna empires to the south, and the roadways to the ancient and medieval Maghreb states to the west.[1]

The three principle regions of Libya are also contrasting. To the northwest, in Tripolitania are the Nefusa Mountains that are still occupied by the native Berber people. To the northeast is Cyrenaica with its own Green Mountains (Jebel Akhdar) of significant historic note for the famed resistance of Omar Mukhtar and the homeland of the Senusiya religious brotherhood. To the far south, deep in the Libyan section of the Sahara, is the Fezzan region embracing the towns of Sebha, Germa, Murzuk, Ghat, and Kufra on the tracks up to the foothills of Tibesti plateau, rising to Emi Koussi in Chad at 11,023 feet and the Ahaggar Highlands rising to 9,849 feet at Mount Tahat. These great elevations do not generate enough orographic cooling to generate rain, so Libya is very arid except some Mediterranean climate along the coast.

Archaeologically, Libya appears in the late Paleolithic Neanderthals found at Haua Fteah in the Jebel Akhdar region of Cyrenaica. The Mesolithic Capsian horizons (7000–4000 BC) of neighboring Tunisia were sophisticated hunters with a ceramic tradition, arrows and flakes tools, who gradually evolved into the modern Berber populations that were also known as Neolithic pastoralist and cultivator evolved into the Berbers at least by 4000 BC who were later on hand to greet the arrival of Phoenicians and Greeks. Such people were later termed as the Garamantes who were the presumed artists of the cave paintings and petroglyphs deep in the Sahara showing hunters, extinct animals, herders, and gatherers.

Geologically, while the Paleolithic Neanderthals were roaming these virgin lands, underground there were budding fields of oil. They didn't look like oil, act like oil, or sell like oil, but millennia had produced the first layers of continental siliciclastics. These solids would transcend Libya, west to what later became Tunisia, Algeria, and Morocco. Buried several thousand feet beneath the feet of the surface dwellers, various troughs and basins were beginning their journey to turning a habitually overrun region into one of the most potent in Africa. Gaddafi's future homeland, Sirte, along with Tibesti and Qarqaf basins and arches would begin their ascendance to oil monarchy. These extremely deep regions, running from 1,000 to potentially 12,000 feet in depth, were glacially absorbing their environment to provide fruits that would provide promise and curse (Rusk).

As the Mesolithic period dawned, the Ghadamis to the west and Murzuq to the southwest, abutting against their immediate neighbors to the west, would capture and evolve what would turn into billions of gallons of economic power. Nature's recipe for creating a commodity that would be as addictive as any drug known to mankind wasn't only evolving in liquid form, but in natural gas as well. Like the understudy for a major Broadway production, natural gas was developing at those elevations and according to the pressures and temperatures exerted on the land that would turn this same solid substance into a different, yet highly useful form of energy. Less stable and more difficult to package and repurpose, natural gas, nonetheless, would form beneath these same sands, and by the time mankind had determined a need for combustible energy, Libya would be sitting on a trillion-plus cubic feet of the stuff. But those are for another chapter.

Nomenclature

Libya derives its name from the generic Greek-recognized Libu people who also were recognized in some of the earliest Egyptian hieroglyphic records under the names: Mashwash, Tejenu, Temenu. These Berber peoples with their emblematic long robes, braided sidelocks, and tattoos were long raiders against the Egyptian oases and river settlements during some 3,000 years of history. Spreading from the oases to Egypt and along the coast they even took control of Egypt itself in the Libyan dynasties XXII–XXIII (tenth to eighth centuries BC).[2]

Another ancient Libyan dynamic is as rivals and threats to the settled people along the Nile, especially during times of political and military weakness. Even when Nubians ruled Egypt and Nubia in Dynasty XXV (eighth to seventh centuries BC), they were trouble by Libyan raiders as recorded in the Kawa temple of Nubian pharaoh Taharka crushing his Libyan opponents in the seventh century BC, not to mention endless squabbles and resistance of Libyans occupying the western parts of the Egyptian delta. Thus we have another set of historical trends of seminomadic Libyan Berbers as long standing rivals to settled populations in Egypt, Sudan and elsewhere. Later Libyan Arabs, also have various efforts to intervene in Chad, Darfur, and Sudan. Most of these are troublesome but ineffective as they represent overextension of Libyan geostrategic security and shortening of Sahelian and Sudanese lines of defense.

OTHER HISTORICAL TRENDS

Aside from the stark desert and seacoast distinctions, there are important urban and rural contrasts between the two major urban regions of Tripolitania and Cyrenaica or Pentapolis.[3] Cyrenaica was generalized to the far south and east to *Ammonium* to embrace the Amun oracle cult center in Siwa oasis that had the historical visit by Alexander the Great in the fourth century BC. Both earlier and later Tripolitania, including Leptis Magna, was struck by several earthquakes, causing substantial destruction. Rich intellectual traditions of Cyrenaica also found root in these early days as the birthplace of some of the great librarians of the seminal Alexandria library, such as the poet Callimachus and the geographer-mathematician Eratosthenes.

Under the dominant Arab veneer of modern Libya are the trans-Saharan Berbers, chronic warfare between various *amghar* (military leaders) and *sof* (heredity factions) and *lef* (larger lineage groups), known to anthropologists as segmentary opposition. This fissile tendency has long made Berbers reluctant to accept authoritarian state control.[4]

CULTURO-RELIGIOUS EVOLUTION AND COMPOSITION

Following the evolution of trends in ancient Greco-Roman Libya, the Berber lands came under German Vandal control under their leader Genseric in 435 AD and converted some coastal buildings to Arian churches. When the Vandals sacked Rome in 455, it was the height of their power, but by 533, Byzantine Christians under Emperor Justinian (ruled

527–565 AD) defeated them and, for a time, restored Christian Roman rule to North Africa.

Within a few years after the death of the prophet Muhammad, this was all to change when Muslim Arabs crossed into Egypt in 639 and moved on quickly to Alexandria, taking advantage of the deeply divided Christian communities (between Egyptian Monophysites and Byzantine Trinitarians). Arabs promptly took Alexandria, approximating the rapid spread of the modern "Arab Spring"; arrived in Cyrenaica and the Fezzan in 642; and spread on to Tripolitania by 647 and then westward to Tunisia, Algeria and Morocco. In 711, Muslims left the Maghreb and moved on to create Moorish Iberia until checked by Charles Martel at the battle of Tours. This began the religious cultural and linguistic homogenization of the former Greco-Roman lands but also of the native Berber populations who often gave local dynastic opposition to these latest foreign invaders. In Libya and Egypt there was greater sympathy with the Sunni Abbasides in Baghdad. At least this was the case until around 910 AD, when the Fatimid Shi'ites took over Egypt in 969 and moved their capital to Cairo in 973. More thousands of Arabs poured into northern Africa in the 1045 "Hilalian Invasions" somewhat parallel to the Moroccan invasion of "Spanish" Sahara in recent decades.

These events were briefly interrupted by Norman invasions in the 1140s. But the puritanical Muslim al-Mohad dynasty displaced them in 1158 until they were themselves replaced by the Hafsid dynasty from 1229 to 1553. During these medieval times, the Tunisian-born historian Ibn Batuta (1304–1369) added fundamentals to the systematic study of history that were regionally influential in his book *al-Muqaddimah* (Prologue). Also of this era was the famed widespread Moroccan traveler Ibn Khaldun (1332–1406), who passed through Tripoli on his caravan and sailing ventures reported in his *Rehla* (Travels). Notable is that he expressed some fears of Bedouin Arabs and preferred to take to the sea on his pilgrimage and travels at a time when the Black Death was ravaging Europe and parts of the Middle East.

The sometimes poisoned relations between Berbers and Arabs disrupted trade and turned friends into enemies as well as made new alliances. Adding more disruption to the evolving Arab world of North Africa was the 1492 expulsion of the last Moors (and Jews) from Europe, and their "golden age" was over. When Sultan Selim I began to expand the Ottoman Empire in 1517, it was only a matter of time before they would arrive in Libya, and by 1553, Tripolitania came under Ottoman Turkish administration. It was under nominal Ottoman rule that the corsairs of the Tripoli *pashalik*'s privateer's fame and controversy in the eighteenth and nineteenth centuries that were central in the formation of American naval strategy. Cyrenaica produced the Sanusiya brotherhood that was linked diplomatically and militarily to the sultanate of Darfur in modern Sudan and did not effectively come under Turkish control until briefly and much later.

ARABS OF LIBYA[5]

Populations noted for their pastoral nomadism, mythical pedigrees, fission, fusion, expansion, shifting dynastic and colonial borders, isolated oases, long-distance Saharan traders, and intermixture with Berbers, Jews, Spaniards, Levantines, Sahelian Africans and even Greco-Romans make it hard to define in clear and unambiguous terms. Especially when the lands of Libya don't have fixed borders of mountains and rivers that might give more definition. Libyan Arabs, in the broadest terms and parallel to the physical geography, include: Cyrenaican Arabs; Fezzan Arabs (such as the Murahidiya and others of Murzuk); Kufra and Wanyanga Arabs (who displaced the Teda people of those oases); Riyah and Busaif Arabs (of western Libya including the Hasauna, Hutma, Magarha, Mozda, Urfilla, and Zintan communities); Sanusi Arabs (embracing the historically significant Sanusi *tariqa* [brotherhood or lodge and other groups of Arafa, Darsa, Abaidat, Awaqir, Hasa, Baraasa, Fayid, and Magharba of the Cyrenaica region and interior to Kufra]); Sirtican Arabs (including the Jamaat, Gadharhfa [of Gaddafi], Awlad Soliman, along the coast near Sirte); and Tripolitan Arabs of the capital region and its immediate hinterland.

Libyan Arabs, sometimes glossed as Bedouin, remain as an important reference point of cultural legitimacy as highlighted by the Gaddafi era and his symbolic nomadic tent meetings with diplomats and visitors. At the same time, the Arabs and their sometimes seasonal transhumance, especially in Cyrenaica, are broadly less educated and less respected by the settled coastal and urban peoples. This makes for a more complex relationship of fission and fusion at times of crisis.

THE BARBARY PIRATES

The pirates of truth don't necessarily follow the legends that bore literature and extravagant films. The "Barbary" pirates were in actuality descended from the Moors who had been booted out of Spain by forces loyal to King Ferdinand and Queen Isabella. Quite coincidentally, as Christopher Columbus was on his voyage of discovery to open new worlds, the men who would become forever linked to that sinister association of barbarianism were highly educated and trained Moors who had, centuries before, ventured into what is present-day Spain and established quite a foothold on the country. Following in their own ways from their homeland of what is now Morocco and Algeria, the Moors introduced forms of irrigaton and agricultural products unseen until this time. For innovation was not a problem for them, just as will be explored with Muammar Gaddafi some 900 years later with his "Great Man Made River" project.

Comprised of Berber and Arab blood, the Moors demonstrated the ability to plan and execute at the community level and on the battlefield, which would allow them centuries of dominance against fractured bands of Christians and other non-Muslims. Architecture was another area in which the Moors transferred their talents to southern Europe. Castles of the type found along the North African coast are very similar to those remaining in Spain (Buckingham).

By the 1490s, like most imperial rules, Moorish influence in Spain had become overtaken by political marriages that yielded predominantly Christian communities who sought to retake what they had held over 700 years prior. Thus, a cultural group who had originally been invited in to defend the Spanish monarch of the 700s, and in turn taken control of Spain, was summarily booted out of Spain to return to North Africa. This context is to highlight the industrious nature of the Moors, and their warlike attributes, as they demonstrated staying power up north. Thus they would demonstrate the aggressiveness along the Mediterranean coast that would befuddle nations for years.

Part of the subterfuge of the Barbary pirate menace was that the nations of Europe were hungry. They were hungry for land, conquest, and trade. This hunger required constant feeding. In order to assuage their appetite, the Europeans were more than willing to pay tributes that the now Ottoman Empire–dominated descendants of the Moors were exacting via boarding of their merchant ships.

Far from hindering significant economic growth of the predominant European communities of the day, the pirates—or privateers, as some studies refer to their activities—kept a thriving marketplace intact as the European powers used these forces to fight a proxy war on their behalf. Eventually caught in the crossfire was a fiercely independent little nation that had just emerged from its own struggle for independence: the United States of America.

Ironically, the very people they were fighting, along the shores of the Mediterranean, were the same people who had been kicked out of Spain by the ruling party who sent Columbus on his voyage that ultimately popularized the discovery of "a new world."

The weapons of privateering, or piracy, were fast and nimble ships and weapons that required speed, not necessarily brute strength. They used sleek, shallow water vessels to prey upon their slower and bulkier victims (Heritage-History). They preferred the cutlass to a broadsword or Brown Bess, as stealth was their ally and close-quarters fighting was their forte. The vigor of attacks would be oft-repeated by Berber, Tripolitanian, Sirtian, and Libyan. The generations would change, but the drive would not. As will be discussed in later chapters, the Libyan fighter was as good as any around, with the proper training and purpose. Like any army, leadership and reason play major factors in influencing the foot soldier, be he a mariner, soldier, or airman, to lay down his life. The rebels would demonstrate this resolve in ways not seen in decades.

EUROPEAN IMPERIALISTS MAKE THEIR MOVES IN NORTHEAST AFRICA

The resolution or transformation of The Corsair privateer issues opened the door for European advances into the region. From 1832 to the 1880s, the French extended their control to the Algerian interior. The royal German explorer Barth ventured southbound from Tripoli to Ghat to Agades and on to Katsina, Kano, and Borno in modern Nigeria and then northbound to Murzuk from 1850 to 1855 and back to Tripoli. Meanwhile, the Italians, dreaming of the glories of the ancient Roman Empire, were making strategic claims along the Red Sea in 1870, when they established a private trade company at Asab in Eritrea. Further European claims were consolidated in 1884–1885 at the Berlin Congress, dividing Africa for European interests and requiring wars of colonial pacification to demonstrate "effective control." That same year, the Italians made a "protectorate on" the Danakil coast of Eritrea, yet in 1887, the Italians were defeated at Dogali, Eritrea. Going back on the offensive in 1889, Italians made fuller Eritrea and Italian Somaliland as "protectorates." By 1893–1894, Italian forces boldly attacked Kassala and Gedaref in Anglo-Egyptian Sudan but were promptly defeated at Amba Alagi, Ethiopia, in 1895 and suffered a major blow at Mekele and Adwa, Ethiopia, in 1896.

Elsewhere from 1896 to 1898, the British mounted a modern mechanized military offensive against the Mahdists of Sudan. Italians, nursing their serious political and military wounds, made Somalia a colony in 1905. At last, in 1911, the Italians were ready to invade the coasts of Libya through Derna, Tobruk, Benghazi, and Tripoli but were immediately resisted as they had been in the Horn of Africa. By 1913, the Italians advanced deep into the Fezzan region at Marzuk but met very strong Sanusi resistance and withdrew. Seeing the Italians pushing from the north, the French from the west, and the British from the southeast, the Sanusi made strategic links with the Sultan of Darfur, but by 1916, the British killed Sultan 'Ali Dinar and annexed that territory to the rest of the Sudan that had already been conquered.

THE LION OF THE DESERT AND SANUSI RESISTANCE IN LIBYA

As European interest, exploration, and penetration of Africa increased in the eighteenth and nineteenth centuries, the initial reception was generally hospitable and of mutual curiosity; but as this evolved, polarization and tensions increased. In this context, Muslims turned to the security of faith and to the Sufi brotherhood tradition of *marabout* (holy men), who in some cases claimed descent from the prophet Muhammad. Across the Sahel and North Africa, religious revivals and jihads unfolded in Guinea, Mali, Nigeria, and Sudan. Increasingly, they assumed populist and antiforeign stances along with piety and religious syncretism, with orthodox respect for the *Quran*, *Hadith*, and *Sunna* but also with local wisdom. So it was with the Mahdist movement in Sudan (1883–1898) with the fortification of the Keira sultanate in Darfur and with the Sanusi movement in Libya in 1843. Indeed, holy wars spread across the Sahelian savanna grassland from Samore Toure of Futa Djalon, Othman dan Fodio (1754–1817) of the Sokoto Caliphates to the Kanuri of Bornu Kanem, Maiurno of Sennar and jihadists in Futa Toro, Masina, and Adamawa in Cameroon, not to mention the earlier Muslim state formations in Mali Songhai and Sennar, the present Islamist uprisings of Boko Haram in northern Nigeria and Ansar in Mali, and Salafist attacks in Benghazi that have been spurred on by the trans-Saharan spillover of small arms and light weapons for the collapse of the Gaddafi regime.

So when Omar Mukhtar (1862–September 16, 1931) was born near Tobruk in Cyrenaica, it was not hard to find models of resistance that were deeply pedigreed in Africa's long political history and founded in the principles of Maliki Sunni Islam with a necessary ingredient of populist Sufism. Cyrenaica, with its remarkable history dating back 2,500 years and, by then, a millennium of Islam, needed no prodding in its collective and prideful self-consciousness. The Romans had been in Libya before and were transformed into Christians during the fourth century. Other foreigners had arrived and were defeated, so it was normal and natural to have another Sanusi resistance leader to mobilize for the First Italo-Sanusi War (1911–1917) in which imperial Italians were often defeated, and only in the Period of Accords from 1917 to 1923 did they have any idea that their colonial state in Libya was making any headway at all.

To make further progress in their colonial ambitions, the Italians bought in more mechanized modern troops and planes in the Second Italo-Sanusi War (1923–1932). Massive population displacement, vast concentration camps, and cordons of barbed wire and brutal repression were deemed necessary to "pacify" the Cyrenaicans led by Mohktar.

From 1924 to 1929, the Italians pushed relentlessly southern in Tripolitana and defeated Sanusi brotherhoods in that region. In 1928, Italians reached Jaghbub near the Egyptian border, and in 1930, they pushed southward in Cyrenaica and finally took Murzuk in the Fezzan and Ghat in the Ahhagar region. At last, in 1931, Italians routed Sanusi resistance at Kufra. In a carefully planned ambush, the Italians finally captured Omar Mukhtar, and on September 16, 1931, Mukhtar was hanged by the Italian occupying army in a public spectacle. After many previous defeats, the Fascist forces of Mussolini finally occupied Ethiopia in 1936.

It was not long after that the Italians were joined by the Nazi Germans in World War II as the Axis powers sought to topple the Allied powers. Once again, North Africa became the battleground from Algeria to Tunisia, Libya, and Egypt as the British and Americans pushed them back and created a bridgehead to retake Italy for the Fascists and Nazis. Fighting raged and waved back across Libya and Egypt from Tobruk to Al Alamein as Montgomery pushed from the east and Patton from the west, finally wresting control of the occupying colonial powers from Italy and Germany.

POSTWAR LIBYA AND THE DAWN OF A NEW ERA

Libya emerged from World War II as shattered as any nation in Europe and the major islands in the Pacific. The population had suffered heavily in the three years of significant fighting that introduced an impressionable Muammar Gaddafi and thousands of other Tripolitanians, Cyrenaicans, and Fezzanis to the weapons of modern warfare; airplanes, landmines, heavy artillery, and tanks. While these had all seen the light of day in World War I, their true devastating power wasn't realized until the likes of Rommel, O'Connor, and Montgomery had mobilized their true destructive force through superbly improvised tactics and a landscape ideal for massive land warfare.

The scars of such devastation weren't long to heal before another wound was inflicted; the consolidation of the three main independent territories into a unified Libya. As the United Nations was, in and of itself, a fledgling body, they meant to do well. They were creatures of the conformist generation. They saw stability in lands with clearly defined, if not ill-mapped, borders. They valued the name on the placard in front of the ambassador. Libya didn't have this as a nonunified entity. Thus, at the hands of the victors, went the spoils of consolidation, and a new nation was "born." Concurrently, the Arab League was forming as those nations, predominantly within the enclave of the Middle East surrounding Saudi Arabia and extending to Iraq, also unfurled their flag (U.S. Library of Congress).

Libya, under King Idris, the Hasan Karamanli of his time, joined the Arab League. This wouldn't be the only time in which Libya and her next-door neighbor, Egypt, would be in alliance. This also helped to cement the bond between a young Muammar Gaddafi and his unknowing mentor, Gamal Abdel Nasser.

The budding United Nations was also looking at "inclusiveness" and felt that the 21 entities that formed "Libya" should be an independent state. By 1949, the UN was mature enough as a permissive governing body to seriously consider the addition of this heavily trod-upon land mass as a separate and equal player. The vote was for independence. The date was by 1952, thus providing them three years to establish all of the procedures, rules, governing institutions, etc. to become what would initially be titled "The Kingdom of Libya."

Membership has its privileges, to include a higher authority for conflict resolution; requests for assistance in times of trouble and need, and a blanket upon which to share responsibilities when other nations are in trouble. However, this same higher authority would have no way of knowing the challenges they were going to face with their newest child in the years to come.

LIBYA AND THE ARAB LEAGUE

Founded in 1945, the Arab League, also known as the League of Arab States, was a collective security, political, and cultural organization along the lines of NATO. They focused on the problems, opportunities, and security concerns that the expanding Muslim countries felt were beginning to come into play. Additionally, as each of the nations involved in the formation of this organization had been under the bureaucratic control of the Ottoman Empire and either occupied or had "hosted" European powers throughout the late eighteenth and early nineteenth centuries, there was a sensation toward expanding their independence and developing their collective bargaining power as a bloc of nations.

Originally there were six nations; Egypt, Syria, Lebanon, Iraq, Saudi Arabia, and Jordan. North Yemen joined a month and a half after this original grouping, but it wasn't until eight years later that the next member would join. Libya became an official member of this august organization in 1953. As one of many nations searching for its identity, membership in this fraternity of like-minded states served to provide Libya with some big brotherly advice and counsel as King Idris tried to navigate his way through the intricate networks of economic, political, military, and social change. Libya's role in the Arab League would remain static for the next 48 years, as Gaddafi engaged in activities throughout the continent and in foreign affairs that, at times, complemented the Arab League philosophies, especially in the heyday of the Palestinian Liberation Organization (PLO) (Libya-Watanona, 1). His militancy was much like that precocious child who needed to be punished, although their actions were not always out of line with the thinking of the adults (Arab League). He would be supported by them when Libya was struck by the United States. He would be ignored by them when he ventured into Chad.

Ironically, when the Libyan Civil War of 2011 began, it was the Arab League's endorsement of air strikes by NATO and allied countries that ultimately provided the foundation of legitimacy for actions in Arab dominated Libya. Had they not provided their endorsement of action against their obstreperous member, significant questions remain whether the U.S. and Europe would have intervened.

LIBYA, FOREIGN BASES, AND THE NORTH ATLANTIC TREATY ORGANIZATION (NATO)

NATO was formed in 1949 as a mutual defense pact to repel the newly created Warsaw Pact nations of Eastern Europe, to prevent a return to European nationalism, and to provide collective economic growth through reductions by any one country to devote a majority of their resources to building and maintaining a standalone military force. Led by the Soviet Union, the Warsaw Pact was also a "mutual defense" treaty, to protect against invasion by any of the Western powers. Mutual distrust and cynicism, just two years after these same nations had fought as allies against the German, Italian, and Japanese forces—how quickly memories fade.

Part of NATO's line of defense was to emplace, or retain use of, ports, airfields, and bases from which they had launched strikes in World War II, for use as jumping-off points or staging areas should they need to attack or defend against attack, from anywhere in Europe, the Caucasus, the newly developing Middle East, or against "proxy war states" on the continent of Africa.

Libya, having been heavily occupied by both Allies and Axis armies and air forces throughout World War II, already had a significant footprint established. Close to deepwater ports and strategically located in the Mediterranean within arm's reach of the major Soviet Black Sea fleet and the Suez Canal, it offered every tactical advantage for "getting there first" if need be, by Allied jet aircraft. Long-range intercontinental bombers used Libya as a refueling and staging area, as this reduced time to target compared to launching from bases in the United States. While proven feasible, the time required reduced response time in the event an event occurred along any of the borders to which NATO was obligated.

The largest site used by NATO, and specifically U.S. forces, was Wheelus Air Force Base. This onetime Italian air base, opened in 1923, had been a hub for Italian occupation and containment of the peoples throughout the three main regions of pre-Libya, Tripolitania, Cyrenaica, and the Fezzan. With the initiation of World War II, Italy and then Germany occupied the base and used it to conduct raids on the Allies sent to expel Germany and Italy from North Africa. By 1943, "Mehalla" as it was called by the Italians, had been captured by the allies and turned into a stepping-off point for follow-on campaigns in southern Europe, mainly Sicily and Italy.

By war's end, the United States had a significant toehold in Mehalla. After World War II, and in concert with the creation of Strategic Air Command, the fledgling U.S. Air Force turned the Mehalla air base into Wheelus Air Base, named after a young aviator killed in Iran. Wheelus would be home to permanently assigned fighter and fighter bomber squadrons, aerial refueling squadrons, and search and rescue units and serve as the transient home to medium-range strategic bombers. One of Libya's many natural graces included a bombing range just to the south that provided crews with a very close opportunity in which to practice their deadly craft. What many would see as a partnering step in mutual security, young Gaddafi saw differently. While U.S. and allied bases remained in Libya, providing for the local economy while using their resources, he saw this as an invasion by other powers.

Wheelus wasn't the only site with its origins in conflict that would turn into either Cold War sites or civilian airports. During the war, the United States occupied no fewer than 13 bases from which they conducted attacks against Germans and Italians in Libya, Egypt, and throughout southern Europe. Several of these later became civilian airports or Libyan air force bases. Chief among these were Benina airfield, later Benina International Airport; Tmed El Chen Airfield (Habit Awlad Muhammad Airport); Martuba Airbase; Darragh Airfield (Nanur Airfield); and Hamraiet Airfield (Ra's Lanuf Airport) (Maurer, 120).

Access is a recurring theme throughout Libyan history, whether at the hands of Ottomans, Italians, Germans, or Americans. By 1970, Gaddafi had enough of outside forces occupying, even with the payment of substantial sums for the privilege, some of his most viable lands. Just as oil fields would become nationalized, so would the fields that had served Libya's liberators for decades. His efforts to boot the Western powers out would meet with the business end of a Colt .45 at the hands of Col. Daniel "Chappie" James, as the two postured, with weapons holstered but unsecured, in a standoff that would have had dramatically different results had Colonel Gaddafi made good on his threat to takeover Wheelus Air Base, forcefully, while under the command of Colonel James. History reflects the outcome, as will be reiterated further in the reading.

The British also maintained land and airbases throughout the Libyan-Egyptian corridor. Their interests were more expansive, i.e., the continued influence over their Egyptian holdings and territories throughout the Mediterranean and Middle East, despite the inevitable diminishment of their empire. Libya had been the domain of the fabled "Desert Rats" (Paterson, "7th Armoured Brigade") who kept the Germans at bay and certainly represented the type of fighting force that the Libyan landscape was most suited for, namely small teams of tight-knit warriors operating independently and with the level of weaponry and tactics that allow them to move throughout the environment with stealth and speed. Gaddafi's son, Khamis, would construct a brigade that, while significantly larger, contained the most seasoned, professional, and adaptable fighters that Libya would own.

Where does this put NATO? Throughout the Cold War, NATO continued to focus on the "Russian Bear" coming across the Fulda Gap in eastern Germany as the fulcrum of activity for the next major war. Therefore, maintaining a massively large presence along that border was the number one priority of the NATO nations. However, as the world was ever shrinking—resources that ran the machinery of business, industry, and war were continually being discovered throughout Africa, and expanded upon in the Middle East and South America—the need for "safety net" bases throughout the southern avenues into Europe remained vital. As mentioned previously regarding the British, they had possessions and holdings throughout the Middle East and Africa. The United States, after being dragged out of an isolationist stance with World War II, went full throttle into amassing bases and stations around the globe that would provide a forward presence and an early warning network in the event of war.

Thus, along with the NATO alliance, staging forces, communications, and monitoring sites along a major avenue of travel, the Mediterranean, provided that early warning network that served the United States and her allies well. Just as we found out when the tactical nuclear missiles were removed from Turkey, in exchange for the Russians removing their tactical nuclear missiles from Cuba, the loss of these bases was important but not catastrophic. NATO continued to operate throughout the Mediterranean, and would make a significant appearance again in 2011.

LIBYA AND THE AFRICAN UNION

If ever there was a philosophically Libyan institution, it was the African Union. September 9, 1999, the date upon which the "Fourth Extraordinary Session of the Assembly, in Sirte, Libya" agreed to establish the African Union, was 30 years and eight days in the making, from the beginning of Gaddafi's reign. A seminal date in the history of Libya and the continent of Africa. Such was the irony that the most economically powerful nation in North Africa, the very same nation that had influenced the major powers in Middle Eastern oil to clamp down on their passivity toward the nations needing their oil; the nation that would raise the stakes on international terrorism through proxies and active pursuit of wanton destruction because they needed to make a point regarding Arab-Israeli

conflicts, and the action, or lack of action, on the part of his Arab neighbors; the country with the most ambitious, and yet potentially feasible,
waterworks project the world had ever seen. This same nation, led by a
man who epitomized "your best friend and worst enemy," was the same
man who conceived of a Pan-Arab and then Pan-African community,
and was able to foster the creation of the African Union.

This wasn't Muammar Gaddafi's first effort at unifying the Muslim
world. Despite membership in the Arab League, Gaddafi didn't feel the
sense of unifying spirit and action with the Arab League. He felt they sold
out to moderates, seeking evolutionary change, when he was adamant
that the only change that would make Muslims of the Arab world a force
to be reckoned with was revolutionary change. As this didn't happen, he
sought other avenues to foster his agenda.

First was the Pan-Arab organization entitled the Federation of Arab
Republics (FAR). Formed from the countries of Egypt, Libya, and Syria,
the organization's aims were to unite their economic, military, and legal
systems under one "roof." The first leader of this new collective was to
be Anwar Sadat. Almost immediately, there was a falling out. First, it
involved velocity. As mentioned earlier, Gaddafi was all about speed of
change. He was a revolutionary in every sense. Sadat was more mature,
older, and seasoned as a political leader. He favored a more measured
approach to this rather significant union of three influential Arab nations.
While Hassad of Syria was content to do his part to bring the countries
together, Gaddafi's insistence on immediate change riled the other two
leaders. Ultimately, without a declaration ever being signed, this first
union fell apart (Gaddafi.info).

Failing to form an Arab union, he refocused his power, consolidating
attentions solely to his home continent. Seeking a "Pan-African" union,
he began making inroads with the likes of Tunisia, Chad, and Angola,
through partnership, military assistance, and economic aid. Besides being
neighbors, in two of the three cases, he believed they were of kindred
spirits. While their leadership either changed (Angola and Chad), or
chose to politely listen and then go their own way (Tunisia), he never tired
of seeking consensus among his Arab brothers.

Alternately passing through the power-grabbing 1970s, in which Libya
made its name, to the downtrodden 1980s, when they were banished to
pariah status for their terrorist leanings and the final backlash on their
economic Draconianism regarding oil, to their penitential 1990s when
they, mostly, focused their energies on internal matters, Gaddafi was
always plotting. As will be shown throughout the book, he was always
one to cultivate allies. If, and/or when, they chose against him, he quickly
dispensed with them and sought new allies.

By 1999, he had repaired enough of Libya's reputation so that he was
able to get a seat at the table of international politics. Part and parcel to

his return was to invigorate the Organization of African Unity (OAU) into a body that was more action-oriented and, to an extent, a rival to the United Nations, or even NATO. Aiding his case was the repeated "assistance" he provided to some of the less economically fortunate nations, via paying their dues, whether to the OAU or to the new AU. Money talks. He had a lot of money.

To read the Constitutive Act of the African Union is to catch part "The Green Book" meets the United Nations, meets, the Constitution of the United States. All 53 nations signed this charter. Right out of the gate, the Constitutive Act mentions its inspiration from "Pan-Africanism" throughout the generations. Certainly, this Afrocentric construct played a pivotal role in the intellectual and emotional development of the young Muammar Gaddafi.

Economics were central, as the Constitution references the mildly effective African Economic Community, of which Libya was an influential member via the *Communauté des Etats Sahélo-Sahariens* (CENSAD). Otherwise known as the Community of Sahel-Saharan States, this organization, headquartered in Tripoli, Libya, provided, and continues to provide, economic collectivism among the 27 member states, ranging from Morocco to the Comoros. Given Libya's relatively consistent economic growth, serving as the headquarters and, ostensibly, the primary influence on policy, wasn't unnatural for Libya.

The constitution to create the African Union contained some interesting provisions that would become controversial just 12 years later. Voting for this constitution, Libya signed up to agree that the AU was chartered to "promote and protect human and peoples' rights"; "take all necessary measures to strengthen our common institutions"; "defend the sovereignty, territorial integrity and Independence" of member States; "promote peace, security, and stability"; and "promote democratic principles" (Constitutive Act, 6, 7). That a nation who would willfully invade their neighbor, and yet sign up to "respect or borders existing" and the "prohibition of the use of force or threat to use force among Member States," speaks to how far Libya had returned from the abyss of individualism throughout her tumultuous 30-year previous run (Constitutive Act, 6).

The onset of the Libyan Civil War in 2011 would severely test this union, as their provisions stipulated "non-interference by any Member State in the internal affairs of another," yet they also allowed the union to intervene in a Member State in the circumstances of "grave circumstances"—i.e., war crimes, genocide, or crimes against humanity. Thus, while Libyans were battling each other, with help from outside players who were contracted to assist in eradicating one side or the other, the AU effectively sat on the sidelines and lamented the situation occurring in Libya.

To be fair to the AU, the decade of the 2000s had not been absent of violence and turmoil throughout the continent—court battles in Liberia and Sierra Leone; civil war in Angola; potentially genocidal actions in Darfur and an ensuing separation of the Sudan into two separate countries. There were suspicions, although none could be proven, that due to Gaddafi's generosity in paying the dues of quite a few of the borderline-impoverished nations, there was a reticence to "bite than hand that feeds." Given that Gaddafi had successfully campaigned to serve as the chairman of the Assembly reflects the schizophrenic power by which he captivated the attention of his peers, while also monumentally confounding those who would seek to have him moderate and become an enduring member of the international community.

What remains to be answered is how the post-Gaddafi Libya will fare with the AU. Will their neighbors have long memories and even longer grudges? Will they forgive and embrace the new nation, reborn from the fires of civil war? Will they nurture the entrepreneurial spirit that Muammar Gaddafi infused in the nascent Libya? We attempt to provide some glimpses of what may be, rather than what may be not.

SUMMARY TRENDS

Geostrategic Foundations

Whether in ancient, medieval, or modern times, Libyan invaders have focused on the coastal corridor, either arriving from the east (Arabs, Turks, English) or west (Germans, Phoenicians, Germans) or directly by the sea from the north (Romans, Italians). Over these ages, Libyan defenders have opted for withdrawal or alliances to the south, or the eastern or western mountains are often featured in Libya's strategic history. Even in the battles of World War II and in the Revolution of 2011, the lack of physical barriers along Libya's coast has meant a good deal of back and forth of the opposing forces.

Libyan Identity and Legitimacy

Aside from the special features of coast, interior, and mountainous regions, the terrain of Libya helps to homogenize a sense of common territorial identity. On account of the long exposure to Islam, from local pre-Islamic and Islamic folk shrines and modern sectarian differences, Libya has a very strong sense of religious unity. It is hard to say how much this might have been true in Phoenicians and Roman times, but ancient polytheism can be rather tolerant of religious plurality. Regarding communication, Libyans have been exposed to various foreign tongues over the years, but for almost a millennium and a half, only the Semitic languages of Arabic and Berber have been widely spoken in colloquial for formal settings, admittedly with some dialectical or regional differences. The only other dimensions of linguistic diversity can relate to class, gender, and educational levels. In short, Libyan people are overwhelming settled along the coast and are remarkably homogenized from a cultural perspective as well as a broadly common history, common enemies and allies, and circumstances. On top of this trend toward cultural homogenization, there are various examples of syncretism or mixture of ancient and modern European and Libyan traditions, of shared Jewish and Berber iconography, and especially of Berber and Arab cultural mergers.

Fission and Fusion

The more Libyans thought of themselves in terms of cultural unity, the more they might manifest rivalry, or hostility to expansive rivals; apprehension toward Egyptians and being quarrelsome with ancient Nubians or modern Sudan along the Nile, as well as a certain degree of potential tension with Tunisia and Algeria. As a result, Libyans have frequent cases of strategic intervention in Darfur, Chad, Tunis, and Algeria even during the time of the Turkish corsairs.

The relations with the majority peoples of coastal Libya were often characterized with xenophobia or prejudicial views toward the minority peoples of the south. Perhaps this was founded on a rural urban or Arab-Berber dichotomy in the mildest form; or when, in medieval times, slaves were force-marched from Sahelian or sub-Saharan Africa, the attitudes were even more stereotyped and harsh. Even in the 2011 revolution, there was a dimension of discrimination or violent hostility shown to Africans in Libya from below the Saharan. In part this was because Gaddafi "recruited" such people as a mercenary force who were despised by the revolutionaries, but also imported labor from Africa in better times also had a degree of ethnic discrimination.

The patrilineal lineal structure in Arab and Berber society gives many opportunities of volatile fission, or temporary fusion during acts of resistance and accommodation to invaders from the sea or coast. These themes will be pursued in later chapters in order to illuminate the present and establish some guides for the future of Libya.

NOTES

1. Comprehensive and illustrated surveys of the cartographic history of Africa, including physical geography, migrations, and key events, are available in Harry A. Gailey Jr., 1973, *The History of Africa in Maps*, Denoyer-Geppert: Chicago; and M. Kwamena-Poh, J. Tosh, R. Waller, and M. Tidy, 1995, *African History in Maps*, Longman: Essex, England. Also the broad survey of African history by Robert W.

July, 1998, *A History of the African People,* Waveland Press: Long Grove, Illinois, is a
handy introductory source.

2. Ancient nomenclature probably complicates the ancient ethnography of
Libya more than it clarifies. Certainly the native Libyan people, known variously
as the Mashwash, Tjehenu, Thamenhu, Temenhu, or Temenu, were of Berber stock
and occupied much of modern Libya as well as ranging into the western desert of
Egypt and Nubia. These terms are used inconsistently and maybe are general
glosses or names of specific lineages or regional groups with unspecified territories. They appear as early as the Dynasty VI travels to Nubia of the Egyptian
nomarch (or *Heka-ib*) Harkuf as he struggled through Tjehenu territory west of
the Nile as indicated in the texts on his tomb in Aswan. In the New Kingdom, Seti
I and his son Ramses II (the first to write the name "lbw") and Ramses III reported
punitive raids into the same lands to block threats to the Nile towns. Indeed, the
New Kingdom iconography illustrated Egyptian pharaohs as "Lords of the Nine
Bows" reflecting the plurality of the "three enemies": Asians to the east; Nubians
to the south, and Libyans to the west. The term *Lebu* was more commonly used
in the Greco-Roman eras and was sometimes generously applied to much of
sub-Saharan Africa and even to the entire continent, much as the tiny part of
northwest Tunisia called "Africa" became the nonindigenous reference to the continent. It was during Dynasty XXII that the Libyans actually took power in Egypt
as a ruling dynasty. But even after, in Dynasty XXV, they were a threat; and in
Dynasty XXVI, pharaoh Psamtik II had troubles with the Temenhu to control trade
in the western desert oases. When the Romans arrived, Trajan and others had to
set up the string of desert garrison and trade forts such as that Dush to protect it
from wide-ranging Berber raids on the southernmost *limes* of the Romans in
Egypt.

3. Tripolitania, is so named because it embraces the "three cities" of *Oea*
founded by the Phoenicians (who called the land "*lby*") in the seventh century
and the Greek-founded towns of Sabratha and Leptis Magna in the general region
of Syrtica. Oea is about at the modern capital of Tripoli, while Sabratha lies to the
west and Leptis Magna further to the east. As archaeological sites, they are among
some of the world's most celebrated example of Roman architecture. Leptis began
as a Punic trade center and as a satellite of the regional capital at Carthage
(founded by Queen Didon in 814 BC). There they traded in foodstuffs, grain,
fruits, nuts, dates, wild animals, ivory, olive oil, and slaves. Homer noted Libya
as part of the *Lotophagii* (lotus eating) lands in his *Odyssey* in perhaps the eighth
or seventh century BC. More concretely, the Greek historian Herodotus (484–
425 BC) gave much regional information, and his map shows a prominent place
for Libya. When the Roman conquest took place in 146 BC, the whole region
became known as *Regio Tripolitania*. Pentapolis is named for the "five cities" of
eastern Libya or Cyrenaica founded by Greek refugees in as early as 631 BC. They
include *Cyrene* (modern Shahat) and its port of Apollonium (modern Marsa Susa);
Tauchera (modern Tocra); *Berenice* (modern Benghazi); *Balacrae* (modern Bayda);
and *Marj* (modern Barca). Under Roman rule parts of Cyrenaica (*Libya Superior*)
were glossed under the term Marmarica (*Libya Inferior*). Romans were among the
first to explore far into the Sahara, with Balbus reaching Garam in 19 BC, Valerius
Festus going deep into Garamantes territory in 70 AD, and Julius Maternius

reaching the Tibesti highlands in 86 AD and going on to Aïr still further south. The Roman emperor Hadrian did order the construction of a formal Roman bath at Leptis Magna in 127 AD. By 193 AD, Septimus Severus, a Roman general born in Leptis Magna, became the emperor of the Roman Empire, suggesting just how important Libya in North Africa had become to Rome.

4. Berbers are named from the Greek *barbaroi* that refers to the twittering or stuttering that was perceived by the Greek ears. So-called Berbers were typically beyond Greek or Roman control and so they were demonized as "barbarians." The Berber populations include the Gadames Berbers of western Libya and eastern Tunisia, the Jalo Berber of eastern Libya and their Berber neighbors in Siwa oasis of western Egypt, the Jofra Berbers of the central Libyan desert, and the Ibadi Berbers of Jebel Nefusa. For at least 3,000 years, the Berbers have been herders, farmers, and traders.

5. Standard anthropological sources that cover the Arabs of Libya can be found in George Peter Murdock, 1959, *Africa: Its Peoples and Their Culture History*, McGraw-Hill: New York; and especially the penetrating, highly informed anthropological book by Edward E. Evans-Pritchard, 1954, *The Sanusi of Cyrenaica*, Clarendon Press: Oxford.

SOURCES

African Union. "Constitutive Act of the African Union." Accessed September 29, 2013. http://www.au.int/en/sites/default/files/ConstitutiveAct_EN.pdf.

Buckingham, Maddie. "The Impact of the Moors in Spain." Accessed September 28, 2013. http://wuhstry.wordpress.com/2011/07/20/the-impact-of-the-moors-in-spain/.

Heritage-History. "Barbary Wars, 1500–1830: Barbary Pirates versus Christian Sea Powers." Accessed September 28, 2013. http://www.heritage-history.com/www/heritage.php?Dir=wars&FileName=wars_barbary.php.

"Libya, What Happened and When?" Accessed September 28, 2013. http://www.libya-watanona.com/libya/libyans.htm.

"Pan-Arabism, African Union and the War in Chad." Accessed September 28, 2013. http://gaddafi.info/panarab.htm.

Paterson, Ian A. "Regiments That Served with the 7th Armoured Division." Accessed July 22, 2012. http://archive.is/Srqbv. (Original website: http://www.ian.a.paterson.btinternet.co.uk/battles1941.htm.)

Rusk, Donald C. "Libya: Petroleum Potential of the underexplored Basin Centers - A Twenty-First-Century Challenge." Chapter 22 in M. W. Downey, J. C. Threet, and W. A. Morgan, eds., Petroleum provinces of the twenty-first century: AAPG Memoir 74, pp. 429–431.

U.S. Library of Congress. "Independent Libya." Accessed 22 January 2014. http://countrystudies.us/libya/27.htm.

CHAPTER 2

Libya before Gaddafi: Arabs, Ottomans, and the Senusiya

As seen in the previous chapter, Libya has always struggled to put its three territorial parts of Tripolitania, Cyrenaica, and the Fezzan together to fabricate a unitary state whether under its own authority, local ethnic or clan leaders, or foreign occupation. Libyan history elides from ancient times with Berbers, farmers and nomads, Phoenician traders, Greek outpost colonies and onto full-scale Roman colonization (first pagans, and later Byzantine Christians). These ancient strategic relations between people of the desert and the Libyan coast and between the coastal occupants of Libya and the Egyptian delta are sometimes collaborative, and sometimes combative. There is a millennial relationship of push and pull between Libya and Egypt and between the settled coastal people and those of the southern Fezzan, as well as relations between Libya and Tunisia that are similar to the give and take of Egypto-Nubian dynamics. When Libya is weak, it gets challenged; when Libya is strong, Egyptians, Nubians, and nomads get expelled or marginalized. Equally, between Libya and Tunisia and traders/raiders to the south, there was a continuous strategic search for balance.

For Libya to be ruled by "true" Libyans, we must really go back to semi-nomadic Berber times, before the Phoenicians, Greeks, and Romans as well as the brief occupation by Spaniards. Even when Arabs and Islam arrive, these were also foreign or exogenous forces, and then the battles between the Arabs (of various dynasties had their capitals far away from Libya) and Ottoman corsairs were, essentially still foreigners fighting over the strategic locations and resources of what became Libya. This historically deep and long-lasting pattern persists to today when foreigners

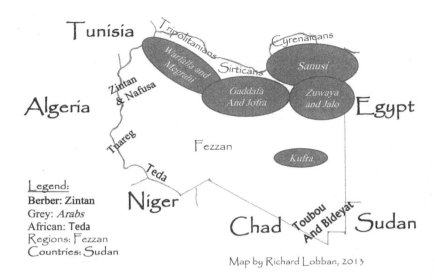

Ethnic Groups of Libya

Map by Richard Lobban, 2013

Ethnic Groups of Libya

fight over their control of the lands of Libya. In short, one might say that Libya has *not* been ruled by Libyans from these ancient times until decolonization. Even then, the Arabized Libyans, such as the Senussi and the Arab tribes have only managed, after 14 centuries, to indigenize themselves to create and constitute the actually heterogeneous and long-standing powerless people, the modern Libyan population.

LIBYANS CONQUERED BY THE ARABS IN THE "GOLDEN AGE"

After the collapse of theologically divided Christian Roman rule in the fifth century AD, Libya fell into something of a religious power vacuum with its own internal forces struggling for a new identity. However, this new identity came in the form of exogenous Islam. Let's take a closer look at Libya in the two main Islamic periods from the arrival of Islam under the Arabs (640s to 1519) and the persistence of Islam in Libya under the Ottomans (officially 1519–1952). After the famed withdrawal or *Hejira* to Medina in 622 AD by the prophet Muhammad, literally the calendar or Middle Eastern events were fundamentally reset. Although the prophet died in 632, Islam fairly zoomed across North Africa after arriving in

Egypt in 639–640 AD, and then pushed west, east, and north and crossed the Straits of Gibraltar (*Jebel Tariq*) in 711 AD. Then the Umayyads marched across Spain, Portugal, and France until finally stopped by Charles "the Hammer" Martel at the Battle of Tours (Potiers) on October 732, only 150 miles from the English Channel. Meanwhile, in 642 AD, the first Arab cavalry under the authority of 'Amr ibn al-'As reached Pentapolis (the "Five Cities" of Cyrenaica), which they renamed from the Greek word to Barca. By 647, under that command of Abdullah ibn Sa'ad Muslims reached Tripoli and western Libya and took it from the Byzantines. The Arab conquest of, at least, coastal Libya was complete by 670 AD.

This ascendance of the Arab and Muslim world was at the expense of Europeans still in their Dark Age that later inspired to the Renaissance and Enlightenment by, in some considerable measure, what the Arabs brought from their capitals and from their translated works of the ancient scholars and scientists, as well as the Arab alliances with the Jews. Each of the major "Golden Age" Arab dynasties brought its unique features, but none was based in Libya, so it began its long-standing political subordination, marginalization, or split affinities with fellow Muslims.

After the bloody sorting out for succession of the Sunnis and Shi'ites, the Sunni *Umayyads* (661–750) ruled their new empire from Damascus, Syria, and as it was consolidated in Syria, it granted semiautonomy to the newly occupied lands of Libya.

The Sunni *Abbasids* (750–1258) carried on with rule from more remote Baghdad, Iraq, but promised commercial security to coastal Libya against Garamantes (Berber) raids from the Fezzan. The remaining Monophysite Copts residing in Barca generally welcomed the Arabs for this reason. During Abbasid times, the western portions of Libya at Tripolitania sometimes fell under the rule of the Muslim dynasties of *Ifriqiya* that centered on Tunisia but elided into eastern Algeria and western Tripolitania. The *Muhallabid* dynasty ruled briefly from 771 to 793; the *Aghlabids* ruled for a century from 800 to 909 AD when the Shi'ite *Fatimids* took over and ruled from Mahdiya, Tunisia, while Sunni Abbasid Muslims carried on in Cyrenaica and Egypt.

The Shi'ite Fatimids (909–1171) gave a considerable tolerant role to the marginalized Berbers in gaining support against their Sunni rivals. By 969 AD, they had sufficient strength to take their rulers to Cairo where they started the great al-Azhar University, the oldest university on earth, and advocated Hanbali *fiqh* (jurisprudence). With the Fatimid capital shifted to Cairo, the vassal Zirid dynasty of *Ifriqiya* took over from 973 to 1048 and became independent from 1048 to 1148 AD as Fatimid power withered and collapsed by 1171.

In the relative weakness of the later times of the Abbasids, the early installation of Fatimid rule, and the strategic drift toward Cairo, the

Maghreb region of North Africa from 1062 to 1147 saw the swift growth of
the fundamentalist and expansionist *Al-Murabitun* (or *Almoravids,* 1040–
1147 AD) and *Almohads* (1198–1213 AD) in Morocco and Algeria that
sought to purify and fortify Islam already perceived to be slipping in
Muslim lands and being challenged in the northern regions of Andalusia.

While the Almoravids never ruled as far east as modern Libya, this was
largely empowered by a Berber dynasty that succeeded in temporarily
blocking the rebirth of Castilian Spain at least as far as Toledo in 1085 that
maintained this long-lasting rivalry between Europe and North Africa.
Empowering Berbers was also something that provoked anxiety in coastal
Libya. The Almoravid alliances with the Sanhaja (Mauritanian and
Senegalese) Berbers and their conquest to ancient Ghana in about 1075
also threatened Algeria and Libya from the south.

The two centuries of the nine Crusades from 1095 to 1291 AD were
clearly the biggest intimidating backdrop for regional politico-military
insecurity. While many of the actual battles were in Europe and the
northern and eastern Mediterranean, the tumult was felt across the entire
Mediterranean littoral. Since about 870 AD when the Aghlabids had
seized nearby Sicily from the Byzantines, the 1072 Norman reconquest
of Sicily must have been very disquieting. The 1191 capture of Cyprus
by Richard I must have added to this discouragement.

When the Almoravids were displaced by the fundamentalist Sunni
Almohad "Unitarians," their empire did reach across Algeria and into
Tripolitania as far as Sirte, but not to Cyrenaica until it withdrew in
1213. In less than two decades, the power vacuum in *Ifriqiya* and western
Tripolitania was filled by their appointed and long-lasting *Hafsid* dynasty
(1229–1574 AD), also based in Berber (Masmuda) people, until finally
having to challenge the expansion of the Ayyubids and later, the
Ottomans. The Hafsids separated completely by 1229 to be fully independent rulers of *Ifriqiya.*

The Sunni Ayyubids (1171–1341) began with the powerful reign of the
great Saladin al-Ayyubi from Takrit in Iraqi Kurdistan who toppled the
Shi'ite Fatimids and restored Sunni Islam and Maliki *fiqh* to the region.
Although centered in Cairo, the Ayyubids promptly established their
authority across coastal Libya up to the Tunisian border where the Hafsids still prevailed.

To summarize this section, one may see the initial era of Islamic expansion of the Ummayads and Ayyubids and the regional efforts of the
Almoravids, Almohads, and Hafsids against Spain and Portugal and then
the period of Crusader fight-back. However, the endless intra- and inter-
dynastic intrigues and conspiracies weakened the Arabs' ability to fight
back effectively for the longer term. Moreover, these Muslim rivalries
often divided Tripolitanian Libya from Cyrenaican Libya by competing
forces from the western Maghreb and forces from the eastern Mashraq

whether in Cairo, Damascus, or Baghdad. These uneasy times of deep distrust and religious fervor on two sides of world civilizations meant military probes, theological exhortations, commercial rivalries, and political tensions. This was the perfect environment for the Christian crusades and Muslim jihads to justify raids and privateering on both sides.

EGYPT AND THE REGION CONQUERED BY THE MAMLUKS, 1250–1517

The "Golden Age of Islam" (Abbasid, Fatimid, Ayyubid) could not be sustained when the serious military leaders were no longer Arabs. Finally, political power of the eastern Mediterranean Muslims turned to the Mamluks, an elite group of Circassian and Georgian slave soldiers who had served the Ayyubid Arab forces of North Africa and the Middle East, especially after 1249 when they played their critical role in defeating the Crusaders forces led by Louis IX of France.

Typically Mamluk rule was mainly of Egypt and Syria and is distinguished with the Bahri (Sea, Nile) Mamluks (1250–1382) and its significant Sultan Baybars I (1223–1277); and the Burji (Citadel Tower) Mamluks (1382–1517), who ruled from Cairo. Baybars I had, by 1260, forced all Mongols out of Arab lands, and by 1291, the last Crusaders were also gone. Despite the fact that Mamluks were not Arabs, at least they were able to consolidate their control and unify the lands under Islamic governance. The weakened and divided Arabs needed the stalwart Mamluks and later Ottoman imperialists to hope for a stronger defense against the Crusades and for their collective faith, especially under serious threats from Crusading Europeans.

1492: THE WORLD TURNS UPSIDE DOWN

After seven centuries of Muslim occupation of portions of Spain, Portugal, and France in western Europe, not to mention Muslim occupation of substantial parts of eastern Europe and Turkey, the tables were about to turn. The great age of Portuguese navigation, cartography, and African coastal exploration headed toward this fulcrum year. The challenges to Moorish rule of Andalusia by the Portuguese and Spanish were persistent, and in January 1492, King Ferdinand and Queen Isabella pushed the last Moors back across the Straits of Gibraltar. Confiscating wealth from Jews and Arabs, the Spanish royalty funded the October 1492 voyage of Christopher Columbus that was to rebalance world civilization. The Mamluks and the Ottomans were to miss the boat!

The deep political, economic, and strategic wounds that had been growing for the previous centuries were only gravely exacerbated by the expulsion and forced conversion in the name of the Spanish Inquisition. The Burji Mamluks of Egypt could hold on for another quarter century to resist these bitter times and humiliated spirit of the North African Muslims. Corsairs, or the so-called "Barbary pirates," were going to re-dress this huge grievance against the West. These state-backed maritime privateers were the proxies of these corsairs, Beys, and Deys who ruled the "Barbary Coast." State privateers versus individual criminal pirates were the proxy naval forces of most contemporary maritime powers, but in the absence of the rule of law or international courts of appeal that could adjudicate the complex issues.

The term "Barbary" is derived from the Greco-Roman words for Berbers (really known as Amaziq or *ber-ber*, meaning, to the Romans, "twitterers" since they could not understand their language or bring them under political or military control beyond the *limes* [boundaries of their empire]). The Amaziq (ancient Garamantes) were mostly living in the mountains and in the Fezzan rather than on the coast. Thus, to refer to the "Barbary pirates" is a triple misnomer, since the corsair "pirates" were mostly Arabs or Ottomans rather than Berbers; they were no more pirates than any other proxy privateers; and all of the circum-Mediterranean nations were amidst the great political and military rivalries of the day. In any case, the words carried more, or less, meaning than intended; the west was committed to call the agents of the corsairs as "Barbary pirates."

LIBYAN (ARABS) AND MAMLUKS CONQUERED BY THE OTTOMANS

In 1453, Mehmet II "the Conqueror" managed to seize Constantinople from the Byzantine Christians and rename the strategic town "Istanbul" and thereby launch the Ottoman Empire. For Libya, the Ottoman era from 1500 to 1800 is also known as the age of the "Ottoman corsairs"; for America of the eighteenth and nineteenth centuries, this was known as the age of the "Barbary pirates," although it had been already underway, even if to a lesser degree.

As a contextual footnote to this period, the remaining part of the Turkish Admiral Piri Reis parchment map of 1513 was an excellent case of maritime intelligence that had clear contributions from the portolan mariner's maps of the Portuguese and the Greco-Roman Ptolemaic maps, but also from the just-earlier voyages of Christopher Columbus insofar as it showed parts of South America in the New World and details of the Atlantic for the first time for the Ottomans. This remarkable map was only rediscovered in 1929, but one may assume that it reflected Turkish mari-time ambitions for much of the contemporary known world. The Piri Reis map was presented to the Ottoman emperor Sultan Selim I, who had very big plans only a few years later.

Sultan Selim I advanced the conquest of Arab lands on August 24, 1516, with his victory at the battle of the Dabiq meadow (*Marj Dabiq*), some 44 kilometers north of modern Halab, Syria, with his strong infantry and cavalry forces against the Mamluks led by Al-Ashraf Qansu al-Ghanri. This was one of those turning points in history that broke the will and unity of Mamluks everywhere. A fearful understanding of rising Ottoman power persuaded the Safavid Persians to make no further claims against them, and the frightening news quickly spread to Mamluk Cairo. In only months, by the time of the January 23, 1517, battle of Cairo, the Egyptian Mamluks capitulated, and Cairo was plundered by the Ottoman forces. Similarly, Libyans, under Arab rule, would also soon see them replaced by Ottoman corsairs. Despites some efforts to revolt and resist, Mamluks were hunted down in Egypt and Nubia (Sudan) in the following spring and were never to return to rule Egypt.

This was a major symbolic turning point in Arab history to be ruled by non-Arab Muslims from a non-Arab capital. Whether slave raids in Sudan, cotton and heavy taxes in Egypt, or privateering in the Mediterranean, the Ottomans had creative financing for their regional empire.

Of the four Turkish Barbarosa brothers from the island of Lesbos, Ishaq was the oldest, Ilias was killed, and Aruj was captured as a slave but escaped and sought revenge for the indignities he faced from the Knights of St. John at Rhodes. Aruj set up a privateer base at Djerba in 1505 and managed to capture Algiers in 1516, all working under the protection of the Ottoman that cause his title to shift from "Sultan of Algeria" to Governor of Algiers. When he was killed in 1518 by the Spanish, his young brother, Kheir al-Din, the "red-bearded" Barbarosa (c. 1478–1546) took over to be one of the most celebrated of the Ottoman "pirates" who worked the Tripolitanian coast in service of Sultan Suleiman the Magnificent.

From the Spanish perspective, Kheir al-Din was one of the most despised. In 1510, Spain pushed its Mediterranean offensive and occupied Tripoli; but in 1534, Kheir al-Din took Tunis, but it was promptly retaken by the Spanish. By 1535, King Charles I of Spain ceded Tripoli and the islands of Malta and Gozo to the Knights of St. John, who had lost their position on the island of Rhodes when this was recovered by the Ottomans. Kheir al-Din was instrumental in helping some 70,000 Muslim *Moriscos* to escape from Andalusia in 1529. Jewish *Ladinos* had also fled to North Africa and Turkey. He also managed in 1538 to defeat the forces of Andrea Doria, who was serving King Charles I of Spain. In 1541, an impressive Spanish navy tried to take Algiers from the corsair forces of Kheir al-Din, but they were not favored by weather, and the corsair managed to keep them out. Kheir al-Din was killed fighting the Spanish in Algeria in 1546. Despite these setbacks, challenges, and victories, the capacity of the humiliated and refugee Arabs of North Africa from

Numidia to Tripolitania was seriously taxed, and seeking umbrella protection from the nascent Ottoman Empire seemed a wise strategic move.

Not less famed and honored by the Turks was Turgut Reis (1485–1565), whose military achievements in the Mediterranean really exceeded those of Barbarosa, who he ultimately replaced as the head of the Turkish navy after rising as a Greek slave to a converted Muslim to the status of Dey and Pasha, and his conquests and very many bold attacks are still celebrated with modern Turkish vessels bearing his name. As much as he was celebrated by the Turks, he was that despised and feared by the Spanish and Maltese. When he became the Pasha of Tripoli in 1551, one may say that the Turkish occupation of Libya began. He was an admiral, administrator, strategist, and soldier *par excellence* and his revenge attacks against Andre Doria (1538 Battle of Prevega) and especially his attack on Gozo island in 1544 netted 6,300 slaves removed back to Tripoli. He was killed in Malta in 1565.

Such violent contests between Spain and Turkey for power and territory in North Africa meant only loose authority for Constantinople in Libya, which the Ottomans under Turgut Reis addressed in their 1551 siege of Tripoli that drove out the persistent Spaniards. In 1565, a Pasha and his junior officer Beys along with janissary troops reestablished Ottoman rule.

Kheir al-Din's later years were contemporary with John Hawkins (1532–1595) and his second cousin Francis Drake (c. 1540–1596) who were both "pirates" and slavers for Queen Elizabeth I. In fact, both were high-ranking naval officers and admirals for the British navy in 1588 when the Spanish Armada suffered a heavy defeat. Clearly one nation's hero is another nation's "pirate."

It was not enough to have the plotting of major foreign powers, but the weak self-governing janissary troops also led to endless mutinies, coups, and conspiracies in the early seventeenth century in which Deys, Beys, and Pashas rapidly rose, fell, and were replaced. Such was the case of Dey Mehmed Sagizli (ruled 1631–1649) and Dey Osman Sagizli (ruled 1649–1672), who finally conquered Cyrenaica toward the end of his reign. The town of Tripoli had some 30,000 inhabitants of Magrebines, Ottomans, and refugee Ladinos and Moriscos from Spain as well as slaves from Europe and the Sahelian Sudan. This was not the end of rivalries when in 1663, the Ottomans extend into Europe even to lay siege to Vienna.

In 1711, the official Ottoman Regency of Tripoli under the new dynasty of Ahmed Karamanli was established. The Libyan Civil War (1791–1795) unfolded when the weak administration of 'Ali Karamanli was toppled by 'Ali Benghal, an Ottoman officer. Seeing a loss of regional power, the Bey of Tunis backed Hamet and Yusef Karamanli to retake Tripoli from Benghal. Installed as Ahmed II Pasha, Hamet held onto power from

January to June 1795 when he was, in turn, overthrown and exiled by his brother Yusuf. Americans tried to seek their advantage and backed the return to power of Hamet in the first Barbary war at the Battle of Derna. They failed and Yusef held the position in Tripoli. In some measure of punishment to the Americans, in 1801, Pasha Yusef Karamanli demanded an increased American tribute to $83,000 per year. Tribute had been paid by Americans since 1796 as "piracy protection." These events not only demonstrated the tumultuous domestic rule of Libya, but also of the inability of the Ottoman to project their authority further west.

Some Mamluk caste soldiers were still on hand in the later "Battle of the Pyramids" when defeated by the French on July 21, 1798, but the French were soon to be defeated by the British by August 1801. Ottoman rule of Egypt persisted, but in name and title only as their power gradually slid into a puppet role for the British. Amid the European global contest for regional control, internal Egyptian politics still meant a rivalry between the Ottoman and the Mamluk holdouts, not to mention the Egyptian peasantry. The March 1811 massacre of Mamluks in the Cairo citadel was one of the most bloody of these showdowns. There was time for one last burst of Ottoman glory with the reign of Muhammad Ali Pasha (1805–1849); while back in Libya, the Karamanli dynasty of Tripoli carried on until 1835, when it officially became an Ottoman *vilayet* (state or province) of Turkey until 1911–1912. The territory covered the coast and the immediate hinterlands of Benghazi, Barca, Jebel Akhdar, and Tripoli, but only slightly into the Fezzan. Southern Libya was virtually an ungoverned territory, penetrated from the east by Egypt and the *viyalet* pushed west into what is today's modern Tunisia.

THE BARBARY PIRATES, TRIPOLI, AND THE UNITED STATES

Tribute was the marketing tool; credibility was the ulterior motive. The fledgling United States faced its first unfamiliar threat since becoming an independent nation. Their previous foes had played by traditional rules with traditional weapons, tactics, uniforms, leadership, and objectives. The outcomes were predictable. Each side amassed their forces in long, majestic lines, shoulder to shoulder, with one ball in the barrel and a long, sharpened bayonet affixed to the end. The forces closed to within 100 yards, whereby they commenced to fire their single shot, followed by bayonet charges and close-in fighting. The casualties were heavy, the battlefield littered with carnage; all very "doctrinal" for the day. North Africa's contesting Barbary States and their warring appendages didn't have that playbook. They wanted something very novel for this period: money. Along with money, they also sought the credibility of being considered power brokers throughout the Mediterranean region, stemming from centuries of success in Spain with the Moors dominating (Buckingham), and becoming the gatekeepers for commercial activity passing to, and from, Asia to the rest of the "civilized" world. It didn't hurt any that the European powers considered the Barbary States and their corsairs to be "proxies" throughout the Mediterranean for keeping each other's fleets on edge and pocketbooks continually opened (Heritage-history).

This proxy war mentality would be repeated in the twentieth century, and some would argue that the Libyan Civil War was a form of proxy war as multiple objectives were sought: an end to Gaddafi's rule; consolidation of rule under one of the several Islamic religious orders present in Libya; and an economic variation as many of the supporting nations rolled out their newest weaponry to demonstrate the capabilities so that nations looking to upgrade their military forces could see these assets "in action."

What would be considered "decimal dust" by today's financial standards was hardly insignificant in the final three decades of the eighteenth century. With a war-driven debt approaching $10 million, the prospect of paying off a shadowy enemy, existing in a far-off land that did not directly threaten any American borders, several hundred thousand dollars a year for the "privilege" of not having their merchant ships captured was considered intolerable.

Initially, the United States dismissed this new threat, as its interests had not been directly impacted. The Barbary States were habitually capturing, ransoming, and returning all manner of European ships. Yet, they hadn't picked on the newest nation in the land. In October 1784, this too would change. The *Betsey* wasn't an unusually large or important merchant ship, just the first under the new United States, to be taken. After nine months for some of her crew, they would be released (Singer). The precedent was that an American ship, versus a colony ship, had been taken. This raised the stakes.

While President Washington agreed with the Senate's desire to raise a navy, he also approved spending over $140,000 for tribute payments. What started out as falling in line with other nations would ultimately lead to a defiant stand by a nascent nation and produce a reputation for stubbornness that would last for another 200 years. Names from Bainbridge to O'Bannon, USS *Constitution* to USS *Philadelphia*, and Derna to Tripoli would forever forge the fabric of our ties to North Africa (Wheelan).

Tripoli's role in this melodrama stems from nothing more than the childish desire to possess what the big kids on the block have. In this case it was ships, money, and prestige. While Tripoli had been a role player throughout the duration of Mediterranean piracy, they hadn't been the main actor. That title went to Algiers. The Bashaw of Tripoli, Yusuf in this case, felt that needed to change. His target was the United States.

His motives were not completely unlike Muammar Gaddafi's; respect of his peers; prestige and power in his region, and the reputation as a power broker among his allies. Unlike Gaddafi, Yusuf Karamanli and the balance of his dynastic family would live to be overthrown and replaced by yet another ruling clan (Boddy-Evans).

SETTING THE STAGE FOR AMERICAN AND TRIPOLITANIAN CONFLICT

Rewinding the clock to 1784, we see that the *Betsey* was captured by the Dey of Morocco because the former had failed to send an official to the latter's nation, thereby serving to link Morocco as the first official recognizant of the United States, a title emotionally sought by the Dey of Morocco. The *Betsey* was his method of capturing the attention of the United States. The fact that he treated the crew more like visitors and ultimately released those who remained alive, for the paltry sum of $10,000, reflected a desire to be an equal versus a scavenger.

Early efforts by Thomas Jefferson and John Adams to negotiate with the Tripolitanian envoy to England, Ambassador Sidi Haji Abdrahaman, led to a tentative agreement, based upon the mandate from President Washington. Ambassador Abdrahaman was a shrewd diplomat and bargainer. He offered a "bargain" to enact a perpetual peace between the United States and Tripoli. This was rejected by the United States on the grounds that not only would the peace be anything but perpetual, the cost of buying peace would not be a final solution, but merely delay the inevitable: confrontation (Wheelan).

With Yusuf Karamanli's ascendance to the throne in Tripoli, and a shift in philosophies within the American presidency—from war-weary George Washington, to the penultimate diplomat John Adams, to the iconoclastic Thomas Jefferson—the cast of characters for this chapter in American-Tripolitanian (Libyan), history was set (Boddy-Evans).

The time-honored tradition, in this era, of the North African Dey's chopping down the flagpole that hoisted the National Ensign of the Ambassador, in this case the United States, resulted in a response he was not fully prepared to meet. President Jefferson made the deliberate, and unvetted by Congress, decision to send a naval squadron into the Mediterranean. He was calling Yusuf's bluff and putting an end to this incessant game of tribute and release.

THE U.S. NAVY ENTERS THE MEDITERRANEAN

Three squadrons would eventually venture into the contested waters butting up against Algiers, Tunis, and Tripoli, and two of them would return home with little to show for their efforts. Chiefly this lay in the lack of aggressiveness by the squadron commanders, commodores whose passion for action had long ago ended, yet because of their seniority within the fledgling navy, mandated they be given command.

Small victories did occur under these first two forays; Lt. Stephen Decatur, a name that would repeatedly surface for gallant action, led the USS *Enterprise* against an Algerian Corsair, ironically, captained by an Irishman turned Muslim. He would also lead a raiding party to destroy the floundered USS *Philadelphia*, one of the largest ships of the line, after her unfortunate grounding while chasing a Tripolitan Corsair, in 1803. His actions resulted in the Tripolitanian Dey losing a large number of pirates, the loss of this valuable prize, both in ransom potential and political value, and yet another example of the pluck displayed by this new generation of naval officers (Boddy-Evans).

Realizing that a naval solution alone wouldn't resolve the ongoing feud with the Dey of Tripoli, the United States devised a plan whereby William Eaton would provide a blow from the east, into Tripolitania, for the express purpose of capturing enough territory to compel Yusuf Karamanli to sue for peace, or capitulate altogether. Eaton had just the resume for such an undertaking. He was a former Revolutionary War enlisted man who became an officer and served under Major General "Mad Anthony" Wayne, an early advocate for unconventional warfare, during the war with the Miami Indians in the Ohio Valley. Eaton was also a teacher and had served in the Vermont State House. Finally, he would rise to be the American consul to Tunis. A man passionate for learning, at ease with Islam as a culture and Arabic as a language, and with all the tools of influence, persuasion, and persistence, William Eaton was charged to put together an organization to go after Yusuf (Seitz, 2).

GENERAL EATON'S EXPEDITION TO DERNA

Despite an austere budget of $20,000, a force of only eight U.S. Marines, although ably led by First Lt. Pressley O'Bannon, and a mixture of tribesman and mercenaries, Eaton led an expedition that far surpassed expectation. Whether by the fact it actually succeeded or despite expending all of their funds, repeatedly running into internal demons of mutiny and hunger, or the vacillations of Hamet Karamanli, the brother to Yusuf and the true heir apparent to the reign, "General" Eaton led his party through Egypt and into lands that would see exponentially more devastation 135 years later, Northern Tripolitania (Libya).

PEACE IS, ALMOST, AT HAND

The attack on Derna, on April 27, 1805, caught Yusuf off guard. He hadn't anticipated a successful land-borne invasion, much less one partially led by his brother and a handful of forces; thus he wasn't prepared for the onslaught. General Eaton and his group were able to take Derna and then hold on for the inevitable counterattack by Yusuf's forces. When that attack happened, Eaton was fortunate enough to receive reinforcement from Commodore Isaac Hull and his ships just off the coast (Navy Department). This attack proved to be the final straw. Within months, the U.S. consul general for the Barbary area produced a treaty whereby the United States made a one-time $60,000 payment for the repatriation of the USS *Philadelphia* captives and agreed to not continue supporting Hamet Karamanli's right to the throne.

What should have been resolved in 1805 was, however, left open due to the lack of will on the part of the United States to impose a presence in the region until Tripolitania "got the message." At the time of the signing of the First Barbary War Treaty, relations between the United States and Great Britain were once again deteriorating. This led to the War of 1812 and a change in priorities by the United States. As a result of the United States removing its naval vessels from the Mediterranean Sea, the Barbary States resumed their pirating activities.

THE WAR FINALLY ENDS

Three years later, upon concluding the War of 1812, President Madison dispatched a squadron under the helm of Commodore Decatur, the same officer who had so frequently disrupted Algerian and Tripolitanian plans, to finally settle the matter with Tripoli. Facing three of the largest ships then plying the seven seas, the Dey of Tripoli, the very same Yusuf Karamanli, made a far more prudent decision to capitulate and accept the American terms for ending all tribute, for all time.

In the same manner that Muammar Gaddafi had repeatedly challenged the United States, whether by his known associations with terrorist organizations throughout the 1980s and 1990s or by his harboring the prosecutors of the Pan Am and UTA airliner explosions, the precedent had been established over 100 years prior for relations between the leadership of Libya (Tripolitania) and the United States to be contentious, at best.

The year 2011 would demonstrate the final scene from this long-running drama, when the United States led a coalition against Gaddafi in order to prevent him from killing his own people, and in turn setting the stage by the National Transitional Council and rebel forces, to end his rule. But we get ahead of ourselves. The year 1815 also put the United States on the map as they established an international reputation for determination and spunk, regardless of the size of enemy or motives. This reputation would continue until the present day.

MORE EUROPEANS ARRIVE

Under Ottoman authority, many explorers of the Sahara started from Tripoli and proceeded southward through the Fezzan. These included Henrich Barth in 1849–1855 whose route dog-legged sharply by starting east, then turned west and then due south to Sokoto in what became northern Nigeria. From there, he went upstream along the Niger River to finally reach Timbuktu. W. Oudney, D. Denham, and Clapperton took a route in 1822–1823 straight south from Tripoli to reach Lake Chad and Bornu.

Gustav Nachtigal, diplomat, doctor, ethnographer and geographer, starting in 1869, took a similar route sweeping slight further east to reach Lake Chad and then to explore the Tibesti range and back south, then turning eastward across the Sahel, then through Wadai and Darfur in 1874 (which was also under Turkish occupation), then on to Khartoum and back to Cairo. Egypt and Sudan were under Turkish rule until taken over by the British in 1882 and by the Sudanese Mahdi in 1885.

The Berlin Partition of Africa of 1884–1885 did not have great immediate effect in Libya since it was under Turkish control and the Turks were not invited, and much of southern Libya was under no one's control in any case. Through what became southern Libya also ran the east-west line that constitutes the northern limits of the "Arms and Spiritous Liquors Zone" that was installed by the Brussels Anti-Slavery Conference of 1899–1890. The zone was defined by 20 degrees north and 22 degrees south, but was so vast and unknown that it had no way to be enforced effectively.

It is clear that when the Ottomans tried to strengthen their rule on Libya, the local leaders lost incentive; and when the local leaders were more incentivized, the Ottomans ruling from Cairo or Istanbul lost their power. This dynamic was further complicated by foreign bids for territory or position in Libya. This ancient pattern holds to this day with well-founded Libyan suspicion of foreigners in general and from their neighbors to the east and west in particular. All of this, when trying to hold the tree piece of Libya into one commonly governed territory.

THE SANUSI PICK UP THE PIECES

For Libyans under the Karamanli dynasty or back under Ottoman authority and influence, it was reasonable to follow Sunni Islam, but also popular was Sufism, which was deeply rooted in Turkish dervish rituals of holy men and spirit possession. The growing perception and reality of steady European encroachment put the Muslim world into a state of intellectual and personal crisis. The wide-ranging Sufi *turuq* (brotherhoods) traditions found a need and gave a foundation for religious revitalization in the quest for restored Islamic order and human dignity.

So it was that the "Grand Sanusi" Muhammad bin Ali al-Sanusi (1787–1859) established his new politico-religious order, especially in northern Cyrenaica, but also trade networks deep into the Fezzan. In 1835, Tripoli, already under Ottoman authority, became an official Ottoman province as they struggled to hold on to their crumbling empire and fractious Karamanlis. The contests for regional and global power that were echoed in Libya from 1835 to 1884 created an environmental of such instability that an Islamic revivalist movement such as the Sanusi was broadly welcomed and perceived in the light of national salvation.

European intentions became utterly transparent in the Berlin Congress of 1884–1885, in which the major European powers, led by France, Britain, and Germany determined to partition the entire African continent for their own national interests. Italy, Spain, Portugal, and Belgium also bid for "their" smaller portions of Africa. One requirement of the multiple European bids for African territory was that these powers had to demonstrate "effective control." This meant invited and bloody wars of subjugation, "pacification," and colonial occupation across the continent. From the east, the (Anglo) Ottomans pushed onto Libya; from the west were the French pushing in from Tunisia; and by 1893, an agreement between Germany and Britain claimed Rabih's Bornu territory in the future Chad and Nigeria. The death of Muhammad 'Ali Pasha on August 2, 1849, started the long, slow decline of the Ottomans in Egypt, not to mention in Libya and Sudan.

The *khalifa* (successor) of the Grand Sanusi was his son Muhammad al-Mahdi (1844–1902), and once he reached maturity, organized a tactical retreat southward to a new regional Sanusi headquarters in Kufra in 1895 to form his *zawiya* (brotherhood lodge) where there was greater security, away from the Ottomans and other threatening foreigners. Gradually a strategic anti-imperialist alliance was being formed among the Sanusi followers of Libya and Chad, the Mahdists of Sudan, and the emerging nationalists of Egypt. Sanusi *zawiya* (lodges) grew in this context of the real fear of foreign ambitions. Muhammad Sharif of Wadai in Chad (ruled 1834–1858) was the first of these Sanusi followers.

On September 2, 1898, an Anglo-Egyptian army crushed the Mahdist state at the massacre of Karreri near the Mahdist capital of Omdurman, Sudan. Sultan 'Ali Dinar bin Zakariya fled to Darfur to claim the throne of Darfur. Steadily from then to 1901, the contenders for the throne of Darfur were eliminated. Meanwhile, the Sanusi was doing the same in southern Libya and Chad. In August 1899, Sayid Muhammad al Mahdi (of Cyrenaica, Libya) moved south from coast to interior at Qiru (Gouro) on the east side of the Tibesti highlands in northern Chad along with his sons Muhammad al-Rida and Muhammad Idris and sons of his late brother and Sanusi leader, Sayyid Muhamad al-Sharif. He was motivated to protect the *zawiya* and expand southward to Wadai and westward to

Lake Chad to trade, defend, and proselytize. It was strategically reasonable to ally with Sultan Ali Dinar to defend against local foreign aggression.

However, in an agreement between Britain and France, the French claimed lands east of Shari River and west of the Nile watershed, including Wadai but not Darfur that would be later claimed by Britain. At this time, the first Sanusi mission to Darfur took place, but so also, in 1900, did the Anglo-Egyptian spy Salih Jibril visit Darfur to report on Sultan Ali Dinar. Tensions mounted, when Adam Asil (grandson of Senusi Sultan Muhammad Sharif) fled to remote parts of Wadai, neighboring Darfur. On April 22, 1900, French forces converged and destroyed Rabih's state at Kousseri to establish a military colonial presence in that part of the Sahel. From April to June 1901, Tuareg (Teda and Kinin) sought refuge from French in Kanem in what became Nigeria. Pushing westward out of the Nile Valley in November 1901, Anglo-Egyptians blocked Ali Dinar in Kordofan and unilaterally told him he was a British client. He did not agree. Back in Libya in the same month, Ahmed al-Ghazali was driven from power by Dud Murra and Sanusis and Sayid al-Mahdi went to Gouro, but from November to January 1902, the French forces added the Sanusi outpost at Bir Alali. This dynamic period had plenty of African resistance, but the great military forces of the Europeans were ultimately going to swing the tide in their favor. And in January 1902, the Sanusi leader al-Mahdi died; but Kufra in eastern Libya was still reasserted as the regional trade and religious headquarters of the Sanusi *zawiya*, and in June, Ahmed al-Ghazali was captured, blinded, and executed. He was a rival to Dud Murra.

From 1902 to 1909, increased French military pressure incentivized the Sanusi to strengthen and rebuild ties with Darfur; but this was easier said than done with military and ecological pressures sometimes closing the regional trade routes in 1904. Under British pressures in 1905, the Kababish of northern Kordofan cut the famed "40-days road" from Darfur. However, the French and British sometimes became overstretched themselves, and in 1905 and 1906, trade ties between Sanusi Kufra and Al-Fasher in Darfur were restored all along 950 miles of long-distance camel routes, even thought it was still another 700 miles from Kufra to the Mediterranean Sea. This remote tactical retreat by Libyans and Furawi protected them from French and British aggression, but only for so long; and in 1906, the French expanded their military camel corps to prepare for further attacks. From 1907 to 1908, the French launched attacks against Sanusi *zawiya* posts, and thus Ali Dinar also felt the pressure and expressed solidarity with the Sanusis. If this were not enough, in 1908, a widespread drought brought further hardship to eastern Libya and western Sudan, in which a fragile and precarious environment is a recurrent problem in the best of times.

The struggles continued. In January 1909, the relief caravan of Muhamad Yunus left Kufra, and in the same month, Ali Dinar captured the Mahdist holdout at Kabkabiya after a 17-month siege. At this point, the Sanusi and Ali Dinar were drawn ever closer at least for tactical reasons, and both thought of the lingering Mahdist presence in Kabkabiya as essentially rebels opposed to Ali Dinar. By March 1909, the Sanusi caravan headed by its ambassador Abu Bakr al-Ghadamsi reached the Fur capital at Fasher. Whatever relief they provided was soon set back on June 2 when the French seized Abesher, the capital of adjacent Wadai. Its leader, Dud Murra, fled north to safer Sanusi areas to coalesce as much anti-French resistance as possible along with support from Ali Dinar. The clock was ticking as the Sanusi at Kufra tried to restores control at Al-Dor. Trade records from Darfur from November 1909 to August 1910 show that the main Darfur export was slaves to Sanusi posts and ivory to the Mediterranean, while arms, ammunition, and luxury goods were imported from the north all under royal monopolies.

Very active military and political contestation continued for all of 1910. Dud Murra (based in Kapka) and Ali Dinar mustered substantial combined forces to oppose the French, but were defeated. In equally turbulent February, the ruler of Dar Masalit invaded Dar Tama on the border to divert French, but the French retook Dar Tama returned a week later, then Ali Dinar's forces restored the original Dar Tama sultan a few days later. In April 1910, Salih Abu Karim fought along with Dud Murra and carried the struggle to Dar Maslait, still fighting with Ali Dinar against the French, but on April 19, Dud Murra was defeated and many refugees from Wadai refugees were welcomed in Darfur, as the French challenged rule of Ali Dinar. However, it did not take long before these refugees were perceived to destabilize Ali Dinar. Meanwhile, the French, struggling for legitimacy, appointed a puppet sultan for Dar Tama at Abesher.

This seemingly endless back-and-forth carried on into 1911, when the Sanusi reclaimed control of al-Dor and restored trade to Darfur and Darmasalit; but by May, the French invaded Ennedi and seized Beskere. Realizing the urgency of the situation, the leader of Darfur sent a large shipment of ivory to get 10,000 rounds of ammunition from Kufra and exhorted the Senusi to "make it fast!" But on September 3, the Senusi statesman Ahmed al-Rifi, former companion of the Great Sanusi, passed away just as a critical time was fast approaching.

THE ITALIANS ARRIVE ... AND A COMPLICATED SITUATION BECOMES MORE SO

On September 29, 1911, Italy declared war on the Ottomans in general and Libya specifically to make it a colony, imagining the great ancient days of Roman North Africa, the new Roman "Fourth Shore." Right away, in October, the neo-imperial Italians seized Tripoli, Benghazi, Derna, and Tobruk. At least by December, this alarming news reached the Senusi in Kufra. In a mixture of amazement and contempt for the intrusive, non-Muslim Italians, a part of eastern Cyrenaica (near Siwa) was ceded to Anglo-Egyptians in tactical hopes of blocking the Italians. In 1912, Darfur traded still more ivory to acquire ammunition to fight the Italians, but by October, an Italo-Turkish peace treaty was signed as the Ottomans knew that was about the best they could do to salvage their diminishing position. At least the Senusi and Ottoman were briefly united in common resistance to the grand Italian plans.

Foreign aggression was enough of a problem, but the great regional famine of 1913 only made Darfur and the Senusi even more vulnerable. The ambush by French military forces of a food caravan heading west to Tibesti only aggravated a precarious situation. And now the weakened Sanusi now had to fight the Italians along the coast, fighting alone without the Turks. In November, the French forces defeat Sanusi fighters at Ayn Kalakla, and by December 14, the French military entered Gouro. In August, the Italians had already penetrated into the Fezzan south from Sirte, on the coast. By December, the Italians reached Brak, while the British started to strategize about the outright annexation of Darfur.

These military and political events across the Sahel in 1913 became dwarfed in 1914 with the outbreak of World War I in European theaters. The Turks in Egypt had steadily withered to British puppet status, being effectively replaced by the British who would eventually clash with Italians. However, the Italians plugged on to the best of their ability. On March 3, Italian colonel Miani's troops reached Murzuq in Fezzan, but further east, the Sanusi still controlled trade to Kufra from northern of Chad. Libyans had not given up the fight in Sirte, and on July 7, eight Italians were killed in Sirte.

At the end of the summer, on August 26, there were more acts of Libyan resistance, and Colonel Miani found himself isolated and overextended to the south, barely making it back to Tripoli. This helped to reenergize the Sanusi forces that could celebrate a badly needed set of victories.

Back in Darfur, Sultan Ali Dinar was gravely worried about getting badly needed arms and ammunition that, in fact, never got delivered. The British were denounced as they were perceived as a steadily increasing threat from the Nile Valley, while the Senusi were threatened by Italians ambitions. This was the moment for Ali Dinar to restore ties to Kufra. After all, Miani had been substantially pushed out of Fezzan with Ali Dinar's weapons.

In 1915–1916, the British occupied the former Ottoman ports in Cyrenaica with a tactical alliance with the local Senusi in order to block the Italians. British intelligence reported that Abu Bakr Ghadamsi was still in Darfur as a Sanusi "commercial agent." Certainly, by this time,

Ali Dinar knew that the British planned to attack and annex Darfur, and in April, he denounced his relationship with Anglo-Egyptian Khartoum. By July, the Anglo-Egyptians made military plans to annex Darfur by force. The Sanusis needed the British to block the Italian threats, while the Furawis needed the Sanusis to fight the threats of the British. Clearly, the torque of this dilemma was not going to be stable or secure; it was indeed a tactical part of the imperial machinations of the application of the age-old principle of divide and rule. In now increasing desperation, in July, Ali Dinar sent his royal caravan to Kufra with 30 military slaves, 100 soldiers, and 200 camels to get arms. British spies in Khartoum were alerted and caused this critical logistics support to return without all the ammunition they sought. Only 30 of the 200 camels got back. Relief forces were also sent to relieve the unfortunate mission as was reported by spies. With some propaganda objective in mind, Ali Dinar exaggerated the number of rifles and rounds as he returned to his palace in al-Fasher.

As 1916 unfolded, on January 29, Ali Dinar congratulated Sanusi on their military successes but appealed again for more ammunition as his intelligence agents reported Anglo-Egyptians would soon be on their way. In March, Anglo-Egyptian forces began their systematic invasion of Darfur, and by May 23, these invasion forces reached al-Fasher. The Darfur sultanate was officially conquered. Sultan 'Ali Dinar and his followers fought on for a few months, but by November 5, Ali Dinar was hunted down and killed.

Far to the north, Cyrenaica became a vast Italian concentration camp with especially brutal methods to suppress the Senusi and other Libyans and terminate the Ottoman rule by 1920. At great human cost in Libyan lives and the first military application of air power by Italians, there was renewed aggression against Libya after World War I, when Mussolini attacked Tripolitania to implant colonial rule.

On the other hand, the Grand Sanusi moved to relative security over the border in Egypt and launched the famed Jebel Akhdar resistance (1923–1932) in Cyrenaica. Thus also was born the first modern national Libyan hero, Sheikh Omar Mukhtar. In 1925, Turkey became a republic as a further historical step away from the imperial glories of the Ottoman era, so now it was Libyans against the Italian invaders and the British against the Italians in colonial rivalry.

In 1929, the Italian fascists advanced into Fezzan with motorized armored columns. In desperation the Sanusi leader Muhamad 'Abid wrote to Muhammad Bahr al-Din, pretender to the throne of Darfur for grain and sheep supplies. Unfortunately, the prince turned the letter over to the British, who then occupied the Fasher palace. The Senusi-Darfur alliance card had already been played out in 1916. Kufra fell to the Italians on January 20, 1931. Shortly later, the heroic guerilla leader Mukhtar was captured, court-martialed, and hanged in public. Musolini's plan for

"Fourth Shore" of the new Roman Empire was complete by 1932, but not for long. In 1937, a Tunisia-to-Egypt highway was completed by the Italians. In due course, this road would prove handy for the British and Germans. By 1940, 110,000 Italians settlers cultivated 495,000 acres of captured Libyan lands.

WORLD WAR II: LEAD-IN TO THE NORTH AFRICAN CAMPAIGN

To the naked eye, Libya's vast northern shelf resembles a canvas without paint; a barren, broad, and inviting expanse. To the trained military observer, northern Libya is the penultimate arena for mobile combat. History has demonstrated the facility with which invading armies could run rampant across the Libyan Plain; French, Italians, and then Germans. Italy had left the most indelible fingerprint through its occupation of strategic portions of eastern Africa, Eritrea, and parts of Somalia. Libya held the inauspicious title of having been part of the ancient Roman Empire; a region Benito Mussolini, Dictator of Italy, sought to regain.

Strategically, Libya under Ottoman rule had precedent for being invaded. In the early 1800s, its pirating ships had bloodied the nose of the nascent U.S. naval fleet, capturing the frigate *Philadelphia* and incurring the wrath of a fledgling U.S. Navy and Marine Corps. Blackmail was the rationale, delicately titled "Tribute" during that time. Fee for safe passage was the price of transiting the Mediterranean Sea to engage in trade throughout the region and to allow nations the opportunity of conducting overland travel into the Red Sea via the land bridge that would become the Suez Canal in a matter of decades.

Libya's strategic location as a mid-Mediterranean choke point just south of Crete, Malta, Sicily, and southern Italy all added to the lore of seeking to control at least Libya's northern portions. By 1939, Italy had attempted to do just that, while dreaming of reconstituting the ancient North African Roman Empire. Great Britain, already engaged heavily in repelling German advances in Western Europe, fighting to keep the French from capitulating, and frantically searching for help from any corner to include the United States, was concerned that an additional strike in North Africa would force a two-front war that it couldn't afford.

FORCES AND COMMANDERS: BRITISH, GERMAN, AND ITALIAN

Prior to the start of the war, Britain had a small Middle Eastern/North African force, roughly 50,000 soldiers, a handful of tanks, and a mixture of thin-skinned World War I–era biplanes and a few modern versions, to patrol the entire Arabian Peninsula and Eastern Africa (Barnett, 21). This force, under General Sir Archibald Wavell, was called into action to stem the Italian tide of occupation and retain free access by Great Britain and her allies to the tiny island nation of Malta. In the ensuing three years, names such as O'Connor, Auchinleck, Ritchie, Alexander, Montgomery, Rommel, and Graziani would gain lasting fame, or infamy; yet all would play a crucial role in the ebb and flow of conflict for a stretch of land, about 1,575 kilometers in length, encompassing three vital port cities, Benghazi, Tripoli, and Tobruk, and casting Libya onto the world's center stage.

The weapons and tactics of this newly emerging war were reminiscent of the previous world war: massed formations of infantry, attacking along large and wide fronts; tanks operating independently as the jousters of new; airplanes providing reconnaissance and close air support, while focusing much of their energy on the aerial ballet of air-to-air combat. Co-ordination of these three entities was amateur at best, catastrophic at worst. Few commanders during the interwar years had made any effort at studying the capabilities, limitations, and options for employing these three vehicles of destruction in any coherent team. Two who had broken the mold of nineteenth-century thinking on this matter were General Sir Richard O'Connor and Field Marshal Erwin Rommel. Both had devoted time in the 1930s, either through self-study or assignment, to studying the art and science of employing combined arms; the incorporation of tanks to lead or support an attack of infantry, with airplanes to serve as aerial cover; interdiction of ground forces; and, more critically, to destroy ensuing supply lines, the lifeblood of any combat force. The opportunity for these two practitioners of modern warfare to engage on the same field would never come to fruition, for General O'Connor would be cap-tured just weeks before Field Marshal Rommel would take the field (Mitcham, 87).

Military engagements throughout history have always contained an Achilles heel. Napoleon's supreme confidence that he would prevail in Russia and again at Waterloo; Lord Cardigan's belief in the cavalry charge against artillery at Balaclava; The Zulus' belief in their tried-and-true tac-tic of placing the enemy in "the horns of a dilemma" by attacking from two corners, thus forcing a peer adversary to focus on one or the other charge. Against British repeating rifles and disciplined fire at Roarke's Drift, they met their match and left nearly 4,000 dead; American fixed coastal artillery batteries against a mobile and multipronged Japanese assault. To such arrogance must be added the failed logic of German high command in resourcing and sustaining the Afrika Korps.

Repeatedly, the German forces, with glimpses of success from their Italian allies, overmatched British firepower and resources by using the same Blitzkrieg tactics that had served the Third Reich so well throughout

Western Europe in the early years of World War II. Yet, the Afrika Korps had to battle a second enemy: supply. Their nearest safe port for offloading and moving supplies, men and machines, was Benghazi, which was over 800 kilometers from their furthest eastern advance into Egypt. The only serviceable, paved road was the Via Balbo. Along this single lifeline, Rommel had to depend on his convoys to safely get through with the thousands of gallons of fuel, millions of rounds of ammunition, and thousands of pounds of rations (Mitcham, 67).

Muammar Gaddafi discovered the same challenge of having the materiel but not the means of moving it to point of need. Yet in the case of Field Marshal Rommel, the flaw in the plan lay on two plains. First was the belief by Adolf Hitler's leadership that Africa was a secondary theater that could be easily vanquished with the few men and machines on hand. Second was the fact that the Axis powers didn't control either the sea or air lanes throughout the Mediterranean and over Libya. This produced an untenable situation as the flow of replenishment never matched the output in fuel, food, ammunition, and broken parts. The result was repeated retreats and pauses just when Rommel had the Allied forces on their heels. Thus, a back-and-forth ebb and flow of action and counteraction occurred throughout the three-year campaign.

Great Britain faced the specter of losing her independence as well as her dominion throughout much of 1939–1942. The loss of France as a fighting ally, the collapse of the entire Western Front, the repeated bombings of London and outlying towns in preparation for an amphibious invasion, the neutrality of Spain and Turkey, and the creeping wave of uncertainty facing Greece's independence, all led Prime Minister Winston Churchill to seek one pillar of strength upon which to bolster Great Britain's hopes. That pillar was North Africa.

TACTICAL VICTORIES, STRATEGIC DEFEATS: BATTLES AND POLITICS, 1940–1941

General Sir Archibald Wavell, Commanding General of the Middle East and the Western Desert Force, controlled a force of about 50,000 infantry, tankers, and armored car cavalry. This force covered was arrayed south to Kenya, east to Iraq, north to Greece and west to Freetown, Sierra Leone. Confronting his force was just under 500,000 Italian infantry, armor, and airmen.

A supreme strategist, General Wavell and General O'Connor had conceived of a six-day plan to push the Italian forces out of Egypt and at least toward Tobruk. What ensued was a six-week campaign that drove the Italian army west and south, past Benghazi and to within 350 or so miles of Tripoli, the last harbor available to replenish Italian losses (Churchill, 483). Tens of thousands of Italian officers and soldiers found their war to be concluded.

General Wavell's singular flaw in the plan was that he didn't forcefully communicate General O'Connor's "game plan" to Churchill until he'd been pressed by the Prime Minister to either act or be prepared to release his forces for duty in Greece much earlier than previously scheduled. This latency in reporting would come back to haunt General Wavell as the delay in reporting would create the time necessary for Churchill's staff to fully develop and push their plan for supporting Greece, to the Grecian Prime Minister. This five-day campaign that became six weeks would have started earlier and been allowed to carry on to Tripoli. But that's for the revisionists to decide. History proved otherwise.

Strategically, this victory had far greater political implications than military results. From the Prime Minister's vantage point, a striking blow to Italy, in her "new Rome," would demonstrate to Turkey, Vichy France, and other nations riding the fence of Great Britain's ability and resolve, especially when the landscape of battle was not in their own geographical backyard (Mitcham, 102).

As a result of preexisting arrangements between Great Britain and Greece, which stated the former would consider any attack upon the latter as an attack on themselves, Churchill denied General Wavell's request to retain the forces slated for Grecian duty, thus ending General O'Connor's impromptu campaign to drive the Italians all the way back to Tripoli. While history can't replay and carry to fruition what might have been certainty reigns that allowing the door of Axis opportunity to remain open provided for the introduction of Field Marshal Rommel's Afrika Korps and a continuation of the North African campaign for two years. The forces sent to Greece were some of the most highly trained and cohesive given their months of continuous battle in arduous conditions. What remained behind were predominantly forces from other portions of Africa and forces new to the continent and without the unforgiving proving ground of combat.

Throughout the balance of the campaign, the Halfaya Pass would play a pivotal role. Its relative ease of passage served as an early "superhighway" for both sides and yet also provided a bottleneck from which many graves would attest to the vicious nature of seeking its possession. The pass also served as the highest observation point to the highway, offering tactical reconnaissance and ambush potential that would repeat itself frequently in two bitter years of fighting.

From 1940 and early into 1941, the initiative was with the British. Despite being outgunned, outmanned, and out-planed, they had better training, discipline, and esprit, which resulted in repeated success against numerically superior Italian forces. Partly owing to distance and partly to the battlefield commander's prerogative, General Wavell didn't always communicate battle plans as quickly as Churchill would have preferred. The outcome of this was an overlapping of plans under the auspices of propping up the Balkans before the Germans arrived in force.

Despite repeated warnings by General Wavell as to the deleterious impact of decapitating the fighting strength of North Africa in order to attempt a statistically risky defense of Greece, the Prime Minister chose the political alliance over the operational victory. The result was the loss of Greece, the loss of initiative in North Africa, and another two years of fighting against Italian and then the Germans.

Unlike Marshal Graziani of Italy, Field Marshal Rommel was an opportunist. Bred in the same mold as General O'Connor, Rommel took every advantage and stretched his lines as far as they could tender without breaking. On occasion he broke them, but not before a decisive victory over the wavering allied force. Throughout Rommel's service in North Africa, he continued to look for the quick and decisive victory, wherever it presented itself. Partly, this tactic was driven by his intellectual makeup; decisive, direct, and determined. Partly, it was related to his knowledge that his supply lines were stretched far beyond what was reasonable or sustainable. Given his need for roughly 25 thousand tons a month, he was receiving barely one third of that, thus his efforts to sustain any form of offensive were stymied by an inadequate logistics network" (Liddell-Hart, 267). Cumulatively, this produced an inability to sustain attacks and forced upon him the objectives of driving toward relatively obvious locations—Benghazi, Tobruk, Sollum, and El Alamein.

Within a month of his arrival, Rommel had the Afrika Korps on the offensive and seeking to retake the losses imposed upon the Italian forces. The counter blow started at El Aghelia and would drive one army, two corps commanders, and thousands of soldiers over a thousand miles back east, past where they'd started, and require a stand or fight engagement at a place called El Alamein. But that's two years from now.

Rommel's aggressive nature and inability to idly watch the Allied forces rebuild and train up their newly arrived forces in North Africa led to bold strikes along many avenues within northern Libya and into Egypt. This tendency to strike and consider the ramifications on his forces would be repeated throughout the course of the ensuing two years. For now, he could get away with bold dashes. The losses in men and materiel hadn't begun to acutely affect his ability to sustain operations. His actions sent a very strong signal to 10 Downing Street, Prime Minister Churchill's home and command post, to compel Generals Wavell and O'Connor to act immediately.

Reluctant adherence to the Prime Minister's recurring proddings for action would prove to be General Wavell's undoing. Two quick strike battles, Operations Brevity and Battleaxe, could well have driven a stake into the heart of the axis. Yet, fate would not favor the allied effort. Brevity, a May 1941 effort, was an attempt to relieve pressure on Tobruk and push back German and Italian forces from Fort Capuzzo and Sollum as a means of recapturing lost ground and creating a salient from which the greater operation, Battleaxe, could begin, which would be the penultimate tank encounter and finally force all Axis forces out of Libya, thus ending the North African campaign. Or so was the plan (Barnett, 65).

To add to an already dire situation, General Wavell's most effective battlefield commander, General O'Connor, was no longer available to execute either operation. He had been captured in April while on a battlefield circulation to advise his replacement. During a lightning strike by the newly arrived Field Marshal Rommel and his forces, General O'Connor and his replacement were both captured by German forces. O'Connor wouldn't surface for two years, when he had successfully escaped from an Italian prisoner of war camp (Churchill, 308).

What should have been a period of refit and retraining, following Great Britain's push to replace the losses from a year of campaigning, turned into an abortive raid on Fort Capuzzo that further diminished the untrained and untested allied men and materiel.

Following the setback in Brevity, General Wavell launched Battleaxe in June 1941. This was to be his shining moment and crescendo for victory in North Africa. What they held in quantity, either of manpower or modern tanks, they lacked in familiarity of tactics and of equipment.

While Rommel was practicing the technique of combined arms, in which tanks and artillery support infantry and move in concert with them, the Allies practiced mass; namely, they matched infantry against infantry and tank against tank. The Allies, suffering from the loss of O'Connor, a rare practitioner of combined arms tactics in the British army, had generals wedded to the last century's mode of fighting in which cavalry (tanks) were sent alone to charge and disrupt. This, unfortunately, opened them up to being taken out one by one as they were the focus of attention by enemy gunners. Gaddafi would practice this same technique to a certain extent, in 2011, as he employed his forces piecemeal to counter a coherent and vicious assault by the rebels and NATO members. The results would also be the same.

By the time Operation Battleaxe had concluded, just two days after it had begun, the die had been cast. Churchill had his justification and Wavell received his walking papers. Churchill stated that Wavell tried his best; but the handling machine at his disposal was too weak to enable him to cope with . . . four or five simultaneous campaigns . . ." (Barnett, 77).

CHURCHILL TRIES TO CHANGE BRITAIN'S LUCK

Replacing General Wavell was General Sir Claude Auchinleck, a man every bit the brilliant strategist and cut of the same cloth as General Wavell. Both were veterans of the entrenchment campaigns of World War I. Both had seen and personally felt the impact of throwing away forces on tactically unsound attrition style massed warfare. General

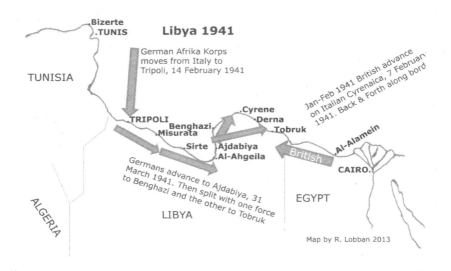

Map of Libya, 1941

Auchinleck brought more of an aggressive approach to the campaign as he benefited from the infrastructure and force increase planning that General Wavell had conducted for the previous four years, while the latter was Commander in Chief of Middle East forces, to include Africa.

His first operation as Commander in Chief was Operation Crusader, a multipronged effort to push Field Marshal Rommel's forces back from Tobruk and to also capture the strategic hub of Sidi Rezegh. The operation would not begin until November 1941, as events throughout the Pacific and in Eastern Europe were capturing a greater quantity of space in the daily news. Crusader was to be Auchinleck's first opportunity to relive the garrison holding Tobruk, and to once again open up the Halfaya Pass to Allied eyes and transit.

Much of the drive by Churchill to compel General Auchinleck to launch Crusader lay in the political realm. Spain was riding the fence of support for either Allied or Axis forces. Churchill fervently believed that an Allied victory in Crusader would ensure Spain's throwing in her lot with the Allies, at least from the standpoint of not allowing occupation by German forces. This would open up Gibraltar as a safe vantage point from which Allied forces could flow into and out of the Mediterranean Sea.

Crusader would capture critical airfields at Sidi Rezegh and El Adem, allowing for the garrison in Tobruk to finally be extricated from that "Alamo" of the desert. Additionally, it would finally weaken yet another pyrrhic dream, the Afrika Korps, to the point of capitulation. The Allies had the technical advantage in terms of armor and air supremacy.

They had recently acquired some of the newer American-made Stuart tanks, which sported a high-powered cannon and were extremely reliable and relatively fast. What had started as a focused strike to relieve Tobruk turned into a violent back-and-forth clash among titans, ultimately resulting in an Allied victory over the German/Italian force and driving them back to Agadabia. The Allies reoccupied Benghazi, and Tobruk was relieved for the moment.

Rommel's greatest mistake during Crusader had been to underestimate his enemy. He didn't accept that the Allies were launching an all-out offensive and therefore he was slow to respond with counterattacking forces. Despite being on his heels, he successfully fought and counter-fought for nearly two months until he was forced to withdraw. Round one to Auchinleck. This would be his finest moment, for the glide slope of 1942 would reverse his fortunes.

The first six months of 1942 would highlight Field Marshal Rommel's efforts to push the Allies back to Cairo. Their primary strike was west of Tobruk at a little town called Gazala. Along with strikes into Gazala, the Axis forces cut south of Tobruk and engaged multiple Allied divisions in a rolling series of tank and infantry encounters; both sides inflicted tremendous damage on the other, but at the end of the day, Rommel and his forces had broken the Allied line and drove them, pell-mell, and east to the Alamein Line. The most significant achievement by Rommel's forces was the capture of Tobruk and the remaining Allied garrison. He would now have the responsibility for holding this critical port city as the Allies would do unto him as he had done unto them: lay siege to the town. Concurrently, had Rommel the supply and personnel reserves to prosecute further action, he may well have ended the Allied hold on North and East Africa, significantly imperiling the looming offensive by a nascent American-led force into northwest Africa. But that's a story for a different volume (Paterson, 6).

What has become known throughout history as Field Marshal Bernard Montgomery's finest victory, the Battle of El Alamein, was delivered, in no small part, thanks to the preparations by General Auchinleck; the tactical tunnel vision of Field Marshal Rommel; the overwhelming superiority in resupply afforded the allies; the complete indifference and begrudging logistical support provided to the Afrika Korps; and time.

Rommel had felt that victory lay in seizing the Suez Canal by holding Egypt. Given the materiel that he had to use, the recent victory that had plunged the Allied force into headfirst retreat, and the knowledge that he had what he had, and no more, with which to prosecute action, he wisely chose to follow victory with effort. His forces attacked the heels of the Allies along the El Alamein Line in July 1942. To the Allies' credit they had prepared the El Alamein line as a solid defensive high-water mark; coordinated minefields with channeling to drive enemy forces into

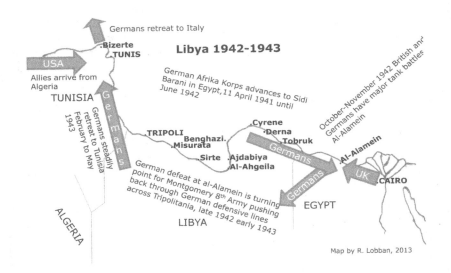

Germans retreat to Italy

Libya 1942-1943

USA

Allies arrive from
Algeria

TUNISIA

Bizerte
TUNIS

German Afrika Korps advances to Sidi
Barani in Egypt, 11 April 1941 until
June 1942

Germans steadily
retreat to Tunisia
February to May
1943

Germans retreat to Tunisia February to May

TRIPOLI
Benghazi.
Misurata

.Cyrene
.Derna
Tobruk

Sirte .Ajdabiya
Al-Ahgeila

German defeat at al-Alamein is turning
point for Montgomery 8th Army pushing
back through German defensive lines
across Tripolitania, late 1942 early 1943

LIBYA

October-November 1942 British and
Germans have major tank battles
Al-Alamein

Al-Alamein

UK

CAIRO

EGYPT

ALGERIA

Map by R. Lobban, 2013

Map of Libya, 1942–43

killing grounds provided for a significantly reduced manning posture to defend this line. Such a force savings would allow for rest and refit of Allied forces while the Axis expended themselves fighting through the few open channels and trying to defeat the minefields. Geography also made a significant appearance, as the Mediterranean Sea blocked a northern end run, and the Qattara Depression, a massive sea of soft, undulating sand, enveloped the southern flank. Thus an invader had a relatively narrow avenue of approach from which to launch an attack (Paterson, 8).

After several days of furious assaults and expert handling of allied forces by General Auchinleck himself, Rommel was forced to call off the attack and conduct a withdrawal so that he could refit and rest what few forces he still had available (Rommel, 248).

ENTER "MONTY": GENERAL BERNARD MONTGOMERY, "VICTOR OF ALAMEIN"

Despite this tactical victory by General Auchinleck, Prime Minister Churchill had already decided to replace the top leadership in the Eighth Army. He selected General Harold Alexander to take Auchinleck's spot and General Bernard Montgomery to command the field army (Barnett, 246).

Success is not always measured purely in wins versus losses. At times, victory is perception. In the case of General Auchinleck, the perception had become that while he was a fabulous planner and leader, his judgment of junior commanders was less than ideal. He had a self-confessed flaw of believing in the abilities of subordinates he selected even when they demonstrated less than appropriate skill for the position. He would protect and guide whenever possible, at times to the detriment of the action. This was born out as General Ritchie, General Cunningham's replacement who had replaced General O'Connor, proved incapable of effectively moving the Western Desert Force around the field and anticipating moves and countermoves by Rommel. While Ritchie was habitually positive and a tremendous motivator to his forces, he retained some of the late nineteenth-century stratagems on employing forces. Additionally, he was a relatively junior general who hadn't experienced large scale combat involving many different forces of varying degrees of skill and weaponry. This all combined to lead to the rout by Rommel in the spring of 1942 and cause Auchinleck to relieve Ritchie.

What Prime Minister Churchill saw from London was a command becoming punch drunk. He felt, as did his general staff, that change was necessary so that they could retain a foothold in North Africa, as they were repeatedly being evicted from battle positions throughout the Western Pacific by the onslaught of Japanese forces.

General Alexander was a stolid man, not prone to significant emotion or rash action. He was patient, political, and calculating. To his calm was the counter of General Montgomery. "Monty," as he became known in legend, was a firebrand. He was a supreme motivator and organizer. In many ways he was a reborn General McClellan of Civil War fame, the one great distinction being that he in fact would act with his forces, rather than continually seeking to amass and train.

General Montgomery was also a terrific "personality." Whether self-promoting or looking for opportunities to shine, he loved the spotlight and relished the attention (Barnett, 250). The victor of El Alamein was a brilliant planner who capitalized on the successes and buildup of his predecessors and the British government. Additionally, he had the advantage of persistent supply lines that by mid-1942 had completely dried up for Field Marshal Rommel. Montgomery infused a renewed sense of purpose into the Allied army. Over the course of the next year, he would embody the finest traits of a planner, organizer, and cheerleader to push through to final victory in North Africa and necessitate the capitulation of Rommel's forces.

Credit for the early victory over Rommel at Alam Halfa, in August 1942, must be shared with General Auchinleck, as he had been working with his staff for months on preparations, both in training of new men to new equipment and in new staffs to the area of operations so that they were integrated militarily, understood the operational situation in this part of the desert, and the command-and-control piece had been refined. Such comprehensive coordination of plan, people, and equipment would elude

Gaddafi 69 years later and lead to continuously disjointed and wasteful holding or rear guard actions.

Such wasn't the case in 1942. Alam Halfa exhausted Field Marshal Rommel's Afrika Korps. While they weren't militarily defeated, they were logistically defeated. Rommel had simply outrun the meager supply lines the German and Italian war ministries were able to sustain. Montgomery's ability to incorporate and refine existing plans along with the newly introduced weaponry of war allowed for him the opportunity to wear out Rommel and begin what would be the final westward push of the Afrika Korps off of the North African plain.

In October 1942, the legend of Field Marshal Montgomery would be fully born. The final assault on El Alamein was launched and so with it, was his immortality. Having trained and resupplied over the intervening seven weeks, the Allied forces had every advantage of Rommel; they were healthy in supplies, weaponry, air power, intelligence, and leadership. Conversely, the Axis forces were depleted by a dried-up 1,000-mile supply line; Rommel was exceedingly ill from two years of constant campaigning and nutritional deprivation; their airpower was eliminated as an effective force by the Royal Air Force, and they were trying to hold a position that was ultimately untenable. Over a weeks' hard fighting, Rommel's forces were reduced to a mere handful of effective armor, 30, and 100 or so Italian tanks, compared to the 600-plus tanks in Allied hands.

What ensued was a race for victory versus a race for survival. Defeat was only a matter of time as the allied invasion of northwest Africa, Operation Torch (Paterson, 1942, 19) had commenced, and Rommel found himself in the eye of a needle. On January 23, 1942, forces under Field Marshal Montgomery attacked Tripoli, completing the journey requested and yet denied by Prime Minister Churchill to General O'Connor back in February 1941. The force in 1941 was a dispirited and ill-equipped Italian army. The force in 1943 employed the most modern equipment and some of the most highly trained and experienced fighters the German army would ever produce. They had lived, fought, and died for two years on that rolling battleground of North Africa. By May 1943, all hostilities had ceased; the Afrika Korps was no more; and the generals commanding would descend upon new venues to continue, or ultimately in Rommel's case, to relinquish, their hold on history.

A CHALLENGING ENVIRONMENT FOR WAR: PRESAGING 2011

World War II in North Africa, specifically Libya, is one of the more interesting studies in military and political analysis. Infrastructure was virtually nonexistent. One road, the Via Balbo, ran border to border.

Airfields were packed sand with burning oil cans for identifying at night. Tripoli, Benghazi, and Tobruk represented the strategic hubs as the chief means for transport due to their ports. The local population wasn't "Libyan" per se; they were Cyrenaicans, Tripolitanians, and Fezzans. They fought amongst themselves and later on against the Italians. They didn't have an identity beyond their community, thus the "Nations" for which wars often are fought to preserve or claim didn't truly apply to this first modern Libyan landscape.

Libya offered unparalleled access to massive force on force tank battles, infantry charges, and aerial bombings. Fear of destroying civilian population centers was statistically insignificant compared to the fighting in Europe. Only the island-hopping campaign of the Pacific War would have equal in terms of raw combat without the same concern for civilian causalities.

Aside from infrequent instances in which local tribes would clean up the battlefield of clothing, food, fuel, and small arms, the engagements of 1940–1943 were fought on their grounds but not by them, for them, or to defend some sacred oath. They were bystanders in a war fought on their land by people who sought access—access to harbors and canals; territory for the sake of territory.

Sixty-nine years later, a man equally as charismatic as either Rommel or Montgomery would raise the anvil of fury to retain power that had long been dwindling. Once again the war would be started by other people for other causes. This time, however, the "Nation" would be under attack; the "Nation" would have to decide on which side the people lay, and ultimately the victor would control Libya. Perhaps there is no irony or accident that the back-and-forth of the TNC with Gaddafi forces in 2011 would have many of the same battlefields and strategies parallel to the engagements between the British and Italo-German forces.

After the war, the last Ottoman traces were eliminated, and the Italians and Germans were defeated militarily. Darfur was conquered and the Senusi was badly trampled by the imperial struggles. Weakened but victorious Britain launched a great imperial debate about what do with Libya. British anthropologist and military intelligence officer E. E. Evans-Pritchard, with extensive ethnographic experience in Sudan, arrived in Libya to write his classic study on the Sanusi in 1949. And, being partial to monarchies, the British created a new Libyan kingdom in 1951 from the UN mandate that officially ruled Libya at that moment. King Idris, the grandson of the Grand Sanusi, became promoted as the new constitutional monarch of Libya from 1951 to 1969. This pre-Gaddafi history concludes in 1969 when a young military officer, Colonel Muammar Gaddafi, toppled King Idris and started a new era in Libya.

In summary, the Senusi in particular, and Libya in general, has long been concerned with the events and polities to the south in the Fezzan,

Chad, and Darfur. Equally, actions in the vortex of regional African events, not to mention European imperial ambitions, usually start simply, and end in complex and unanticipated configurations. The historical and strategic security dilemmas of Libya in the past shed much light on the Gaddafi era as well as the present post-Gaddafi period since his death.

The three internal divisions of Libya—east, west, and south—persist in the political geography of this land. Parallel internal divisions by ecology of the urban coast (easy access versus vulnerability) versus rural desert (isolation versus protection) are also persistent parameters. The desire for Libyan autonomy and independence has often been frustrated by internal succession issues and a limited protective umbrella that could be gain with problematic imperial alliances. But with foreign control or access, there could be external manipulation and intrigue as we have seen over the many centuries of Libyan history. With vast oil wealth, this is only a greater dilemma for Libyans to face during Gaddafi and after.

SOURCES

Barnett, Correlli. *The Desert Generals*. Bloomington, IN: Indiana University Press, 1982.

Boddy-Evans, Alistair. "Tripolitan War of 1801–05." Accessed May 2, 2013. http://africanhistory.about.com/od/militaryhistory/ss/Tripolitan-War1.htm.

Buckingham, Maddie. "The Impact of the Moors in Spain." Accessed September 28, 2013. http://wuhstry.wordpress.com/2011/07/20/the-impact-of-the-moors-in-spain/.

Churchill, Winston S. *The Second World War: The Grand Alliance*. New York: Houghton Mifflin Company, 1977.

Evans-Pritchard, E. E. *The Sanusi of Cyrenaica*. Oxford: Oxford University Press, 1949.

Heritage-History. "Barbary Wars: 1500–1830. Barbary Pirates versus Christian Sea Powers." Accessed September 28, 2013. http://www.heritage-history.com/www/heritage.php?Dir=wars&FileName=wars_barbary.php.

Hitti, Phillip K. *History of the Arabs*. 10th edition. New York: Palgrave/Macmillan, 2002.

Hourani, Albert. *A History of the Arab Peoples*. New York: Grand Central Publishing, Hachette Book Group, 1991.

Mitcham, Samuel W., Jr. *Triumphant Fox: Erwin Rommel and the Rise of the Afrika Korps*. New York: Stein and Day Publishers, 1984.

Navy Department Library. "Battle of Derna, 27 April 1805: Selected Naval Documents." Accessed May 2, 2013. http://www.history.navy.mil/library/online/barbary_derna.htm.

New Cosmopolitan World Atlas. New York: Rand McNally, 1965.

Paterson, Ian A. "Engagements 1941." Accessed June 12, 2012. http://web.archive.org/web/20070819154436/http://www.ian.a.paterson.btinternet.co.uk/battles1941.htm#Brevity

Paterson, Ian A. "Engagements 1942." Accessed June 12, 2012. http://web.archive
.org/web/20070818221505/http://www.ian.a.paterson.btinternet.co.uk/
battles1942.htm.

Rogan, Eugene. *The Arabs: A History.* New York: Basic Books, 2011.

The Rommel Papers. Edited by B. H. Liddell-Hart. New York: Harcourt, Brace,
Jovanovich, 1953.

Seitz, Barr. "Barbary Glory, Barbary Shame." Accessed May 2, 2013. http://
military.com/NewContent/0,13190,041905_Barbary,00.html

Singer, Jonathan. "The Pirate Coast: Thomas Jefferson, the First Marines, and the
Secret Mission of 1805." Accessed May 2, 2013. http://contemporarylit
.about.com/od/history/fr/pirateCoast.htm.

Spaulding, Jay, and Lidwien Kapteijns, *An Islamic Alliance: Ali Dinar and the Sanussiyya, 1906–1916.* Evanston, IL: Northwestern University Press, 1994.

Wheelan, Joseph. *Jefferson's War: America's First War on Terror 1801–1805.* Public
Affairs. New York: First Carroll & Graf, 2003.

Wolf, John B. *The Barbary Coast: Algeria under the Turks.* New York: W. W. Norton,
1979.

CHAPTER 3

Rise to Power, Domestic Policy, and Practice

INTRODUCTION

Muammar Gaddafi (born June 7, 1942, in Qasr Abu Hadi, near Sirte) emerged from his humble desert origins motivated to seize power from the Libyan king and reassert his ideas of a proud Arab people and nation. However, with a penchant for bizarre costumes that defined a military dictator, he nonetheless sported an ideological zealotry to redress the inheritance of colonialism and reclaim Arabism. He forged a nonstate *jamhouriya*, guided by his *Green Book* and resultant "green revolution," and an eclectic mélange, centered on "peoples" committees. Avoiding the stereotypical dictatorship, his unique leadership style, coupled with a mixture of nationalism and Sufi mysticism, resulted in a state that exploited its own natural resources to exponentially improve the average standard of living of its citizens, while concurrently producing progressive domestic policies and effectively sidelining international influence. Yet, his syncretic nationalism merged with delusional visions and parochialism and notions of international revolution that finally hobbled his international aspirations and brought him to his ignoble death and display of his corpse in a refrigerated room in Sirte followed by an anonymous burial in his beloved Sahara.

GADDAFI'S BIRTH, ADOLESCENCE, AND POLITICAL CONTEXT

In the very year of his birth, in September 1942, German, Italian, and English imperial rivals were actively at war in Libya and across North

Africa. No doubt the signs of war were evident to this infant, who was nourished on fearsome and horrible tales of Italian conquest, soaked in the blood of mechanized assaults and lopsided engagements and the horrendous concentration camps sprinkled throughout Libya. Actions contested virulently by the "Lion of the Libyan Desert" Omar al-Muktar, himself an excellent guerilla fighter. This early heroic figure in Gaddafi's catalogue of heroes would meet his end in a most public hanging on September 16, 1931. Even when this war was over and the Axis powers were defeated by the English and Americans, the three lands of Libya were cobbled together under the authority of a Libyan king who was never known in Libyan history.

Really, it was bad enough to have your lands and towns destroyed by foreigners, but to then have your nation managed by an imposed king by a foreign monarchy was another sort of outrage to a nomad Arab family. One inevitably presumes that Muammar Gaddafi took in this seminal and turbulent history in his earliest years and through his informal conversations with family and friends. Such was the context of Libya in the 1940s and 1950s.

Muammar Gaddafi was reportedly born in an Arab herdsman's tent in the vicinity of Sirte. World War II was actively underway in Libya; Rommel's final advance into Cyrenaica and western Egypt went through much of 1942. And from November 1942 to February 1943, the major counteroffensive of the British Eighth Army marched and motored across northern Libya while British air and naval power sought to disrupt Axis supplies coming to this Italian colony.

Gaddafi was three years old in 1945 when the German forces were finally defeated and the British occupied Libya. No doubt peace was welcome, yet, only shifting from one foreign occupying power to another, also dictating the governance of Libya, was a mixed blessing that was to mark Gaddafi's long and complex love-hate relationship with Britain. By 1948, when Gaddafi was six, the state of Israel was born, out of British mandatory Palestine. This culturally painful event in the Arab world would prove to be an enduring and central issue, for the many decades to come, either serving as a humiliating defeat of the Arab communities and nations or as an excuse and diversion to justify repressing their own populations. By 1949, when Gaddafi was seven, the Peoples' Republic of China was born and the Libyan constitution was drafted, by the British and Sanusi leaders. While the Arab world was generally more attracted to the Soviet orbit, the anticolonialist and radical independence of China was duly noted as an attractive political option that could be applied to their situation. However, given the relative impotence of the fledgling Libya to the world powers, the connivance by the British in writing their history was reluctantly accepted.

In 1951, Gaddafi turned nine. He would be witness to the adoption of the constitution and the British installation of King Idris, on December 4. Idris would be the first and only king in Libyan history. Libyan independence was declared on December 24, 1951. King Muhammad Idris bin Muhammad al-Mahdi as-Senussi (March 12, 1889–May 25, 1983) did have a strong Libyan (Jaghbub and Kufra Senussi) and Sufi pedigree and did resist the Italian occupation in the 1920s, but his necessary tactical collaboration with the British was perceived negatively by the new generation of Arab nationalists. His rule was tolerated and even welcomed at first, but his long-standing inability to produce multiple sons meant that the end of his reign found him in both declining health and political ineffectiveness. Indeed, when Gaddafi brought it to an end, he was enfeebled and receiving health treatment in Turkey. His son, Prince Hasan, was to have taken over on September 2, 1969 as King Idris was supposed to abdicate, but this was too little and too late.

Gaddafi was not quite 10 in July 1952 when he heard about the Free Officers in Egypt (led by Gamal 'Abd al-Nasser) toppling King Farouk, a nominal Ottoman and British puppet king whose mandate was to secure British interests in long-staple Egyptian cotton and the strategic Suez Canal. Unquestionably, this act of Arab nationalism and anti-imperialism was an inspiration for the young Gaddafi, who would later appear with, and endlessly frustrate, al-Nasser as a parallel military head of government.

Gaddafi was just a tender boy of 11 in 1953 when the Anglo-Libyan Treaty was signed by King Idris. This was perceived by some Libyans as a sellout to the British, eager to secure their own strategic interests. The brand new Arab nationalist Republic of Egypt was declared on June 18, 1953. The Libyans installed a king, while the Egyptians had overthrown theirs. There was no question which route was favored by Gaddafi.

Gaddafi was 12 in 1954 when the National Liberation Front (FLN) of Algeria launched its long and bloody war of national liberation against French settler colonialism. The notion of armed struggle against European colonialism in Africa and the Middle East was added to the ideological baggage of this soon-to-be Libyan teenager. The regional turmoil had another jolt with the 1956 Suez Crisis between his role model Egypt, who was pitted against the Europeans and the newly born state of Israel. Only the intervention of the American war hero General Dwight Eisenhower (1890–1969) prevented this from getting unraveling into a wider conflict beyond the relatively narrow Suez Canal area.

Such a clearly defined and contained role of President Eisenhower (1953–1961) was appreciated in the Middle East, but the "Eisenhower Doctrine" was driven by a Cold War outlook and binary polarity that was not shared by an Arab world more concerned with Israeli and Arab governance. Eisenhower's overthrow of the democratically elected government in Iran in 1953, backed by American oil interests, and sending thousands of Marines to Lebanon in 1958 to block a Nasser-inspired revolt was certainly not appreciated in the contemporary "Arab street." Then there was the Russian milestone in successfully making it to space first, in 1957, that evoked the "enemy of my enemy, is my friend" dialectical, which tipped radical Arab nationalism toward the Soviet Union, while conservative and monarchical Arab regimes were nudged even further toward the anti-Communist West.

Gaddafi was an impassioned 20-year-old in 1962 when the classic Cold War Cuban missile crisis took place as showdown/standout between President Kennedy and his Russian counterpart Nikita Khrushchev. If these instrumental and pivotal events in Gaddafi's biography were not enough, he was still only a very young adult of 25 in 1967 when the "Six-Day War" between Israel and the neighboring Arabs broke out. This fundamentally defined the borders and complex issues that remain until today with the American "tilt" toward Israel bedeviling American relations with the entire Arabo-Muslim world. Libya is, once again, no exception, nor was Gaddafi.

GADDAFI COMING TO POWER AND TRANSFORMING THE LIBYAN *JAMAHIRIYA*

On May 25, 1969, Colonel Gaafar Muhammad Nimieri (January 1, 1930–May 30, 2009) and his Revolutionary Command Council overthrew the ineffective, but democratic, government of Isma'il al-Azhari in Sudan. Nimieri was repaid in kind as his government was toppled on April 6, 1985, in a popular revolt that restored democracy to Sudan. He had ruled for 16 years, first as a national socialist, then as a capitalist, and finally, as a "neo-Islamist," at which time he had run out of options. The balance of his life was spent in in exile in Egypt, but he would eventually return home to Sudan whereupon, at age 79, he died. At least once, Nimieri, Gaddafi, and Nasser met for a photo opportunity, and there was a short-lived, yet, divisive attempt, in 1970, to unify the three nations.

Muammar Gaddafi was just 27 in 1969 when he overthrew the politically weakened and physically ill King Idris, the day before his son, Prince Hasan, was to take the reins of the Libyan monarchy. The king officially abdicated on September 8, 1969, and mostly lived out his exile in Cairo. In this most busy year of 1969, yet another government fell. On October 21, 1969, the government of Somalia was overthrown by General Siad Muhammad Barre (October 6, 1919–January 2, 1995). He would eventually be overthrown, as was the accepted method of transferring power among less historically established nations, in January 1991, paving the way for Somalia to enter into the abyss that becomes a failed state—a status for which Somalia can't claim to have overcome. He ruled for 22 years as a Somali nationalist and orthodox socialist, amidst the Cold War alliances and proxy wars. He would live out his 76 years in exile.

All three revolutionary Muslim nationalists were supposed to launch new progressive eras in their respective nations, joining the still extant revolutionary nationalist government of Gamal 'Abd al-Nasser in Egypt. These Cold War–context military coups were the local versions of the tide that was still sweeping the decolonized Third World, which was joining with the political struggles in Asia and Latin America to link the world working class along with the socialist camps that had important divisions between Beijing, Tirana, and Moscow. Such ambitious plans were not destined to last. Within a year of Gaddafi taking power—September 28, 1970, to be specific—Nasser was dead of a heart attack, and within two decades the Soviet Union had collapsed, and Barre and Nimieri were replaced. Only Gaddafi survived this epoch, and he would remain a beacon of individualism, extremism, and contravention until his extraction from a culvert and humiliating murder in Sirte. Where his life began, so would it end. The final straw on the camel's back of this revolutionary nationalist trifecta; the man whose rule spanned two generations, 42 years, of his nascent nation's population; frustrating, confusing, yet charismatically inspiring and drawing admiration from his power, had ended.

In 1969 or 1970—accounts and history vary—Muammar Gaddafi married Fatiha al-Nouri, a schoolteacher, and mother of his first son Muhammad. They were soon divorced, and her present location and status is not publicly known. In 1970, he married Safiya Farkash, a nurse and mother of (alphabetically) Ayesha, Hannibal Muammar, Khamis, Mutassim, Saadi, Saif al-Arab, and Saif al-Islam. She was reportedly in exile in Staoueli, Algeria, as of August 29, 2011, but may have moved since. Muhammad (born in about 1970), son of Fatiha, was the head of post, telephone, and communications in Libya during the Gaddafi era. He was also a leader in the Libyan Olympics Committee. He fled to Algeria during the 2011 revolution and was not indicted by the ICC.

Regarding Gaddafi's actions to "retake Libya from outsiders," soon after Gaddafi seized power, he personally approached the U.S. general who presided at the comfortable and vast (23 square miles) American Wheelus Air Force Base in Tripoli. This moment could have changed Libyan history, for, you see, the general who was confronted by Gaddafi at Wheelus was none other than four-star USAF General Daniel "Chappie" James, Jr. (February 11, 1920–February 25, 1978). "Chappie" trained the famed World War II Tuskegee pilots, saw combat in over 100 missions in Korea and Vietnam, and was the first African American to reach the rank of four-star general. He was not a man to be trifled with.

After Gaddafi had launched his coup in Benghazi, he went to Tripoli and drove his half-tracks provocatively through Wheelus and stationed howitzers on the perimeter. General James, an experienced diplomat and warrior, and recently installed in command of Wheelus, was not about to surrender to Gaddafi. Having full confidence in his American forces, and several squadrons of the latest F-86 fighter jets, he personally confronted the new leader of Libya. With both men resting their hands upon their revolvers, Chappie instructed Gaddafi to "drop it." Later, Chappie admitted that had Gaddafi moved to draw his weapon, it would have been his last. Wheelus was shortly returned to Libya, the last forces leaving on June 11, 1970. "Chappie" James would die from a heart attack just three weeks after retirement in 1978. He was buried in Arlington National Cemetery. So goes history, one round from changing it all.

Wheelus was the former Italian military airport of Mellaha, first constructed in 1923 to provide air support for their innovative military air campaign against Libyans. Again, some Libyans saw this base as a tangible reminder of King Idris's "selling out to the Americans." After it was retaken it was briefly renamed Uqba bin Nafi Air Base, in honor of the seventh-century nephew of Amr ibn as-'As, who brought Islam to the African continent and for whom the famed mosque of Kairouan was built. Today it is called the Mitiga International Airport. Ironically, at times it served American interests and at other times it was bombed by Americans. The history of this airport and its nomenclature is truly a micro-history of modern Libya; that is, a substantial part of Gaddafi's Libya.

After pushing for unity between Libya, Sudan, and Egypt in 1970, going so far as to issue a 2-*piastre* postage stamp, there was opposition to such a move, and in 1971, a short-lived coup took place against General Nimieri by Hashim al-Atta in Sudan. Gaddafi forced down the British Overseas Airways Corporation (BOAC) VC-10 plane in Benghazi, Libya on July 22, 1971, and sent Lieutenant Colonel Babiker al Nur Osman and Major Farouk Hamadallah, colleagues of Hashim al-Atta, on to Sudan, whereby they were executed. This was in support of the British, Saudi, American, and Egyptian effort to topple Al-Atta and bring back Nimieri.

Gaddafi's second son, Saif al-Islam, was born on June 25, 1972. He graduated from the London School of Economics (LSE) with a PhD in 2008. He initiated the Gaddafi Foundation pledge to the LSE of £1.5 million, but it is believed that only £300,000 was ever donated. Before the 2011 revolution, he was heir apparent to Muammar as a "reformist" spokesperson. During the revolution, he was captured in November 2011 on his attempted flight to Niger and as of this writing was being held by the militias of Zintan in a political struggle between Tripoli, Zintan, and the ICC, over jurisdiction.

Gaddafi's third son, Al-Saadi, was born on May 25, 1973, and was a notorious playboy and football (soccer) player. He was also Commander of Libyan Special Forces. He fled to Niamey, Niger, where, as of this writing, he was wanted by the new Libyan government through an Interpol "Red Alert" arrest warrant.

In 1973, Anwar Sadat unleashed the October War against the long-running Israeli occupation of the Sinai Peninsula that was heralded across the Arab world as a major military success and gave great credit to Sadat. While this redressed the Arab dishonor of 1948 and 1967, even this was not to save Tripoli-Cairo relations.

Gaddafi's fourth son, Mutassim Billah was born on December 18, 1974. He was executed on October 20, 2011 by rebels in Sirte on the same day as his father, Muammar was killed. He was head of National Security and thus responsible for much of the counter-insurgency killing in the revolution. Mutassim was considered as a rival to power against his brother Saif al-Islam. He was noted for his flamboyant extravagance such as a $1 million fee to singer Mariah Carey for a party in the Caribbean. He was responsible for many of Libya's major arms purchases.

Gaddafi's fifth son, Hannibal Muammar was born on September 20, 1975 and was a "businessman" in maritime shipping. Like his brother, Al-Saadi, he was also an ill-behaved playboy son of Muammar, noted for scuffles abroad in Switzerland the England, domestic abuse and abuse of servants by his wife. He fled to exile in Algeria.

Gaddafi's first daughter, Ayesha, was born in 1976 and she became his "goodwill ambassador" and trained lawyer for her father. Her husband (Muammar's cousin) was killed in a French attack in July 2011 along with two of their three children. She fled to Algeria during the revolution where she gave birth to a daughter, Safiya (named for her mother) in Algeria on August 30, 2011. She worked on the defense team of Saddam Hussein in Iraq.

President Gaddafi was 35 when the March 2, 1977, Sebha Declaration of People's Authority pioneered his effort to remake the political economy of Libya and to create a supposedly new model of governance.

It was also in 1977 when the brief Egypto-Libyan war broke out. While this war was indecisive, regrettable, and unnecessary, worse was to come when Arab "unity" was further broken apart with the September 8, 1978, signing of the Camp David Accords between Menachem Begin's Israel and Anwar Sadat's Egypt. The Arab world saw this as a fundamental betrayal. Despite the very well-publicized dissent in the Arab world, on March 26, 1979, these accords between Israel and Egypt were finally signed by Sadat. Gaddafi, Barre, and Nimieri saw this as a gross betrayal of Arab nationalism as they continued with their own political experiments.

Meanwhile, the 1978–1987 Libya-Chad war limped onward with Gaddafi keen to spread Libyan influence and acquire uranium-rich lands in the Aouzou Strip of northern Chad. This went on until Gaddafi's forces were defeated in the Battle of Maaten al-Sarra in 1987, the aptly titled "Toyota War" due to the proliferation of Toyota pickups as machine gun platforms, which was the primary vehicle and weapon system. The revolutionary fervor of the period was also seen in Shi'ite Iran when, on January 16, 1979, the pro-Western and dictatorial Shah of Iran was forced into exile. His theocratic replacement, Ayatollah Khomeini, arrived in Tehran on February 1, 1979. While Sunni Arabs were nervous observers of this transition to Shi'ite power, the anti-Western and anti-American aspects were lauded.

Gaddafi was 37 during the October 1–3, 1979, Libya Popular Congress when he stated that "all Libyan power is from, and to, the Libyan people." He was increasingly disillusioned about his effort to foment world revolution, and to exemplify that disillusionment, Gaddafi's armed support of the Irish Republican Army (IRA) came to an end as he increasingly turned inward to the African continent to try and gain a leadership position there, especially among the poorer nations that needed his financial assistance. He was 39 on June 27, 1981, when the African Charter of Human Rights was signed. Later that year, in a military parade celebrating the Great October war, Egyptian President Anwar Sadat was assassinated on October 6, 1981, by representatives from *Takfir wal Hegira*, an Islamic extremist group. This news was celebrated by Gaddafi and his instruments of mass public media noted that "the people stopped talking, and the rifles started talking."

Gaddafi's sixth son, Saif al-Arab, was born in 1982. He was also noted as a "businessman" playboy and lover of fast cars, in Germany. He was killed during a NATO airstrike in Tripoli on April 30, 2011, along with three of Muammar's grandchildren. This turbulent period was followed by the Israeli invasion of Lebanon 1982 that in turn provoked the bombing of the Marine Corps barracks at the Beirut Airport on October 23, 1983, during the Lebanese civil war. This resulted in 299 French and Americans killed, making for the deadliest single day in Marine Corps history since the 1945 Battle for Iwo Jima, in World War II, that saw 220 Marines, 18 sailors, and 3 soldiers die on a single day.

Gaddafi's seventh son, Khamis, was born on May 27, 1983, and became the commander of the notorious "Khamis Brigade" (32nd Brigade) that was responsible for the early killing in Benghazi and elsewhere. He was also a minor film producer and an ardent and brutal defender of the Gaddafi regime. It is likely that he was executed on August 29, 2011.

Floating in a sea of oil wealth in lightly populated Libya, Gaddafi was 41 in 1983 when the first plans were launched for the Great Man Made River project that would mine the underground water resources of Libya and expand agriculture throughout this historically subsistence-based agricultural land. In the following year, his engineers began the work on this massive artificial "river." Gaddafi-backed attacks at the Rome and Vienna airports on December 19, 1985, and his episodic support for such groups as the Abu Nidal faction, the Red Army faction in Germany, the Red Brigades in Italy, and the IRA, among many others, poisoned Libyan relations with Washington and Europe. The Gaddafi-backed attack on American servicemen at a Berlin nightclub on April 5, 1986, led to the First Gulf of Sidra punitive attack in 1986 on Libya. Gaddafi was 44 in 1986 when U.S. forces bombed his Tripoli compound and other sites.

Gaddafi's adopted daughter, Hanaa al-Gaddafi, was alleged to have been killed in an American airstrike on Tripoli in 1986. No physical evidence was ever produced, however, and rumors persist that she may be working as a medical doctor. Also, Milad Abuztaia al-Gaddafi was adopted after he allegedly saved Muammar's life in 1986.

Emboldened or angered, Gaddafi turned 46, and on June 12, 1988, the Great Green Charter of the *Jamahiriya* was launched at al-Bayda to create the Libyan Popular Assembly. This syncretic and idiosyncratic mixture of socialism, nationalism, Arabism and Islam captured the untutored but inspired mind of this Libyan military man.

GADDAFI AND *THE GREEN BOOK*

Gaddafi's *Green Book* addresses three topics: (1) the solution to the problem of democracy; (2) the solution to the economic problem; and (3) the social basis of the Third University Theory. These audacious if not imaginative tasks are, essentially, typical Gaddafi. He sincerely wanted to tackle such fundamental questions with his very considerable economic resources in Libya; however, his utter lack of formal training meant something of a hodge-podge of reductionist ideas that could not really get implemented.

This book has no footnotes, references, or bibliography; it is assertive and analytical only in the sense that it tries to address important contemporary issues, but it certainly lacks a systematic or scholarly academic approach. Mostly it is a window into the mind of Gaddafi amidst its many twists and turns—the contradictions, failed opportunities, and indeed, some of his delusions about the nature of the state and his role in it. In any work of a major leader, it is always hard to determine just how much was believed versus how much was projected to his citizen-followers, willing or not. It addresses issues covered by history, political science, anthropology, administration, and economics, but it does not build upon any specific or existing framework or database.

The English-language translation of *The Green Book* is smooth and clear. It is easy, well structured, reading designed to be accessible, at least in terms of the intended meaning. It is also polemic and argumentative and tempts a comparison with Mao Tse-Tung's *Red Book*.

The first part deals with governance and is rather neo-Marxist in terms of his ideas that history unfolds by class struggles, but he then concludes that one side will lose, even by democracy, and this can only generate more conflict and "defeat of the people." Majority rule means that a large portion of the electorate is governed by people or parties they oppose. This is well known, but practices of accountability, transparency, balance of powers, terms in office, and elections certainly address this apparent contradiction. Nonetheless Gaddafi advances in his critique that parliaments and representative assemblies serve as "barriers" to hear the peoples' voices. Otherwise, such democracies are "outdated" and "power should be entirely for all the people." Political parties, according to Gaddafi, are "contemporary forms of dictatorships," and partisanship "betrays society." Moreover "referendums make a mockery of democracy." Gaddafi's "solutions" to these political dilemmas were to form "Peoples' Conferences" and "Peoples' Committees" everywhere across his model of an utterly decentralized nation. Issues of legislation are also addressed in this theoretical model.

Despite the fact that there is no mention of Islam in this part, the model is certainly influenced by the *Shura* council model of consultative governance that exists in some Islamic states. Its green color is emblematic of the positive value of that color in Islam or in the flag of Libya during the Gaddafi era. There is also no provision to determine who might be the head of the government or head of state or how power and authority could be acquired, transmitted, or removed. Such omissions were typical of the four decades of the Gaddafi administration and, presumably, were responsible for its opposition and its ultimate collapse in 2011.

The second part of *The Green Book* focuses on economics and is introduced with his version of "socialism" as his solution to economic injustice. Wages paid to workers, even with union leadership, are never really adequate; the wage systems must be abolished according to Gaddafi, to end workers' enslavement. Human freedom is always compromised if needs are controlled by another. People may own their own homes, but no more. This led, in practice, to the confiscation of second or more homes in Libya. Income should be on a partnership or share basis, not as wages. Land must not be private property, he insisted. Inequality in wealth is unacceptable, said Gaddafi. Domestic servants should be abolished since such people are virtual slaves. Well, however, good, bad, or utopian such goals might be, they were certainly observed in the breach by Gaddafi and his family that steadily acquired more and more property and wealth and, especially for the playboy children of the head of state, were notorious in their conspicuous consumption and reckless personal behavior.

The third and last section formulates the social basis of Gaddafi's "Third Universal Theory," which is equally utopian and was much more observed in its absence than in its effective implementation. Interestingly, he recommends that all societies should have religion, but he does not mention that Islam might be that faith. National and minority identities are parts of continuing struggles, and the family is more important than the state. Two sections deal with the social group he terms as "the tribe"—that is, a cohesive extension of the family. There is also some criticism of how the "tribe" might also be divisive in achieving a higher sense of national unity. Gaddafi addresses the topic of gender by stating that women are equal human beings, but each should "perform their assigned roles" and "understand their natural differences." Gaddafi believed that childcare and nurseries were not natural. Also, according to Gaddafi, "black people will prevail in the world" despite the tragic history of slavery. Remarkably, the "lassitude of black people" is due to living in "constantly hot climates." His thoughts on learning were "to force a human being to learn a particular curriculum is dictatorial." And "ignorance will come to an end when everything is presented as it really is."

Although the Gaddafi concepts of a "socialist *Jamahiriya*" are not developed in *The Green Book*, they are founded in it. One will never know whether these ideas were really believed, or simply never practiced as they were so utopian and impractical that, from the outset, they were delusional and, in any case, they are now dead with him. Despite four decades of their currency, they were more of a smokescreen for abuse of power, and until Gaddafi's last moments, perhaps he truly thought that he was not really the head of government and that the people really were in charge. Perhaps, in the end, the Libyan people were in charge as he was being killed along with his son Mutassim?

TERRORISM IN THE SKY

Sadly, *The Green Book* somehow gave a "reason" to Gaddafi to justify the Lockerbie bombing of Pan Am Flight 103 that took place on December 21, 1988, in which all 259 passengers and crew on board were killed while an additional 11 died on the ground in Lockerbie, Scotland. Gaddafi and his instruments of "state security," such as his brother-in-law Abdullah Senussi, were likewise implicated in the parallel bombing of the Union de Transports Aeriens (UTA) Flight 772 bombing on September 19, 1989, over the Sahel, taking the lives of 170 crew and passengers, including the wife of the U.S. Ambassador to Chad. Something had to be done to curb these acts of terror against innocent civilians, so a second Gulf of Sidra challenge took place along the "Line of Death" in which Libyan jets attacking American naval vessels were shot down in 1989. At least this seemed to make a temporary standout, but it would be more bad news for Gaddafi when he turned 48 in 1990 and his chief foreign ally and source of arms, the Soviet Union, collapsed and the Cold War dimension of Middle Eastern politics was abruptly concluded. However, this was the same year in which the forces of Iraq's Saddam Hussein invaded Kuwait, launching a Coalition response resulting in the First Gulf War (1990–1991). Egypt and the United States, under President George H. W. Bush, collaborated to protect Saudi Arabia and save Kuwait. Gaddafi viewed Egyptian President Hosni Mubarak as an American puppet and the United States as the aggressor against Iraq, which had had historical claims to the region. Elsewhere, events remained on a brisk pace as we saw the final defeat of President Muhammad Siad Barre by General Farrah Aidid in Mogadishu, Somalia, in May 1991. This would tragically lead to more than two decades of misery, famine, piracy, and conflict in that failed state in the Horn of Africa, by the Islamic Courts Union and its violent successor, al-Shabab.

LIBYA AND THE UNITED NATIONS

At least 16 United Nations Security Council resolutions have been passed regarding Libya, as shown in Table 3.1. All but one, the very first, was focused on the Gaddafi years.

Table 3.1

United Nations Resolutions regarding Libya

Resolution	Date	Vote	Purpose and Notes
UNSCR 109	Dec. 14, 1955	8–0–3	Libya's membership application to the UN. Abstaining: USA, China, Belgium.
UNSCR 731	Jan. 21, 1992	15–0–0	Condemns Libya for PA 103 (Lockerbie) and UTA 772 (Niger) air bombing.
UNSCR 748	Mar. 31, 1992	10–0–5	Embargo on civil aviation and arms to Libya. Abstaining: Cape Verde, China, India, Morocco, Zimbabwe.
UNSCR 883	Nov. 11, 1993	11–0–4	Sanctions imposed because of no Libyan cooperation on UNSCR 731 and 748. Abstaining: China, Djibouti, Morocco, Pakistan
UNSCR 910	Apr. 14, 1994	15–0–0	UN Reconnaissance Mission for Aouzou Strip exemption from UNSCR 748.

Table 3.1 (*continued*)

Resolution	Date	Vote	Purpose and Notes
UNSCR 915	May 4, 1994	15–0–0	Establishes UN Observer group for Aouzou.
UNSCR 926	June 13, 1994	15–0–0	Terminates UN Observer group for Aouzou.
UNSCR 1192	Aug. 27, 1998	15–0–0	Recalls UNSCR 731, 748, 883 and calls for Sanctions and trials for bombing suspects Khalifah Fhimah and Abd al-Basset al-Megrahi.
UNSCR 1506	Sep. 12, 2003	13–0–2	Lifts sanctions against Libya. Abstaining: USA, France. Resumption of normalized relations.
UNSCR 1970	Feb. 26, 2011	15–0–0	Sanctions proposed against Gaddafi for suppressing the 2011 revolution.
UNSCR 1973	Mar. 17, 2011	10–0–5	Establishing a Libyan "no-fly zone" and the right to protect civilians. Abstaining: China, Russia, Brazil, India, Germany.
UNSCR 2009	Sep. 16, 2011	15–0–0	Establishes UN Support Mission for Libya.
UNSCR 2016	Oct. 27, 2011	15–0–0	Terminates military intervention in Libya.
UNSCR 2017	Oct. 31, 2011	15–0–0	Notes need for custody of small arms and SAM7s proliferating in post-conflict Libya.
UNSCR 2022	Dec. 2, 2011	15–0–0	Extends mandate of UN Support Mission in Libya.
UNSCR 2040	Mar. 12, 2012	15–0–0	Enforcement of arms embargo for Libya. Extends smaller 'panel of experts' mission for 12 months.

Almost all of these resolutions were approved unanimously by member nations, with a few important exceptions. When modern Libya was created, the United States, China, and Belgium abstained. Other abstentions in some cases involved either issues of superpower politics or of nations either beholden to Libya for various reasons, or with their own issues relative to African governance, such as Morocco. The volatile politics of Libya is also apparent as it moved from pariah issues to "normal" and back to very wide opposition to the brutality in trying to suppress the 2011 revolution. As a parallel matter are the ICC interests and positions vis-à-vis the airplane bombings and the post-conflict trials for war crimes and crimes against humanity for some of the surviving top figures in the Gaddafi administration. Gaddafi's wars in Africa and his support for various insurgencies and foreign nations were, in general, failures.

GADDAFI TRIES AGAIN

Gaddafi was 54 in 1996 when his great engineering project, the Great Manmade River began functioning with two huge aqueducts and 4,000 kilometers of pipes to bring water from the desert to the populated areas along the northern coast. While ecologically dubious, it certainly had short-term gains for the people. But this was not all, because in 1998 he sought to build the Community of North African States with his financial resources. Nonetheless, the political heterogeneity of this region did not lead to any fruitful results for his imagination. The Surt Declaration of September 9, 1999, tried to move this forward, but also without substantial result. Buffeted by these unfavorable political winds Gaddafi pivoted to the larger parts of the continent on July 11, 2000, at the Constitutive Act of the African Union and hosted the Surt Summit on the African Union. In this 60th year, on July 10, 2002, the Durban Declaration launched the African Union with Gaddafi bankrolling the poorer states to purchase friends and influence in this pan-African organization.

Gaddafi also had a fresh start in 2003 when he initiated secret security and financial collaboration with the United Kingdom. The following year, an official American delegation visited Libya to slowly pave the way toward normalization of relations. The UNSCR 1506 was the historic milestone for the birth of the "new" Gaddafi as then President George W. Bush signed the Libyan Claims Resolution Act to draw a line under Lockerbie, Berlin, UTA bombings, and the U.S. bombing of Tripoli. He signed the act, effective August 4, 2008, to take effect on June 28, 2009, to restore official diplomatic relations between Tripoli and Washington and to reestablish the diplomatic mission in Benghazi. But this was all too little and too late, for his reforms, the patience of the Libyan people and the world had worn too thin. President Muammar Gaddafi was almost 69 in 2011 when he was killed in Sirte in violent revolution against him, his family, and entire administration and mercenary forces.

GADDAFI'S DOMESTIC POLICIES AND PRACTICES

The mercurial, syncretic, and unaccountable nature of President Gaddafi makes him simultaneously charming and deceitful, impressive and disappointing, admirable and criminal, as well as global and parochial, generous and wasteful, focused and delusional. In short, one never knew with certainty just where he stood or what he might do next. The inventory of UN Security Council resolutions pretty well tracks these vicissitudes.

Domestically, he celebrated those who supported him and publicly hanged those who opposed him. He greatly improved the health and education of the Libyan people. His Great Manmade River Project was an indelible expression of using the oil-rich nation's resources to serve the people. The grotesque Abu Salim Prison Massacre of June 29, 1996, deserves special mention. Filled with political prisoners and prisoners of conscience, this prison was faced with a revolt, protest, or escape attempt depending on which sources are consulted. For certain it held a large number of Libyan Islamic Fighting Group (LIFG) Islamists whom one may term "terrorists" as some (such as Abu Sufian bin Qumu, who was also held at Guantanamo) had traveled to Iran, Iraq, and Afghanistan to fight with insurgents there and returned to Libya to do the same against Gaddafi. But there were certainly a wide variety of other prisoners. The allegations by Human Rights Watch is that 1,270 prisoners were killed on this date. Denials by contemporary Libyan authorities made this impossible to confirm with precision. Moreover, even after the 2011 revolution, there were claims by Al-Jazeera that mass graves were found, but some of the images of bones shown were questioned for various reasons. One imagines that as Libya restores security, then a proper accounting and forensic exhumation may take place to let the victims be better identified and rest in peace. Gaddafi may also claim to be the first to have a suit with Interpol against Osama bin Laden after his agents assassinated al-Qa'eda enemies in Libya. But at the same time, there is massive brutality by Gaddafi military forces and mercenaries in the 2011 revolution when he tried, and failed, to suppress his civilian populations. One must also not forget the many informal assassinations (domestically and globally) and formal executions as well as the plots to bring down civilian airlines.

GADDAFI'S FOREIGN RELATIONS: NEIGHBORS

Gaddafi's relations with his neighbors were equally volatile and problematic. For example, Gaddafi applauded the assassination of Anwar Sadat in Egypt. Libya even had a pointless border war with Egypt. Libyan intrigue took place in adjacent Tunisia as it became a haven for the growing opposition. Sometimes Libya and Algeria were unified on common security and political interest, as evidenced by their support for the Western Sahara guerrilla movement that naturally antagonized their common competitor, Morocco, the occupying state.

The Libyan military adventures in Chad that kept the Libyan-Chad war going from 1978 to 1987 with the Islamic Legion represented another bloody phase of Gaddafi's reign. Admittedly, the Aouzou dispute had other dimensions, including arbitrary European colonial borders and uranium deposits. Libyan-Sudan relations ranged from Gaddafi's air force bombing Omdurman in March 1984 with some "idea" that would aid rebels in South Sudan or help to undermine Nimieri; to his support of some Darfur rebel factions; to his failed effort to host a peace conference in Sirte in October 2007 and building his remarkable hotel and conference tower in Khartoum.

GADDAFI'S OTHER FOREIGN RELATIONS IN AFRICA AND THE MIDDLE EAST

Further afield, Gaddafi's whimsical and highly personalized foreign policies and practices buffeted from place to place and from time to time as he faced isolation and frustration with little progress in establishing influence on the Middle East issues. Therefore, he turned his interests and great wealth toward the other regions of the African continent, especially as he sought to purchase his way into leadership of the African Union. He knew he could influence the poorer nations through paying their AU dues, as long as they voted for Gaddafi. Ethics and human rights records were no problem for Gaddafi, as he espoused neither, beyond his *Green Book*. Such examples include Ethiopia where he supported the brutal head of the Dergue, Mengistu Haile Mariam, until he was overthrown and exiled to equally problematic Zimbabwe. In Uganda, Gaddafi sent Libyan troops to support the harsh and murderous rule of Idi Amin in the Uganda-Tanzania war in October 1978. When defeat was a certainty, Gaddafi provided refuge for "The Last King of Scotland," which lasted a year, until Amin moved on to Saudi Arabia where he died. In the Central African Republic, Gaddafi aided "Emperor" Bokassa, who was internationally renowned for his bizarre behavior. In the Saharan Arab Democratic Republic (Western Sahara) and its liberation movement Polisario, Gaddafi and Algeria both supported Polisario's war against Morocco until this dispute stagnated into the current intractable mess.

Liberia broke relations with Libya under coup-maker Sergeant Samuel Kanyon Doe, but Libya renewed relations with Liberia under Charles Taylor in 1997 after Doe was executed. Liberia once again broke relations with Libya in April 2011 in the revolt against Gaddafi. After the Libyan elections of July 7, 2012, Liberia renewed relations with Tripoli on July 16. Linked to Charles Taylor, Gaddafi also bears some responsibility for the horrible civil war and civilian atrocities in Sierra Leone for which Taylor was convicted of war crimes by the International Criminal Court.

While no one could blame Gaddafi for creating any of the Middle Eastern problems in Palestine, Lebanon, or Iraq, neither could anyone find any justifiable interventions to credit him with in this contentious and violent region. Not surprisingly, Gaddafi supported Saddam Hussein and opposed the Western war to liberate Kuwait (Huntington, 248). Really, none of these foreign policy adventures could be considered as successes.

GADDAFI'S TERRORIST ADVENTURES IN EUROPE

In the Eastern European enclave of Bosnia, Gaddafi provided arms and funds to the rebels (Huntington, 28, 281) and there were reports of Libyan aid in Chechnya, Tajikistan, and in the Trans Caucasus. In Italy, Gaddafi was said to have supported the "Red Brigades," and in France and Germany, Gaddafi supported the so-called "Red Army" as well as the bombing of the "La Belle" nightclub in Berlin, Germany, on April 5, 1986, in which three were killed, and 229 injured. As early as 1973, Gaddafi sent the Provisional IRA a shipment of Soviet arms to aid in their cause against English rule, and in April 1984, the Libyan Embassy was the site for the assassin shooting and killing of the policewoman Yvonne Fletcher in London. Needless to say, as noted above in the UN resolutions covering the Pan Am crash in Lockerbie, Scotland, in 1988 and the UTA bombing in 1989, both were coordinated by the Libyan Secret Service, often headed by Abdullah Senussi, brother-in-law of Muammar Gaddafi. The blood was undeniably on Gaddafi's hands. The challenge was in trying to understand what he intended to "accomplish" with these acts.

GADDAFI'S OTHER VENTURES WITH TERRORISM

Aside from inspiring or supporting the conflicts in Sudan, Niger, Chad, and Uganda, Gaddafi was developing various (perhaps nuclear and chemical) weapons of mass destruction at his facilities in Tarhuna and Rapta, Libya. At least one serious assassination attempt backed by Libya against the Saudi royal family is known, and the Japanese terrorists who carried out the Lod Airport Massacre in Israel were praised by Gaddafi on October 7, 1972. In the Philippines, several thousand insurgents of the Moro Liberation Front were trained in Libya according to Huntington (274). Likewise there were reports of his aid to rebels in the South Pacific, Venezuela, and Kashmir as well as his friends in Cuba.

GADDAFI'S SUPPORT FOR NGOs

In addition to his support for armed insurgents, Gaddafi endlessly tried to maneuver for influential positions in the Arab League, the Organization of African Unity, and the African Union. He also financed a host of nongovernmental organizations (NGOs) such as the World Muslim

Congress (Pakistan), Muslim World League (Saudi), and many other parties and movements and causes (Huntington, 176).

SUMMARY

The remarkable, turbulent, and yet volatile life of President Gaddafi came to a screeching end when he was dragged out of a roadside culvert in Sirte and killed by his captors on October 20, 2011. This signaled the end of the 2011 revolution, at least the physical dismemberment of the Gaddafi regime. This would also include Abdullah Senussi (born December 5, 1949, in Tripoli) and the brother-in-law of Muammar Gaddafi. Senussi was Gaddafi's notorious intelligence chief who may know who was responsible for the 1984 killing of Yvonne Fletcher in London. He may also have been involved in the 1988 Lockerbie bombing in which 270 died as well as the 1989 UTA air crash over Niger that killed another 170 passengers. Senussi was allegedly responsible for the 1996 massacre at Abu-Salim prison in Tripoli in which 1,200 were killed. He is also alleged to have plotted the attempted assassination of Crown Prince Abdullah in Saudi Arabia. During the 2011 revolution, Senussi organized much of the repression against the rebels, including the hiring of mercenaries to fight with Gaddafi's forces.

As the revolution unfolded, Senussi fled from Libya to Morocco. Then an ICC warrant for his arrest, for crimes against humanity, prompted him to move to Mauritania. But with incentives and political pressure applied in equal measure, the Mauritanian authorities handed him over to custody in Tripoli for trial. The issue of fair and free trials in Tripoli was still being raised by the ICC as of this writing, and it was feared or anticipated that the grave allegations against Senussi would lead to his execution.

Ahmed Al-Gaddafi al-Qahsi (died July 26, 2011), was a cousin of Muammar Gaddafi and he married Muammar's daughter Ayesha. He was a colonel in the Libyan army and was killed during a French airstrike in 2011, along with two of their children. Another relative was Hasan al Kabir al-Gaddafi, the cousin of Muammar Gaddafi and commander of the Revolutionary Guard Corps of Libya. Musa Ibrahim was perhaps another Gaddafi cousin. He was a Gaddafi spokesman in any case. He was captured in Tarhuna but may have escaped to Germany with his wife. He gained a PhD from Exeter University in England.

Other important figures who also fell with the death of Gaddafi are Musa Kusa; although not a Gaddafi relative, he served as Gaddafi's intelligence chief from 1994 to 2009. In March 2011 during the revolution, he fled to Tunisia, then to the UK, for reasons that are unclear, but it is known that he worked with British intelligence MI-6 probably over rendition of terrorist suspect to Libya. Kusa was also instrumental in the demobilization of the WMD that were held by Libya. Presumably these acts gave him some "credit" with British intelligence. From England, he then went to Doha, Qatar. He currently resides in Amman, Jordan. He also served at Libyan Foreign Minister. He is alleged to have personally tortured prisoners at the infamous Abu Salim prison, and the execution of 1,200 took place during his administration.

In 2011, the Gaddafi era came crashing to a bloody end, much like the great bloodshed during his rule. After breaking the Gaddafi state into pieces, the task ahead is to put the pieces back together.

SOURCES

Brynen, Rex, Peter Moore, Bassel Salloukh, and Marie-Joëlle Zahar. *Beyond the Arab Spring: Authoritarianism and Democratization in the Arab World*. Boulder, CO: Lynne Rienner, 2012.

First, Ruth. *The Barrel of a Gun: Political Power in Africa and the Coup d'Etat*. London: Penguin Books, 1970.

Gaddafi, Muammar. *The Green Book*. Tripoli: The World Center for the Study and Research of the Green Book, 1980.

Gaddafi, Muammar, with Edmond Jouve. *My Vision*. London: John Blake Publishing, 2005.

Huntington, Samuel P. *The Clash of Civilizations and the Remaking of World Order*. New York: Simon and Schuster, 1996.

Ronen, Yehudit. *Qaddafi's Libya in World Politics*. Boulder, CO: Lynne Rienner, 2008.

Vandewalle, Dirk. *A History of Modern Libya*. New York: Cambridge University Press, 2006.

CHAPTER 4

The Arab Spring in Libya

INTRODUCTION AND CONTEXT

On June 25, 1950, nine nations voted to intervene in the North Korean invasion of South Korea. Among those in favor was the People's Republic of China. Russia was absent and Yugoslavia abstained. Had either voted against the resolution, then the United Nations would have been legally bound to not intervene. They did not choose to attend or vote. There was war. Three years later, there was an armistice.

By contrast, on March 17, 2011, 10 nations voted in favor of establishing the no-fly zone—emplacing an embargo on all goods entering and exiting the country, and blockading the ports except for humanitarian traffic. Five abstained; the People's Republic of China, Russia, Germany, India, and Brazil. What changed?

Economically, all five stood to potentially lose influence, if not financial gain, by not endorsing what was otherwise seen as a legitimate use of international influence. None of the five is a predominantly Muslim nation; thus religion wasn't a sticking point. None of the five had long-standing historical ties, as did Italy and the United Kingdom. So why not vote either for or against action? What they missed by not participating boggles the mind: 26,000 individual flights by aircraft encompassing 21 nations; 17 million tons of bombs dropped on 3,565 targets; hundreds of millions of dollars, euros, pounds, and francs, expended to relocate, base, fly, gas, bomb, photograph, and float 26 ships, 273 aircraft and helicopters, and 17,498 service members (Rogers). In a corporate boardroom, these figures would produce incredible forecasts of profit for any given quarter. In combat, when the objective is prevention of the incumbent leader, Muammar Gaddafi, from eradicating his delusional threat of the month, his own people, this is a trifling figure compared to the human suffering it prevented.

The conflict to remove Gaddafi from power was couched within two United Nations Security Council resolutions, 1970 (UNSCR 1970) and 1973 (UNSCR 1973). Both held extremely limited and surgically written objectives: the former to seek Gaddafi's respect for human rights, including the right to protest, and to cease hostile action towards his citizens; the latter to emplace a no-fly zone, embargo, and stated purpose to protect innocent civilians from Gaddafi's brutal measures of repression. Unlike the United States' efforts in Iraq and Afghanistan, in which regime change was never a "stated" objective, such a limitation on the purpose for the operation was made perfectly clear in Libya. The United Nations wanted Gaddafi out. The African Union, Arab League, and neighboring states generally wanted Gaddafi out. This was a collective effort, despite the usual national caveats, to diminish the power base of Muammar Gaddafi and to remove him from power in Libya (Blanchard, 23).

Previous chapters have carried the intellectual water along the path of Libya's ascendance to nationhood, along with the rise of a young, ambitious, exceptionally charismatic Muammar Gaddafi to power as "a citizen among citizens." He was the man who was going to deliver Libya from the depths of servitude and manipulation into the stratosphere of world supremacy, if not equality, utilizing a vast array of efforts to mold Libya into a power to be reckoned with; they had money, resources, weapons, and dangerous friends. He chose paths of righteousness, empowering women through *The Green Book*'s philosophies, while emboldening terrorists throughout Northern Ireland, Nigeria, Eritrea, Chad, Venezuela, and many other nations. He lived a relatively modest lifestyle for a national ruler, while expanding the cultural, educational, economic, and military status of the Libyan people and nation. If ever there was a schizophrenic nation, it was Libya under Gaddafi. His commitment to good was outweighed by his destructive tendencies. By 2011, the scales of political, civil, and legal justice had vastly weighed against him.

All nations endure some forms of protest, while the causes may change. The United States saw the Vietnam War divide the nation and lead to riots and protests in 1968 that shook the nation to its roots. Czechoslovakia also endured a revolution in 1968, coming apart at the seams and narrowly hanging onto its national identity. Germany saw the collapse of the Berlin Wall as the Cold War between the United States and the Soviet Union ultimately cracked the German foundation and produced a reunified, albeit politically and culturally confused, single Germany once again. Kenya sought reconciliation as a democratic nation by employing the principles of open elections and "the voice of the people," only to see the results of their presidential election turn into several days of bloody protests and rioting. Only a professionally trained police and armed forces cadre, unwilling to engage in "coup" actions, allowed an extremely bloody conflict to resolve in relatively short order. Thus intranational problems aren't new. Nor are they always a completely counterproductive exercise in national maturity. It's how they're handled by the ruling body that differentiates costly but resolvable conflicts from the recurring nightmare of overthrows, coups, and countercoups.

Libya lived on the precipice of a choice until the "Arab Spring" erupted all around their borders. For months they remained safe as first Tunisia, then Egypt, Syria, Yemen, and other nations, equally possessing predominantly Muslim populations, imploded. What set Libya off were political protests in February 2011, whose root cause lay in the previous year's imprisonment of political rivals to Gaddafi's regime, for what would be considered by most nations as normal political protests (RUSI, 2). Gaddafi had a history of ruthlessly crushing any form of dissent within Libya's borders. This was the final straw. Rather than allow peaceful conflict to subside, he mistakenly turned the nation against him by employing draconian measures of oppression against any form of protest, just as the Internet and YouTube were popularizing the Arab Spring throughout North Africa and the Middle East.

By early March, the United Nations, and the world were tired. They had seen enough violence and wanted it to cease. While the nations surrounding Libya regained control or provided the concessions necessary to quell most of the violence, Gaddafi turned up the heat on suppressing or destroying any form of opposition to his "people's" rule. This ultimately resulted in the two UN resolutions that empowered the United States and 20 other nations to intervene.

Operations in the first weeks of deliberate foreign intervention carried many banners—Operation Odyssey Dawn, Ellamy, Freedom Falcon, Harmattan, and Karakal. Operating under predominantly U.S. direction, these independent yet loosely aligned missions involved suppressing Libya's loyalist forces long enough for the nascent rebel movement to gain a foothold in Benghazi and Misurata; even the odds against Gaddafi's firepower, albeit ranging in age and technology from early 1970s until the early 2000s (Combataircraft.com); and reduce Gaddafi's ability to engage in wanton violence against his own people. While regime change wasn't a fashionable phrase for the end state of these initially independent actions, the ultimate objective remained strikingly clear: reduce or eliminate Gaddafi's authoritative hold on Libya, after a 42-year reign of violence, insecurity, economic instability, and political schizophrenia. Never was the objective to capture and kill the only ruler a large portion of Libya had known. Daily news briefings made that caveat painstakingly clear. This wasn't personal, unlike Iraq the second time around. This was all business. The business of getting rid of a ruler whose time had passed; whose influence had diminished and turned against his own people;

whose interests lay in the retention of power for the sake of, rather than the practice of good stewardship, that differentiates good leaders from despots. The means and methods were to be carefully crafted to ensure the newly established rebel groups, headed by the Transitional National Council (TNC), were always in the lead for any ground action and final moves against Gaddafi personally. The Coalition of the Very Willing, both Christian and Muslim, Eastern and Western nations, served to corner, cut off, collapse, and diminish the power base, resources, weaponry, and fighting strength of Gaddafi's loyalist forces.

UNSCR 1970 was approved on February 20, 2011. It asked Gaddafi to stop what he was doing. It also set the stage for the Coalition to mobilize forces and resources and to negotiate bases and strategies to convince Gaddafi that further action against his own people was not in his best interest. Observing that Gaddafi paid no heed to UNSCR 1970, the Security Council turned up the heat with UNSCR 1973 (Blanchard). This granted the right to establish and enforce a no-fly zone, freedom of navigation for commercial vessels, and active measures to prosecute an air and naval campaign against Gaddafi's forces. The intent was to prevent him from seemingly genocidal actions toward his own people, regardless of their Fezzan, Cyrenaican, and/or Berber heritage. By March 2011, his ruthlessness knew no bounds. What was explicitly forbidden in UNSCR 1973 was the introduction of ground forces for purposes of offensive action. This didn't prevent advisors from assisting the neophyte TNC and rebel forces, with military tactics, employment of weapons and communications, and the understanding of strategy in building a military campaign against Gaddafi. It prevented two significant emotional events from occurring. The first was the perception of rewinding the clock to 1884-5 when the Berlin Conference subdivided the continent of Africa into compartments, owned by leading European nations, with total disregard for the ethnic, cultural, spiritual, and economic heritage of the indigenous peoples. The second was a crystal-clear message that this was not the Crusades revisited, ergo a religious engagement of Christianity against Islam (Quartararo).

The fact that throughout the conflict the United Arab Emirates, as well as the Arab League, provided wholehearted support financially, militarily, and politically, reflected their faith in the principles upon which the resolutions were based, and the integrity of the Coalition's objectives. These two caveats created significant tension in terms of allowable actions by the providing nations; yet at the end of the day, the synchronization of efforts, although challenging at times, produced a steady pulse of action against Gaddafi's forces that allowed the rebel fighters to make consistent strides against the loyalist forces, and ultimately to capture or kill the ruler, Muammar Gaddafi.

The ultimate testimony of this conflict lay in the immediate postwar results when no nation came forth, including the newly liberated Libya, with accusations of collusion by the West; corruption by the providing powers; or manipulation of the TNC for political gain by the UN or surrounding nations to Libya. This was considered a clean result with a clearly established and relatively stable new governing body that was accepted by the average Libyan.

THE WAR UNFOLDS AND THE STARTING LINEUP IS SET

Starting on March 19, 2011, the United States executed Operation Odyssey Dawn (OOD). This was the inaugural campaign for the Coalition, and a time in which the United States would bring to bear the latest in technology and weaponry. It was the opening salvo designed to thoroughly knock Gaddafi down, until the UN forces were ready to assume command and control of the operation.

Authority to execute Operation Odyssey Dawn rested in the hands of the newest Combatant Command in the U.S. Department of Defense, U.S. Africa Command (USAFRICOM). Established in 2007, USAFRICOM was the new kid on the block whose charter specifically focused on a command staffed and resourced for the primary purpose of conducting engagement events with the independent nations throughout the continent of Africa. As "A different kind of Combatant Command," they weren't equipped or trained to focus on the traditional kinetic operations, armed intervention or resistance to attack; rather, they were heavily resourced to engage—one nation at a time, one tribe at a time—to prevent conflict vice resolving such conflicts (Quartararo).

Commanding USAFRICOM was General Carter Ham, a 30-year veteran of the U.S. Army. He had been through combat in Iraq and performed peacekeeping duties in Macedonia. He served as an advisor to Saudi Arabia and as the Head of Operations for the Joint Chiefs of Staff, performing the delicate act of balancing service-level priorities with Joint-level requirements. He was a patient, studious man who graduated with distinction from each of the civilian and service schools he attended. He knew the environment, the politics, and the passion of the region. He had the temperament and the patience to manage the expectations of those within Washington who considered USAFRICOM another traditional Combatant Command, thus ready on a moment's notice to strike out and eliminate any threats (Quartararo).

The only glaring shortfall in USAFRICOM's ability to conduct operations that might involve fighting was the fact that they weren't resourced with the units, personnel, or equipment that typically populates such commands. For his airpower, General Ham had a very small air force contingent that was administratively under the command as the 17th Air Force, commanded by Major General Margaret Woodward. Their available aviation assets were controlled and maintained by the Third Air Force, based in Ramstein, Germany. The Third Air Force was also under the administrative control of the U.S. European Command (EUCOM). This required General Ham to officially request permission from Admiral James Stavridis, Commanding General of EUCOM, for his combat and heavy-lift aircraft. Just as complicated was the chain of command to obtain naval support. Since AFRICOM didn't own any ships, but they were in charge of the area and the initial engagements, General Ham needed the services of the U.S. Sixth Fleet, headquartered in Naples, Italy, and under the operational control of Admiral Samuel Locklear. He was also designated as the overall U.S. Commander for Joint Task Force Odyssey Dawn (JTF Odyssey Dawn) forces. For Marine Corps contributions, he relied upon coordination with Brigadier General Paul Brier, then Commanding General of Marine Corps Forces Africa. Concurrently, Brigadier General Brier served as the Deputy Joint Force Maritime Component Commander to Vice Admiral Locklear. To access ground forces, if events proved catastrophic thus requiring a persistent ground-based presence, he had to coordinate through Brigadier General Brier and U.S. Army Forces Africa under Major General William Garrett III.

While complex, the close regional proximity of these leaders, coupled with historically close working ties with NATO's commanders and nations that would ultimately play out in the Libyan War, resulted in a swift and relatively efficient transfer of forces or capabilities to General Ham and Admiral Locklear. What Libya would see was a fusillade of airborne and sea-launched weapons, precisely targeted to minimize civilian casualties while taking out Gaddafi's tracking, targeting, and command-and-control networks. Strikes would focus on reducing, if not completely eliminating, Libya's ability to launch aircraft, surface-to-air missiles, or conduct electronic jamming. While roughly 2,000 American ground forces were in the region due to President Obama's strict policy of not introducing any ground forces into the conflict, they were a resource to be left on the shelf.

General Ham and USAFRICOM's greatest contribution to this conflict, other than their intimate familiarity with the environment and forces at play, was to provide the steady hand of supervision; while Admiral Locklear and his staff, heavy with USAFRICOM service members and civilians, conducted the day-to-day planning and operations.

BOLD ASSUMPTIONS AND OPENING SALVOS

The assumption going in was that USAFRICOM and the provided forces were solely to enforce both UN resolutions and, effectively, provide top cover, until the United Nations Coalition forces could arrive, stage, fuel, arm, plan, and begin operations. This all happened within a remarkably short time frame of 12 days. Operation Odyssey Dawn officially began with the launching of cruise missiles from the U.S. destroyer USS *Barry* just after midnight on March 19, 2011. The impact area for these missiles was command-and-control sites, weapons storage facilities, and large troop formations (Quartararo).

On the heels of these missile strikes were low-altitude penetration raids by F-15 Strike Eagles, F-16 Fighting Falcons, and FA-18 Hornets, all armed with laser designated, precision guided bombs. Within 12 hours, dozens of aircraft from the U.S. Air Force, U.S. Navy, U.S. Marine Corps, Britain's air arm, France's air force, and Canada's air force had turned Gaddafi's initial gains into stalemate, while sustaining zero casualties.

Operation Odyssey Dawn proved to be a timely speed bump to Muammar Gaddafi's efforts at forcibly reunifying, or cleansing, Libya. While the rebel faction grappled with newly achieved victories in Derna, Benghazi, and Ajdabiya, they struggled just as heavily with consolidating their power under a centralized command structure. The most militarily advanced nations on the planet have had generations to refine command structures to ensure good order and discipline, to establish a chain of command and clearly defined roles and responsibilities, and to train a cadre of leaders and young soldiers who will immediately and unhesitatingly carry out the orders of the civilian leadership. The rebel Libyan faction had days, weeks at most, in which to formulate a battle plan; establish a chain of command and appoint leaders; obtain the weapons, munitions, and communications equipment for waging war; and train their forces. The fact that a band of forces, much akin to colonial soldiers of 1775 in the budding American Revolution, held their own against a professionally trained and led force, speaks to a level of dedication and zeal to a cause that allowed them to overcome what would otherwise have been challenges too great for a less fully enveloped cause (Clarke et al., 11).

As a strategist, Muammar Gaddafi finally paid the price for his own lack of attention to studies when attending military academies and the British Communications School in the mid-1960s. Had he bothered to focus on how to develop a force, using time-tested methods, incorporating modernized weaponry and communications, and establishing a coherent command structure, he may well have found himself able to repel the initial rioting that occurred in February 2011.

As it was, he was becoming the recipient of the same groundswell of change that he too had advocated some 42 years prior. Fearing a repeat of his own revolution, Gaddafi had purposefully chosen to minimize the level of training and education that his armed forces received. The weapons were first rate, the users were bush league. They knew the basics, from commanding forces to maneuvering ships. They weren't schooled in the nuances of adapting to a battlefield in which the adversary changes tactics, from traditional force on force, to the modern-day version of fighting from among the population. His incessant fear of his own demise led to systematically dumbing down the abilities of his increasingly educated workforce, which formed the majority of his fighting forces. True, he employed other nation mercenaries on a regular basis, but they were an exception, not the rule. Thus, the core of his ability to repel any invasion, let alone manage a series of disjointed riots, was sorely lacking.

GADDAFI'S APPROACH

Gaddafi had held 40-plus years of opportunity to mature all elements of his force—from the infantry, to mariners and the aviators, to the armor officers—through military engagements he chose to involve Libya in, throughout the continent. From invasions of Chad in the mid-1980s to providing company-sized elements in support of Idi Amin in Uganda, Gaddafi repeatedly sought opportunities to expand his influence and help his so-called friends, as they too felt the sting of revolution. In the case of Chad, Gaddafi felt there was territory, the Aouzou Strip, that historically belonged to Libya, and therefore needed to be brought back inside their borders (Vira, 22).

Unfortunately, he recurrently ended up on the losing side, and over the generations, his forces developed a sort of marginalist attitude. They were marginally trained to handle low-level conflict, against inferior forces or bands of armed civilians. And their adversaries didn't hold significant advantages in weaponry or tactics. As a matter of fact, Chad relied upon French intervention to repel the Libyan forces. In Uganda, Idi Amin was forced from power and Gaddafi's warriors had to beat a hasty retreat lest they become embroiled in the post-Amin infighting and rampant violence.

What is so ironic is that Gaddafi had brilliantly planned his revolution against King Idris, taking years to develop his trusted network and manipulating the educational system to gain access to the advantages of British-operated military schools and Libya's own institutions of higher learning. He very surreptitiously identified, gained allegiance from, and collated the young men who would form his inner circle when September 1969 was ready to occur. Every element of planning this event, he totally neglected once he was in power. Possibly realizing that his own hold was as fragile as that of King Idris, he stopped planning for the future and began to plan for the here and now. That required dispensing with adversaries or untrustworthy subordinates. That also required ensuring that while technically sophisticated, his armed forces weren't so well integrated that they could coherently form against him and overturn his regime.

He devoted monastic time to compiling the stories for his *Green Book* that became the bible for Libya. Yet, that same messianic zeal to which he applied his ideals for a Libyan utopia, he blatantly disregarded when it was time to determine the course of his armed forces, both at the local level and those capable of action beyond Libya's borders. Thus, every move he made to take power from King Idris, he failed to implement for the long-term health of his reign.

Some may argue that Gaddafi trained and corralled his forces precisely in the manner in which he sought; namely, to protect him, not the nation. That is a valid perspective. What is left out is the realization that scoping the military arm to be the protector of Gaddafi leads to a rift among the ranks between those who blindly follow their leader and those who see the armed forces as protecting the nation, to include fighting beyond the borders when necessary.

Therefore, over the ensuing 42 years, Gaddafi developed two generations of fighters who couldn't think beyond the simple self-preservation tactical piece. They didn't see "what's next." They remained as loyal, whether publicly stated or not, to their tribal affiliation and region, as to the regime. Therefore, when the opportunity presented itself for them to make a choice about their future, Gaddafi began to see the unraveling of his armed forces, into pockets of loyalty with gaps created by defectors.

Violating the first principle of commanding a large force, unity, Gaddafi had independent brigades, led by his sons or cronies, who weren't obligated to synchronize their efforts with a central commander. Gaddafi was the leader of the people and ostensibly the commander in chief of the armed forces, but when the time came to organize his forces to quell the burgeoning discontent that was spreading from the Nafusa Mountains along the Tunisian border, to Benghazi en route to Egypt, he had no established communications plan or military strategy for dealing with the situation. He let the forces operate independently, just as his small revolutionary force had done so, in 1969. As that method was good enough for him to oust King Idris, he didn't realize that this time it was different. The outbreaks weren't coordinated. They weren't led from a central figure. They were mini civil wars in separate communities, all fed from the surrounding regions' emotional surge of energy that was the Arab Spring. He wasn't fighting just a small group of zealots seeking power; he was fighting an idea whose time had come. He wasn't prepared for that type of engagement.

What started out as oft-repeated localized violence, burning cars, trash cans, and anything else the rioters could find, was met with the typical police force response; rubber bullets, real bullets, night sticks, tear gas, and beatings. Unlike previous riots, this time, Gaddafi didn't have the luxury of being able to concentrate his known loyal forces into one specific area. The violence was all throughout the country. His police and military forces were spread thin. A growing number of those police and military forces used these riots as an opportunity to slowly peel away from the central government's authority and to link up with the various rebel movements.

Gaddafi had not anticipated such a large defection of forces and leaders, including his own Minister of the Interior and a senior general in the armed forces, 'Abd al-Fatah Younis. Along with the losses of his best-trained and longest-standing commanders, this dealt a blow that had long-term implications. Despite the apparent mismatch between government forces, possessing hardware that was more than adequate to suppress a rebellion, the rebel forces had several advantages on their dance card (Younis Obituary).

First was the fact that they had popular support. The Internet and immediate communications generation served as their command-and-control network. With the sparking of Arab-on-Arab actions throughout the Middle East and North Africa, the rebels initially had the advantage of popular sentiment working on their side. Videos posted to the Internet allowed one enclave to see and therefore become part of another side's actions. This, coupled, with a herd mentality that often overcomes any large organized movement, allowed, from Zlitan to Tobruk, to simultaneously erupt into protests and violence for which Gaddafi and his forces were caught completely off guard. Gaddafi's delusion of a content populace, therefore not requiring tighter security measures, proved to be his undoing. Unwittingly, the rebels created so much confusion throughout the northern third of Libya that Gaddafi's initial steps further fueled the resentment toward his regime. Using time-honored, draconian tactics of police states, his cameras captured his loyalist military and police forces ruthlessly quelling riots wherever possible. This allowed an otherwise unorganized movement to retain momentum, unlike his quiet revolution of 1969 that was bloodless and short-lived.

THE GAME CHANGES

Thanks to the miracles of modern technology, the unrest throughout the Middle East and North Africa was garnering the attention of the United Nations. As violence spread throughout the region, a more focused lens turned to Libya, chiefly due to the publicized actions by the government toward its citizens and the historical enmity that the UN held for Libya.

Riots that persisted from hours to days to weeks, finally forced the United States to seek a political solution through UN Security Resolution 1970. As Gaddafi failed to heed the limitations imposed by this resolution, collective action by the UN and lead efforts by Great Britain, France, and the United States were applied to put more pressure on Gaddafi and put a halt to the increasingly violent and persistent clashes in Libya. UNSCR 1973 finally tipped the hand of the international order as enough was enough. Gaddafi had played his final hand, and the rest of the world didn't like the cards he had dealt.

Recognizing that the United States possessed the most rapid response to stunt the suppression of the rebel movement, the President engaged the U.S. Africa Command, via the Joint Chiefs of Staff, to establish a task force that would serve to intervene until a UN force could be assembled. What Operation Odyssey Dawn achieved was time. There was time for the UN to mobilize a joint force; time for the rebels to consolidate some of their gains and lick their wounds from some of their losses; and time for the international community to decide whether Libya was a problem worth solving, or one better left to internal dynamics. Fortunately for the Libyan people, this became a unified effort. It wasn't Christian versus Muslim or Berber versus Tobu. It was independence versus ongoing oppression.

A CHRONOLOGY OF DISORDER AND DECISION

February saw a disorganized series of protests with violent clashes along the Mediterranean population centers that normally would have been short-lived and decided by overwhelming government firepower. However, as previously discussed, the lack of consistent training and maturation of skill in planning military activities began to unravel the government efforts to keep a lid on the budding revolution.

The expansion of violence in March that resulted in both UN resolutions being published reflected a quick maturation in the fighting skill of the rebels. Additionally, by March 5, the first publicly professed ideas by the Transitional National Council were becoming known outside of Benghazi. Led by the now former Minister of Justice to Libya, Mustafa Abdul Jalil, they publicly declared their right as the only legitimate government of Libya. This in turn set off yet another dilemma for Gaddafi as he now faced a two-front war: the first among his own people to retain authority as the leader of the Libyan people, and the second to stare down an organized enemy who was gaining support from the international community in political and military circles (RUSI, 2).

While the United Nations was contemplating action and the TNC was slowly building to their inauguration as the self-proclaimed legitimate government of Libya, what had been disorganized and low-level rioting turned into full-scale combat that had not been witnessed in Libya since 1942. Action in the Nafusa Mountains by Berbers clashing with Gaddafi's National Guard and police forces initially brought that region under the control of the rebels. Meanwhile, further east, Ras Lanuf and Benghazi were garnering heavy attention from combined air and ground forces, including modern Russian T-72 main battle tanks, Sukhoi-22 fighter-bombers, and a myriad of Eastern bloc small arms (Vira, 29). Facing this onslaught, the rebels amassed any weapon they could find. These ranged from World War II–era bolt-action, single-shot rifles, to relatively modern AK-47/74 assault rifles and rocket-propelled grenade launchers (Vira, 45).

Ras Lanuf held strategic value for both sides as it served as the primary oil refinery and shipping port. Benghazi had a long-standing history because of its role as the eastern anchor to Libya, it being the second-largest city in the nation, as well as the "Philadelphia" of the Libyan revolution. Ras Lanuf would see a frequent shift in ownership as first the rebels removed the loyalist forces from the city, followed by Gaddafi's forces retaking the town and pushing the rebels out. With this resurgence, the rebels routed the loyalist forces and were able to withstand yet another attack from Gaddafi's forces. The tipping point during the rebel's final occupation of Ras Lanuf lay in timely provision of close air support from U.S. and NATO fighter bombers. Independent of outside assistance, it is logical to presume that the rebellion would have burned itself out over the ensuing month as resources and training to keep the TNC-led fight alive would have been cut off by Gaddafi's forces (Simon).

The intervention by the United States in Odyssey Dawn provided the breathing room the TNC required to consolidate their leadership among the rebel factions throughout the nation; to establish a rudimentary command-and-control system; and to begin the process of turning street fighters into a coherent fighting force that could withstand charges by better-equipped and somewhat better-trained forces of Muammar Gaddafi. South of Benghazi was the same sort of back-and-forth effort, with the same reliance upon allied air power to reduce the imbalance in weaponry that otherwise faced the rebels. By March 31, 2011, the U.S.-led, Coalition-supported campaign to stem the tide of Gaddafi's forces, and prop up Jalil's ever-growing rebel movement, had been offi-cially handed off to NATO, under the moniker Operation Unified Protector (OUP).

A NEW LINEUP, THE SAME MISSION AND DESIRED END STATE

As March turned into April, the rising tide of engagements along the economic highway of Libya became a barometer for the effectiveness of the Coalition efforts and the persistence of the rebel forces. Benghazi became a stronghold for the rebels. Ras Lanuf was in their corner. Misurata flared up. Sirte became a battleground. Adjadbiya turned into a bloody morass. Al Brega became hotly contested. Tripoli remained the single, predominantly government-held outpost.

The formalizing of the Transitional National Council and the initial rec-ognition granted to them as the official government of Libya, by France, produced another wave of inertia that was realized in the form of popular uprisings in heretofore quiet towns such as Zintan and Sukhan (Cowell). Larger venues, Sirte among them, also felt the renewed sting of rebel activity. By early April, the NATO mission had found its rhythm, and the forces that were going to participate had arrived and begun operations. Reconnaissance jets from Sweden and jet fighters from The Netherlands. Aerial refueling aircraft from the United States and surveillance planes from the United Kingdom would make the critical difference. This was an all-in effort by forces that had devoted 64 years together, except Sweden, to the principle of a common defense against a common enemy.

Led by Lieutenant General Bouchard of the Royal Canadian Air Force, the combined air forces of 14 nations were brought to bear, launching from Decimomannu, Sigonella, Giola Del Colle, Souda Bay, Rota, and as far away as Royal Air Force bases in England. Their mandate was very straightforward; engage the enemy to protect civilian life. To that end they had to be very cautious in the manner to which they executed their mission. They had the weapons, trained crews, intelligence, and support structure necessary to carry out a very surgical campaign. Comparisons abounded concerning the last major NATO action, in Kosovo, in which national politics and caveats created an overly bureaucratic and inefficient command-and-control network. Such would not be the case this go-round (JFCNAPLES).

Lieutenant General Bouchard's right-hand man was the Royal Navy's Rear Admiral Russ Harding. An electrical engineer by trade, he had spent his career as a surface warfare officer and had become a naval aviator. His expertise in balancing the requirements of the air and surface components provided perspective regarding the participating nations as all sought to align their capabilities with their caveats and maximize their contributions while minimizing their risks (JFCNAPLES).

Nine years of international conflict had taken a heavy toll on the civilian populations of several nations, and Libya would prove to be as microscopically observed as any major conflagration. To that end, all of the participating nations employed the latest in weapons technology, from targeting, using global positioning systems, to final impact confirmation infrared technology that can divert the missile away from the target if the potential for collateral damage is too great. No longer were unguided, "dumb" bombs even considered for use by coalition forces.

Providing nations adhered to unitary taskings, short of national caveats that prevented or restricted the types of operations they could engage in. Sweden, as an example, deployed only reconnaissance aircraft. Their only weapons were self-defense air-to-air missiles and guns. Despite this limitation, Sweden's role in Operation Unified Protector was very significant as they provided the preponderance of battlefield photographs and targeting data, critical to allowing the forces to drop bombs, and to do so with much greater accuracy and significantly reduced instances of collateral damage (AFP/Swedish Wire). That created an entirely unexpected problem throughout the conflict, namely, the speed with which the smart weapons would be consumed and the danger some of the smaller providing nations would run into regarding their ability to remain relevant to the mission. The result was that larger nations provided spares to the smaller nations, or in some cases, additional emergency purchases were made to replenish stocks. Throughout the campaign, over 9,600 missions designed to destroy targets were launched out of a total of about 26,300. When the Operation Odyssey Dawn portion of the war is included, those totals rise to over 10,000 strike missions and over 27,000 missions of all types (NATO).

The officer charged with commanding what would result in the above mission totals was Lieutenant General Ralph Jodice II. A U.S. Air Force officer with 36 years in uniform, he was familiar with joint operations, fighter and ground attack air employment, and operations involving a heavily diplomatic component on top of military options. He was well versed in managing expectations and maximizing the potential of forces assigned.

THE WEAPONS OF WAR

Weapons technology wasn't the only arena in which nations paraded their latest and greatest. Aircraft were also introduced into the war that had not seen service prior to this conflict, although they had been on active service for at least a few years. The Eurofighter "Typhoon" made its combat debut over the skies of Libya and demonstrated a level of capability and precision that rivaled that of American tactical jet fighters. Designed with the latest in all-weather targeting capability, the Typhoon proved to be a critical component to the Coalition aerial strategy, and was one of the leading stars in the early days of OOD, when the French and British were the main two players against Gaddafi's forces. As the Typhoons were making their grand entrance, the distinguished elder statesman of British jets, the Tornado, was a front-row contestant throughout the campaign. Approaching 30 years of operational age, the Tornado had been upgraded to provide for the most precise targeting and penetration abilities. This team would be a mainstay throughout the six months of daily bombing sorties.

France also introduced their "Rafale" fighter, a twenty-first-century technological marvel that was replacing the venerable Mirage series of air-to-air and ground attack jets. Working alongside the latest British jets, the Rafale provided persistent air-to-ground coverage that reduced many of Gaddafi's Russian-made tanks, trucks, armored cars, aircraft, and missiles, to so much metal and dust.

Because of the withdrawal of the United States from kinetic operations at the end of March, these aircraft, operated by crews from many of the nations involved, carried the fight to Gaddafi and provided the cloak of security to the budding rebel forces that allowed them time to organize, train, and obtain weapons either from captured Libyan stockpiles or from nations willing to provide such assistance.

Air support wasn't relegated to fixed-wing tactical jets. NATO provided the ageless E3A AWACS (Airborne Warning and Command System) to monitor and direct aerial operations throughout the Mediterranean area of operations and from border to border in Libya. The Royal Air Force provided tactical electronics aircraft, built upon the Canadair Regional Jet airframe, that delivered invaluable intelligence to ground controllers and flight crews alike, allowing the planners in Italy to clearly identify targets and provide instructions to the crews that left no room for confusion.

At sea, the Italians participated and contributed with the ubiquitous Sea Harrier Jump jet. A 1970s platform with short duration, it had the distinction of being the only in-service aircraft that can take off and land like a helicopter, then transition to a fixed-wing, ground-attack airplane. These jets conducted some of the earlier strikes against Gaddafi's forces, prior to the public announcement of Italy's participation in OUP.

Britain employed its sole amphibious ship and its complement of Apache attack helicopters. Highly touted for their ability to identify, track, and destroy targets, the Apaches had been serving since Operation Desert Storm and had refined their abilities throughout Operations Iraqi Freedom and Enduring Freedom.

Flushing out the "who's who" of military aircraft, there was the distinctive F-16 Fighting Falcon; FA-18 Hornets; CP-140 Aurora anti-submarine warfare aircraft, a propeller-driven master of long-range, open-ocean aerial surveillance; multiple variations of the KC-135 aerial tanker; and a host of attack and transport helicopters (OUP, IISS). All contributed to suppressing any urge Muammar Gaddafi had to launch his air force, and served to turn his ground forces and equipment into so many burning hulks.

Victory in Operation Unified Protector was by no means limited to aircraft operations. A very significant naval presence was brought to bear on the situation. The first strikes of the Libyan War, under Operation Odyssey Dawn, were conducted by submarines of the United States and Britain, firing Tomahawk cruise missiles. Because of their range, in excess of 500 miles, and their pinpoint accuracy, they were a natural choice for opening the supporting efforts of the Coalition. Recognizing that a significant disparity existed between Gaddafi's forces and the rebel movement, the targets selected were critical to Gaddafi maintaining his tactical advantage, command-and-control centers, airfields, and large concentrations of armor, ammunition dumps, and communications sites.

Initial results were impressive. All airfields were successfully struck with no Coalition casualties. The few airplanes that attempted to take off did so after the initial strikes, and then only to defect. Airpower, which had caused so much consternation for the rebels throughout February and early March, had ceased to be a factor in the war.

Command-and-control nodes were significantly harder to dispatch. As they ran the gamut from fully established brick-and-mortar facilities to highly mobile vehicles with a radio and an antenna, their elimination was far from complete. Throughout the course of the seven-month conflict these assets would repeatedly be targeted and destroyed.

While Gaddafi's communications network was somewhat dated, reliant upon Soviet-era technology and upgrades, his armor presented a significantly greater problem. As the first rule of imperial rulers is to stay in power, that requires a level of sophistication in weaponry, if not forces, to ensure protection of the ruling body. He maintained and upgraded his armor capabilities to rival the best in the West, in his T-72 tanks (Vira, 21). While they may not have had the precision targeting capabilities that Western models brandished, they certainly had the firepower to eliminate any threat the rebels could pose against their skins. He used these to great effect early on in the fighting for the eastern cities, especially Ajdabiya and Ras Lanuf.

Prior to the initiation of Operation Odyssey Dawn, Gaddafi conducted combat in the traditional urban way; employ combined arms of armor, artillery, and infantry, and mass the effects to push back or destroy the enemy. As OOD progressed and his mechanized forces increasingly drew the attention of the Coalition, he brilliantly adopted the tactics of his foe. He went into hiding. Rather than out-in-the-open engagements, he moved his armor and artillery into protected sites, frequently comingling weapons of war with civilian populations (Simpson, 1). By no means is this considered "fair" by the rules of war, but Gaddafi wasn't known by reputation as a fair man, nor as one who greatly cared for his people, despite the renderings of his mantras in *The Green Book*. He went underground to preserve his fighting strength, and this proved to be a significant change in the dynamics of the war that extended its duration by months. Rooting out pockets of resistance became much more difficult for a Coalition that had very tight rules of engagement regarding damage that could occur to nonmilitary targets.

By April, he had completely discontinued the use of open land warfare and had adapted to the rebel "pickup truck" method. Regarding Gaddafi's indirect fire strength, much had been made of his SCUD missile inventory. Although these presented a significant threat from the standpoint that they could carry both conventional and chemical munitions, given that he had never had occasion to fire one of them, his technical skill in maintaining them was suspect, and suitable targets for employing them were few and far between; they served more as a weapon of fear than a true threat. That said, by late August, as he was exhausting his resources in trying to retain power throughout Libya, and focusing on concentrating it in his hometown of Sirte and the capital, Tripoli, he in fact did launch a couple of SCUD missiles, but to no effect. They landed out in the desert with no harm to humans (Vira, 34).

His artillery presented a greater threat. He had 1960s-era GRAD rockets. Picture a pickup truck with 16 rails on the back for unguided rockets to launch from. These were indiscriminate killers and frequently found their way into communities, schools, mosques, and pretty much anywhere but where they intended the rockets to strike. A weapon designed for open land warfare, against massed formations of soldiers, had no military value in this civil war. It did produce a tremendous number of civilian casualties and therefore was the target for rooting out by the Coalition for destruction. These weapon systems were easily hidden, thus they were a focal point of strikes throughout the seven-month campaign.

Since the Coalition had deliberately decided to not engage in a land war, the ground weaponry available to the rebel cause lay in those items that were recovered from the war dead; obtained via attacking arms caches and supply dumps, and occasionally supplied by one or more of the participating nations. France in this case did provide small arms and ammunition to besieged forces in eastern Libya, but this was the exception (Birnbaum).

Interestingly, throughout the conflict, firepower disparity was seldom defined as the compelling reason why the rebels fell back during an engagement. Numbers rarely played in their favor, but not a lack of firepower. They didn't take possession of armored cars and tanks until the late summer, by which time the odds had turned to their favor. They fought, and succeeded, by finding the weak spots in Gaddafi's human armor. They knew early on that force on force would not favor their objectives and purposefully used modern-day urban fighting techniques. Namely, they normally used hit-and-run tactics, relying upon the speed and mobility of their machine gun–mounted pickup trucks, and the use of channeling actions to force Gaddafi's forces into areas in which they would be hard pressed to escape when confronted by the rebel forces.

The rebel cause also had one distinct advantage; 'Abd al- Fatah Younis. Born and raised Libyan, a member of Gaddafi's inner circle for many years, and appointed to be his Minister of the Interior, General Younis knew his adversary well. He knew how Gaddafi thought, how he planned, how he calculated. General Younis was a critical linchpin to the initial successes of the rebel forces, and until his unfortunate death in July, he was a key member of President Jalil's cabinet. Much speculation exists surrounding the perpetrators of Younis's death. That can be debated by others. During his brief association with the rebel forces, he provided the forces with the fundamentals essential to building a credible force that could withstand Gaddafi's attacks and hold out long enough to compel the world to pay attention (Younis Obituary).

True to the adage that no service fights alone and no capability desires to be left out of the battle, naval forces of both sides played a critical, if unheralded, role in the war that was Libya. Gaddafi's naval strength, on paper, represented a credible non-oceanic-oriented, coastal defense force. He had purchased corvettes, frigates, motor torpedo boats, frigates, and minesweepers, and he had even obtained from Russia four of their older diesel-powered submarines. Thirty-six boats in all; this was impressive for a nation with a coastline facing one of the busiest commercial highways in the world, the Mediterranean Sea. On paper, this was a force capable of threats, action, and terror. On paper, a force that was rapidly deployed and not easily identified. Yet, paper didn't fight the coalition. Flesh and blood did. In reality, he had fewer than 50 percent of his fleet operational. The most fearsome weapon, his submarines, amounted to one serviceable asset. This ship, along with other combatants, was captured relatively early on in Benghazi.

Gaddafi did engage in repeated torpedo boat attacks and attempts to harass the smaller coalition ships as well as stalking the refugee ships that carried away citizens seeking protection from the war zone along the coast. For the first time in several decades, naval surface fire was brought to bear on an adversary ship as the Canadians and British replied to hostile intentions by Gaddafi's gunboats with shelling from their destroyers (Harding).

As air power prevented Gaddafi from providing an aerial screen or combat air patrol, to use the Western parlance, he was unable to mobilize his fleet for coordinated, offensive action against the ships facing off against him. To be sure, there were soft naval targets available as the Coalition required the use of replenishment ships and minesweepers, both relatively lightly skinned ships, for use along the northern Libyan coast.

Squaring off against Gaddafi's naval forces, the Coalition mustered 43 ships in total, with at most 21 on station at any given time. These ranged from cruise missile–carrying submarines from the United States and Great Britain, to guided missile destroyers, stealth frigates from France, aging but still potent frigates from Turkey and Bulgaria, minesweepers, amphibious assault ships from the United States, France, Great Britain, and Italy, and smaller destroyers from Bulgaria and Romania.

Aside from the nuclear submarines, these ships were specifically geared for close quarters and littoral missions. Commanding this relatively impressive array of ships was Italy's Vice Admiral Rinaldo Veri. During peacetime, he was the Italian Chief of Staff to their Joint Operations Headquarters. Thus, commanding a collection of a contributing nation's assets, with differing capabilities, weapons systems, and sensor arrays, was not an uncomfortable position for VADM Veri to occupy (JFCNAPLES).

Nautical rules of engagement are significantly different from those airborne and when soldiers square off face to face. The NATO mission helped to create a unique balance of power as they retained their peacetime maritime rules of the sea. They were obligated to answer ships in distress, be they friend or foe. While the latter never required their assistance, Libya did recurrently launch refugee ships to sea as part of an effort to occupy the time and energies of the contributing nation's fleets. Approximately 600 refugees were picked up; almost 300 ships had been boarded, with 11 being turned back due to suspect documentation or cargoes. The fate of these refugees would be far more positive, compared to their contemporaries making the same journey just two years later. That will be covered in Chapter 7.

Concurrently, the Coalition navy was asked to retain freedom of navigation for the oil tankers authorized to enter Libyan waters as they were providing critical revenue streams via the oil they retrieved from Libya's vast wealth and transporting it to markets ready to receive. The millions of dollars this income generated served to enable the rebel forces, later termed the Free Libya Forces, to continue arming, equipping, training, and transporting their forces throughout the nation. It is in this arena that Gaddafi's forces posed the greatest threat. Fortunately, they never ventured close enough to what some might have been justified in claiming was an ironic "line of death"—the 12-mile zone whereby ships are in international waters from that point. The exclamation point on the navy's efforts during the war could legitimately have been in September when a Royal Navy destroyer, the HMS *Liverpool*, escorted a former Libyan navy frigate, *Al Hani*, into Tripoli Harbor (Navy News). While on land and in the media, Gaddafi continued to profess his resistance to takeover, at sea he was quietly, yet forcefully, being choked off by his own resources, with the subtle yet pronounced assistance from Libya's savior during the Second World War.

The forces brought to bear, the weapons of war, have been illuminated; the battles that could add their names along those of Tobruk, El Alamein, Sicily, including Bani Walid, Sirte, Ajdabiya; the lineage of operations. But what was happening with the Libyan leadership? They were instrumental to the success of the operation, yet were virtual unknowns to the world prior to February 17, 2011.

THE TRANSITIONAL NATIONAL COUNCIL'S DECIDED ADVANTAGE

While no Robespierre or Rommel can be as intimately linked as "the face of the war," several members of the government established the foundation for a new Libya. Interestingly to the formation of the new government, faces were less pronounced as being central to the formation, as much as the title of the organization became the beacon of hope. The TNC was a conglomerate of economists, engineers, lawyers, and activists. They were rebels in spirit and humanists in soul.

Mustafa 'Abd al-Jalil, the former Minister of Justice under Muammar Gaddafi, was the first to publicly declare his allegiance with the rebel cause. Breaking away from the government due to the enduring violence associated with protests over human rights, political activism, and lack of inclusion in the affairs of state, he was selected to serve as the first Chairman, equivalent to the Presidency, of the TNC. Having served under Gaddafi for 30 years, he had a price on his head of $400,000. Ignoring such distractions, he set out to form a coalition whose aim was to keep Libya together once the war ended (BBC News, August 22, 2011).

Serving as Jalil's right-hand man was 'Abd al-Hafiz Ghoga, another lawyer and avowed human rights activist. Selected to also serve as the voice of the TNC, he had gained prominence from his defense of victims of a 1996 mass shooting at a Libyan prison. Not known to hide in the shadows, he provided a staunch backdrop to Mr. Jalil's passionate yet quiet leadership (Gritten).

To fund the war, the TNC found an expatriate economist in 'Ali Tarhouni. Departing Libya in 1973, he had devoted 30 years to teaching and research. When the opportunity emerged to return and try to create the Libya he still loved, Mr. Tarhouni leaped at the chance. His contribution was in the ability to find funding where it had been locked away or gone missing. Not only was he persistent, but he was creative, up to the point where he orchestrated breaking into a central bank in Libya to take just over $320 million, a pittance in war terms. On a grander scale, he appealed to the international community while on a fund-raising drive in Italy, seeking access to the frozen funds, to the tune of $160 billion in U.S. dollars (Fisher). While nations were reticent to provide a blank checkbook, they did begin honoring his request for the credit, with Italy stepping up first with $504 million and the United States falling in line with an additional $1.6 billion. His actions throughout the war would be remembered as he was voted to assume the office of President in the new, transitional Libyan government. He was the first of the postwar Prime Ministers and his role, albeit brief, would provide a foundation upon which his successor, 'Abd al-Rahman El-Keib, could build.

Probably the most polarizing figure was the former Minister of the Interior and now Major General in the new Libyan rebel movement, 'Abd al-Fatah Younis. Defecting within days of Mustafa Jalil, General Younis served as the senior military officer in the new administration, providing the technical expertise so critical to a nascent military force that was void of organization, uniforms, a rank structure, or an established

chain of command. He was responsible for corralling the zeal and frag-
mented efforts of the multiplicity of militias throughout Libya, to turn
them into a consolidated force that would turn Gaddafi's forces back
and ultimately provide the security forces necessary to maintain the peace
while the TNC transitioned to their expected role of the victorious, peacetime, Government (Younis Obituary). Fate would work against General
Younis, as he was killed on July 28, 2011. While the verdict has never been
fully determined, the rumors persist of an insider job by an arm of the
militia that didn't condone his stance on the nation's future.

Another figure of notoriety was 'Abd al-Rahman El-Keib. An electrical
engineer by trade, an activist by heart, and expatriate professor at the University of Alabama, Mr. El-Keib worked with the TNC in a supporting
capacity until his selection to become the interim Prime Minister in
November 2011. His posting would last until November of the following
year (Al-Shaheibi).

What this group of men lacked in long-standing military and governmental service, they more than made up for in heart, intelligence, and
wisdom. Starting a movement from scratch, in the modern world of
instantaneous communications and exit poll mentality, is not something
for the faint of heart. That this small body of businessmen, academics,
and lawyers cohesively welded together a fractured battlefield, determined as much by local militia forces as any central uniformed group,
speaks to their patriotism and to the ideals they believed Libya possessed,
those of equality, humanity, and prosperity.

LESSONS LEARNED

The Libyan War of 2011 will not garner the level of study and remem-
brance of conflicts long silenced, in the same region and fought on the
same ground. The names of Zlitan, Sabha, Bani Walid, or Brega won't
make for cinematic films and multipart novels. The tombs will be visited
by the close family. The scars of shells and missiles will be painted over,
torn down, or repaired. The images of Muammar Gaddafi will be the
most highly sought after by collectors, or most diligently targeted by
those seeking to forget. There will be a minority who will, for whatever
reason, long for the days when he ruled the land. Maybe this was because
of their name, or their family connection in business. This is inevitable
and has been demonstrated throughout history.

What lessons does this recently concluded war provide to us? First and
foremost is that despite two generations of autocratic, despotic, and frequently incalculably confusing rule, there will also be members of any
particular nation who see beyond the immediate flaws. That so disparate
a band as the men who formed the TNC, coming from all corners of the
globe, retained a common cause for 40 years and descended upon their

homeland at the right time, speaks to the innate ability of good people to wrestle the reigns of authority from evil.

We saw nations not recently in the vanguard for advocating global action, Great Britain and France, vigorously stepping into the fray to deliver millions of citizens, few of English or French heritage, from the bonds of a rapidly disintegrating dictator. Neither nation was so deeply embedded in the economy of Libyan oil that they were in danger of economic collapse should Libya implode. They saw an opportunity to provide stability in a region that had undergone a stunning spring of turmoil, and they wanted to stem the flood before there was no turning back. Their efforts, alone and unafraid, helped mobilize nations big and small, from the United States to Bulgaria, into action (Clarke).

Thus, being the largest power in the land doesn't necessarily mean they are the only power. The United States was hesitant to jump in, partly from fatigue of 10 years in Iraq and Afghanistan, partly out of fear at being labeled "anti-Muslim" in their prioritization at what conflicts to engage in, and partly out of uncertainty as to their ability to influence action in historically European parts of the world in which French, English, Italian, and even German influences had deeper historical roots. Yet, once the decision was made, the United States, along with the other nations participating, took to heart the UN resolutions and determined that stopping Gaddafi was the only course of action available. Not with forces on the ground, as those were plentiful among the Libyans themselves, but with supporting arms that allowed the ground forces time to form, time to learn, and time to succeed.

Technology proved to be an overwhelming advantage, yet an Achilles' heel, during the war. Due to the fervent need to minimize civilian casualties, stockpiles or "smart weapons" that had been designed and built to confront massed formations and structures housing first-world forces were employed, with devastating effect, in Libya. Yet, those stockpiles, because of their cost and sensitivity, were rapidly depleted, and there was a bit of a crunch to purchase additional weapons' components to make new smart weapons. In the absence of sufficient stocks by some nations, the burden shifted to those nations with greater industrial capacity to produce replacements. Thus, Denmark, employing just a handful of fighter-bombers and yet flying a statistically significant portion of the missions, went through their stocks rapidly, yet they remained in the fight and were buttressed by allies who compensated them for their costs (Wenande).

Command and control was once again highlighted as a success story. While European nations did employ a few of their special forces units, they did so primarily to provide an air-to-ground conduit to be used for ensuring air strikes hit their intended target, not veering off course or inadvertently targeting the wrong facility, à la the Chinese Embassy in Kosovo. They had the additional benefit of providing small unit training to those militia forces in the east, to which they were attached. Their impact was minor but significant. They provided a catalyst for the forces to continue growing in numbers, weaponry, and training.

Politically, we learned that Libya wasn't Egypt, Syria, or Iraq. Because of Muammar Gaddafi's past, there was a somewhat odd laissez-faire attitude to the events of 2011. Nations in the UN Security Council who had voted for intervention in Korea some 60 years earlier either voted against intervention, or abstained. Russia was the main focus. They didn't believe this was a fight to be had. Yet, unlike 1950, rather than walk out, de facto, abstaining, they made a point of not voting for or against, yet using the media to voice their objections. China, a supporter of intervention in Korea, also abstained. Yet they provided warships and transports to evacuate their people and made no efforts to intervene on the side of the loyalists, as they had with North Korea. Germany, taking a decidedly pacifist stance—and to be fair to them, not a completely inappropriate stance given their last occasion of visiting Libya—did in fact come around by early summer and take on a supporting role at the headquarters level (Marquand).

Much can be made of the abstinence by Egypt, Tunisia, and Chad, in avoiding open conflict or choosing sides with either of the parties to this war. While the borders of the eastern and western nations remained open to refugees, they did monitor them with military activity to ensure the war remained confined to Libya. They did have their own internal problems, but history has shown that at times, the government can seek to minimize its own troubles by intervening in another conflict, to serve as a temporary distraction.

At the end of October, when the billions of dollars, millions of rounds, thousands of bombs, and hundreds of casualties had been counted, this war was about a nation finding the time right to reclaim its identity, which had been stolen and corrupted in September 1969 by a cunning, persuasive, and charismatic leader, Muammar Gaddafi. The challenge of tomorrow is far greater than the struggle of the past. The once knowingly simple routine of conformity to the People's Committees now became the unknown of a country controlling its own destiny, making its own rules and setting its own guidelines. Will they succeed where others have failed, and build upon a legacy of tribal bonding, or will they remain distracted by local alliances and prevent a rejoining of Cyrenaica, Fezzan, and Tripolitania, into a unified Libya that sits as an equal at the table of government, commerce, and society?

SOURCES

AFP/Swedish Wire. "Sweden Sends Eight Fighter Jets to Libya." Accessed July 21, 2013. http://www.swedishwire.com/politics/9146-sweden-sends-eight-fighter-jets-to-Libya.

Al-Shaheibi, Rami. "Abdul Rahim El-Keeb, New Libya Prime Minister, Balances Demands of Rebels and West." *Huffington Post World*, November 1, 2011. Accessed July 21, 2013. http://www.huffingtonpost.com/2011/11/01/abdul-rahim-el-keeb-libya-_n_1069198.html.

BBC News Africa. "Libya Crisis: Profile of NTC Chair Mustafa Abdul Jalil." BBC News Africa, August 22, 2011. Accessed July 21, 2013. http://www.bbc.co.uk/news/world-africa-14613679.

Birnbaum, Michael. "France Sent Arms to Libyan Rebels." *Washington Post*, June 29, 2011. Accessed July 6, 2013. http://articles.washingtonpost.com/2011-06-29/world/35235276_1_nafusa-mountains-hans-hillen-libyan-rebels.

Blanchard, Christopher M. "Libya: Unrest and U.S. Policy." Congressional Research Service. Accessed June 6, 2013. http://www.loc.gov/crsinfo.

Clarke, Michael, Malcolm Chalmers, Jonathan Eyal, Shashank Joshi, Mark Phillips, Elizabeth Quintana, and Lee Willett. "Accidental Heroes: Britain, France and the Libya Operation." Saqeb Mueen and Grant Turnbull, eds. Accessed June 9, 2013. http://www.rusi.org/libya.

Cowell, Alan, and Steven Erlanger. "France Becomes First Country to Recognize Libyan Rebels." *New York Times*, March 10, 2011. Accessed July 6, 2011. http://www.nytimes.com/2011/03/11/world/europe/11france.html?_r=0.

Fisher, Max. "Ali Tarhouni." *The Atlantic*, October 3, 2011. Accessed July 21, 2011. http://www.theatlantic.com/magazine/archive/2011/11/ali-tarhouni/308670/.

Gritten, David. "Key Figures in Libya's Rebel Council." BBC News, August 25, 2011. Accessed July 21, 2013. http://www.bbc.co.uk/news/mobile/world-africa-12698562.

Harding, Thomas. "Libya: Royal Navy Warship HMS Liverpool Comes under Heavy Fire." *The Telegraph* (UK), August 4, 2011. Accessed June 21, 2013. http://www.telegraph.co.uk/news/worldnews/africaandindianocean/libya/8682572/Libya-Royal-Navy-warship-HMS-Liverpool-comes-under-heavy-fire.html.

Joint Forces Command, Naples. "Unified Protector." Accessed October 27, 2012. http://www.jfcnaples.nato.int/Unified_Protector.aspx.

"Libya." Combataircraft.com. Accessed June 9, 2013. http://www.combataircraft.com/en/Military-Aircraft/Libya/.

"Liverpool Conducts Historic Escort Mission in Libya." Navy News Reporting Service (UK). Accessed June 21, 2013. https://navynews.co.uk/archive/news/item/1031.

Marquand, Robert. "Germany Plays Catch-up after Being on Sidelines of NATO's Libya Campaign." *Christian Science Monitor*. Accessed July 23, 2013. http://www.csmonitor.com/World/Europe/2011/0825/Germany-plays-catch-up-after-being-on-sidelines-of-NATO-s-Libya-campaign.

"Operation Unified Protector—Allied Assets Deployed to Libya." *International Institute for Strategic Studies*. Accessed May 19, 2013. http://archive.is/cKiH.

"Operation Unified Protector Final Mission Stats." NATO Operational Media Update, November 2, 2011. Accessed July 21, 2013. http://www.nato.int/

nato_static/assets/pdf/pdf_2011_11/20111108_111107-factsheet_up_facts
figures_en.pdf.

Quartararo, Joe, Sr., Michael Rovenolt, and Randy White. "Libya's Operation
Odyssey Dawn: Command and Control." *PRISM*, 3, no. 2 (March 2012).

Rogers, Simon. "NATO Operations in Libya: Data Journalism Breaks Down Which
Country Does What." *The Guardian* (UK). Accessed July 23, 2013. http://
www.theguardian.com/news/datablog/2011/may/22/nato-libya-data
-journalism-operations-country.

Simon, Scott. "In Libya, the Fight for Ras Lanuf." NPR.org. Aired March 5, 2011.
Accessed November 23, 2013. http://www.npr.org/2011/03/05/13428
8525/In-Libya-The-Fight-For-Ras-Lanuf.

Simpson, John. "Libya Crisis: Gaddafi Forces Adopt Rebel Tactics." BBC News
Africa, March 30, 2011. Accessed November 4, 2012. http://www.bbc.co
.uk/news/world-africa-12911904.

Vira, Varun, and Anthony H. Cordesman. "The Libyan Uprising: An Uncertain
Trajectory." Center for Strategic and International Studies, June 20, 2011.
Accessed July 21, 2013. http://csis.org/files/publication/110620_libya.pdf.

Wenande, Christian. "Air Force Makes Redaction Blunder in Libya Report."
Copenhagen Post, October 12, 2012. Accessed July 6, 2013. http://cphpost
.dk/news/international/air-force-makes-redaction-blunder-libya-report.

Younis, General Abdel Fatah, obituary, *The Telegraph* (UK), July 29, 2011. Accessed
July 6, 2013. http://www.telegraph.co.uk/news/obituaries/politics
-obituaries/8671455/General-Abdel-Fattah-Younes.html.

CHAPTER 5

Libya and Oil: Curse or Blessing

In the vernacular of popular television, it was "black gold" and "Texas tea." To the founders of the Organization of Petroleum Exporting Countries (OPEC), it was winning the lottery. In the eyes of the seemingly brilliant strategist and yet concurrently delusional dictator, it was both a sword and a ploughshare.

Muammar Gaddafi was born into economic and national identity poverty; both played significant influences on his state of mind as a Libyan and ruler of his nation. He devoted tremendous energy toward projecting humility, while secretly hiding away well in excess of $200 million in assets, both cash and material. Among his many robes were those of pure silk from the finest Persian tailors. The security force consisted of "Amazonian" beauties with a deadly eye for accuracy. His security entourage was outfitted with the latest in weaponry and vehicles. Yet this same man sought to equalize the masses; provide free education for all who sought a better life; and construct waterways that would tap into resources in central Libya for the agricultural and personal needs of the citizens along the very densely populated northern shore.

DISCOVERY OF OIL AND THE INITIAL CONTRACTORS

Nature had blessed the North African coastal region with abundant prehistoric life that devolved over time to turn into energy. As discussed in Chapter 1, the evolution of plant and animal life from the Miocene Era through the Jurassic Era produced reservoirs of energy, both oil and natural gas, which would provide the foundation for enormous wealth or extravagant waste, according to the finders of this vast underground wellspring.

The same speed with which natural resources were forming could have been subscribed to the development of technology and human intellect surrounding the discovery and extraction of these resources. Civilizations hadn't required any significant quantity of combustible material for any means other than cooking and the occasional torch to keep ravenous wild-life at bay. Centuries played out in which a mere wax candle, possibly a hay-based torch or a whale oil–burning lantern, more than adequately sufficed to light, heat, or power, the machine of the times; the human.

By the late nineteenth century, fledgling discoveries of oil began to pop up. Most notably, Titusville, Pennsylvania, claimed the top spot as the first known discovery of significance. Aside from the novel distinction of being "the first," this lent itself to nothing more than the stepping-stone to further explorations throughout the American Northeast, and progressively into the South, where the truly remarkable discoveries would arise. These discoveries would turn Oklahoma, Texas, and Alaska into boom states for natural resources and cement their reputations for predominantly single commodity successes.

Meanwhile, back in sleepy Tripolitania, Cyrenaica, and the Fezzan, agrarian life remained as pastoral yet difficult, as from the previous 1,000-plus years of known human existence in this region. However, in one small village just south of Sirte, a Bedouin family was producing generation after generation of farmers who would one day produce a son. This son would recall his humble roots as he ascended to power; nonetheless, he would ascend and capture the riches that accompany such power. He was Muammar Gaddafi.

He didn't realize he was living on top of the 13th-largest oil repository of extractable oil and natural gas in the world (Libya Oil Almanac, 42). Recent estimates place reserves in this one "pond" at 117 billion barrels of oil or "oil equivalent," to use the jargon of the natural gas industry. That alone would keep Libya, and outside investors, busy for centuries to come. But, that's assuming the technology and calculated consumption rates remain at their 2013 levels of about 1,470,000 barrels of oil taken daily from the earth.

This bubbling brook of opportunity was discounted by scientists and geologists as late as 1931, after oil had been a known resource in close proximity to Libya. An Italian geologist, Ardito Desio, of the Royal Geographic Society of Italy (Whaley, 2), prospected from Libya to the western frontier of the Sudan and pronounced that no significant deposits of oil/natural gas existed. While he would later discover some oil at the subsurface in Libya, he found greater resources of artesian waters than oil. Not to paint him as incapable—he was a highly trained and well-respected geologist of his day. The technology wasn't to the point where prospecting with rudimentary tools, charts, and local knowledge could produce reliable measures of potential for resources.

In yet another twist of fate, Adolf Hitler's North African campaign, led by Germany's most highly respected and feared general, Field Marshal Erwin Rommel, which focused on eliminating the southern threat of the Allies, eliminating their access to the Mediterranean and the strategic oil transportation route via the Suez Canal, and providing a stepping-stone for continued Italian participation in World War II, netted absolutely none of these goals. The British, Australians, and New Zealanders, with logistical assistance and intelligence aid from the occasional local tribesman or clan, held off Rommel's forces long enough for the United States to enter the conflict and open a second front via Morocco. Additionally, Allied air and sea power reduced the Italian fleet and German-chartered merchant ships, manifested with crucial supplies of oil, ammunition, and rations to feed Rommel's resource-starved force, to freshly established sunken reefs for the aquatic life, thereby opening up the Mediterranean and the Suez Canal to the mostly free flow of traffic; virtually eliminating Italy as a militarily credible ally to Germany, given their significant investment in resources and personnel, and providing Germany with the net gain of no territory. Italy would remain a vital cog in delaying the Allied advance through the southern channel into Europe, but Benito Mussolini's days were numbered, and Italian armed forces could muster no more than cursory resistance.

Despite every tactically brilliant, battle-hardening move, and early philosophical advantage, oil, and the Afrika Korps' voracious appetite for it, was the ultimate downfall for Field Marshal Rommel. His counterpart, Field Marshal Bernard Montgomery, certainly could lay claim to finally outsmarting Rommel; however, the straw that broke Rommel's back lay in the lack of accessible oil. While it lay just 2,000 feet below the surface, especially in the critical Sirte Basin, no one was aware of its existence in any meaningful quantity, nor had any exploratory wells been drilled prior to the war. So close, yet so far. Thus, for every precious gallon Rommel did receive in support of his thousands of tanks, ammunition carries, trucks, airplanes, and cars, he lost nine other gallons to enemy action. He required 80,000 tons a month, yet was lucky to receive 25,000 tons (Topedge.com).

MATH THAT WOULD NEVER END IN HIS FAVOR

The war would end. Muammar Gaddafi would continue to age and be further educated on the failings of his tribal and political forebearers; he'd personally witness the devastation wrought by open and total warfare; he would witness the "spoils of war" as the victorious Allies would officially seek to partition Libya into the three predominant regions, under the title of Libya, via the newly established United Nations.

Governance would be handed off to a benevolent dictator and friend of the Allies, King Idris, who would establish the underpinnings of the first oil revolution in Libya.

By 1951, technology, machinery, and a demonstrated thirst for the power of oil was beginning to show signs of maturing throughout Libya. Exploration was beginning to discover the intimations of potential, while the dollars and pounds that had subsidized World War II were now searching for new homes to harvest the benefits of industrialization and modernity. While Libya was still a recipient of aid, in exchange for basing agreements and access to the Mediterranean and trading routes, this not-so-tiny nation was on the verge of an economic revolution. However, even they did not know what was about to happen.

In 1953, oil, in significant quantities, was discovered in Algeria. So what? True of some things, but given the lack of impermeable subterranean borders among the nations of Africa, and the close proximity in terrain that marked Algerian, Tunisian, and Libyan "borders," a find in one was inevitably to lead to finds in the other nations. Such was the case. While Algeria thought they were the big dogs on the block, they were but a mere sideshow to what Libya would find and begin producing just three years later (Whaley, 2).

The year 1956 would see the first exploratory wells drilled, and three years later, as if to announce to the world that oil was to become the commodity of kings and a strategic bargaining chip, the first commercially viable well was discovered in the Zletin oil field in the Sirte Basin (Libya Oil Almanac, 14), as an American Airlines Boeing 707 streaked across the sky from coast to coast. The first widely purchased and employed commercial jet airliner and her four shrieking turbo jets announced the arrival of a completely new era (HistoryOrb.com).

The politics of the day declared that the major oil companies were chiefly American (Conoco, Standard, Hess, Marathon, Occidental), British (British Petroleum), French (Total), and a smattering of other smaller corporations from throughout Europe and Canada. They had the experience, several gaining their reputations from the late 1880s; they had the capital, roughly $1 million by 2013 valuations for each well; and they had the labor force well seasoned by generations of wildcatters and oil men.

The onrush of oil companies brought about a double-edged sword. On the one hand, this relatively sudden surge in economic potential began to release Libya from the historical shackles of fiefdom that had so long occupied the "tribes" and communities of Libya's disparate ethnographic regions. Where they had once been the doormat upon which the military, economic, and political boots of invading and conquering nations and kingdoms had stepped, they now had their own resource for wielding the same economic and military stick. They could now choose with whom they sought to associate, with whom they allowed access to their airfields, ports, roads, and resources. They had options. King Idris was a gracious, if not mild-mannered, ruler. He saw no reason to rock the boat; thus the initial agreements put in place with internationally sourced oil companies tended to be more generous in favor of the oil companies. Within 10 years, this would completely turn on its head.

Thanks in large part to persistence by the initial oil giants, the Kingdom of Libya, by 1965, had become the world's sixth-largest exporter of oil (Whaley, 2). The company that put them on the map was Occidental Petroleum, run by Dr. Armand Hammer. His pedigree was business, not oil. But to an industrialist and entrepreneur, oil was just another commodity. As an independent, Dr. Hammer didn't have institutionalized memory of how the oil industry was supposed to work. He viewed it as opportunity. With Occidental down in the economic dumps, he infused the funding to make it an international powerhouse. His shrewd dealings with the Libyan government cemented his place as a maverick and trend setter. For a time, Occidental was the largest producer of oil in Libya. Libya put Occidental on the map, and Occidental put Libya on the map. Yes, there was mutual benefit and mutual gain, to a certain extent. However, that would change dramatically in just a few short years (Pace). What was not known at this time was that Libya was sitting on the largest reserves of oil on the continent of Africa, roughly 46 billion barrels, and over 54 trillion cubic feet of natural gas. More about natural gas later.

By comparison, the proven—i.e., "recoverable" at reasonable cost— reserves of oil in Nigeria and Algeria, numbers two and three respectively, amounted to 37.2 billion and 12.2 billion barrels, respectively (*Petroleum Insights*). Financially, this allowed Libya to evolve, almost overnight, from a subsistence-driven economy, depending overwhelmingly upon the external infusion of financial and occupational resources, into an equal player in the resource import and export business. Not to mention the exorbitant cost of importing food staples to allow the roughly five million people to live out their lives in something resembling modern comfort and with improved health.

Oil's price of 90 cents a gallon allowed a nation of 1.5 million citizens to emerge from living as one of the poorest on earth to becoming overnight high-rollers in the economic game of life. From humble economic origins at the outset of Muammar Gaddafi's reign, when the per capita earnings of Libyans stood at just over $2,100 (Vandewalle, 2), until throughout the economic boon and then sanctions-created bust, Libyans consistently saw a rise in economic potential that few nations could match. Their "bubble" didn't hit in 2008. It arrived three years later at the hands of Gaddafi's henchmen in attempting to suppress the protests by the citizens tired of being isolated and scouted throughout their daily lives. Recovery would take time, but as Libya has demonstrated her resilience, the economy has slowly rebounded.

But, as goes the price of oil, so go the fortunes of the people. September 2, 1969, would turn this nation on the rise into a nation on its head, as a young signals officer from the Bedouin region of Sirte, would mobilize a force of disaffected youth and turn Libya into one of the most potent, if not confounding, nations on the planet. So how did they take riches and turn them into rags? That involves Gaddafi's penchant for turning gold into dust, or commerce into collectivism.

NATIONALIZING THE OIL INDUSTRY AND LIBYAN POLITICS

Oil's rise in the world economy was met with a mixture of disdain and glee. On the one hand, nations possessing stocks of this valuable commodity weren't mature enough in their business acumen to appreciate its strategic implications. While World War I had introduced mechanized warfare as a staple of conflicts present and to come, it wasn't until the Second World War that this resource became an end unto itself. Japan required virtually 100 percent of its oil via import and the known reserves throughout the Pacific region presented the easiest means of obtaining this commodity. So much so that they purposefully chose to strike the largest adversary, rather than seek a diplomatic and economic solution, as a means of obtaining secure access to oil as well as exerting their desires to become a world power militarily. On both fronts, their successes lasted but a decade, starting with their incursion into China and ending with their receiving atomic destruction delivered via fuel-burning machines. Germany also knew the value of, and necessity for securing, oil fields. Theirs were located much closer, in the southern European region; nonetheless, their efforts to obtain and retain these strategic oil fields, Ploesti in Romania the most highly publicized, also resulted in short-term gain and long-term destruction.

The Middle Eastern players remained conspicuously absent throughout this international conflict. As mentioned earlier, Libya was completely unaware they sat upon the largest reserves on the continent. Saudi Arabia and Kuwait were not militarily strong enough, nor interested enough, to actively participate in the war. They were content to be a provider, as their contribution to the end of the war brought in a level of income they'd not previously held, and this was good enough for them.

Once Libya learned of their newly found riches, they rather quickly set out to establish at least some rudimentary policies to help govern this wealth. The Petroleum Law of 1955 laid out the framework for oil companies who wanted to do business with Libya. While Libya didn't have an extensive corporate history, they were astute enough to establish a formality by which the corporations with decades of experience could contract with Libya, and not completely take the Libyan for an economic ride.

A significant component of the 1955 law was that participating oil companies were only able to lease 75,000 square-kilometer blocks. This served two purposes. First, it prevented any single entity, or small grouping of companies, from monopolizing the resources, thereby opening the door to price fixing at artificially low levels for the Libyan sponsors. Competition would be maintained, and ultimately, better prices for the product would be secured. Secondly, reducing the size of blocks allowed also prevented various companies from leasing but not exploring or developing these chunks of real estate. Why this would have been a concern is that given the volatility in the price of oil, with few companies holding large blocks, the opportunity for those companies to "sit" on their blocks would have been easy, and it would have had a second order effect of preventing others from exploring and extracting the oil, and it would have reduced the flow of cash into the Libyan government (Oxford Institute, 5).

With oil was selling for $1.93 per barrel in 1955, the industrialization of the world following World War II and the roaring 1950s presented a very clear picture of the value of fuel as the means of continuing the drive of the international economic "engine." Beginning with the first production quantity of oil flow from Esso pipelines in 1961, Libya was now officially a player in the gas and oil business. In 1962, they joined the Organization of Petroleum Exporting Countries (OPEC). Little did the other nations of OPEC know that this upstart would turn the oil industry upside down and provide them with the inertia to seek greater rewards for what nature had buried deep under their soil.

By 1965, Libya had become the sixth-largest producer of crude oil in the world. The government knew they weren't reaping "market rates" for their product, but the philosophy of the Idris administration was that of introducing and sustaining competition and of a nation that had been poor and now was no longer. Thus, any profit and improvement in quality of life was immeasurably better than the alternative. That theory, unfortunately, didn't translate to the masses, as they began to sense that the profits received from their oil weren't flowing as freely to the common citizens as they were into the hands of a relatively few government officials. One quiet, yet potentially powerful agent was born in 1968, the Libyan National Oil Company (NOC). What would start out as a semiprivate business would soon gain prominence as the ultimate power-wielding giant in the oil game.

The year 1969 would ignite the fuse as Muammar Gaddafi and his cronies chose to upend the existing administration and begin their revolution to wrest back their country from the corrupt or inept. One of Gaddafi's first actions, in early 1970, was to nationalize the NOC. This had the effect of redirecting all profits into the government treasury, ostensibly for redistribution to the masses. A second order effect would be the financial potential this nationalization had on Gaddafi's grand dreams of liberating all of his people and breaking free from the economic chains cast by the international oil companies.

The first, and arguably most radical, nationalizing step was the introduction of participatory agreements, replacing concessions. The NOC transitioned all existing agreements into these new tools, whereby the oil companies became "contractors" rather than owners. The land and contents reverted back to the NOC and Libya; the oil companies performed all of the labor associated with finding, extracting, shipping, loading, and moving the oil. The NOC was the landlord and would receive fees for the opportunity by the contractors to access the Libyan oil. Concurrent with transition to participatory agreements, the price, taxes, and royalty fees, all skyrocketed. What had been an oil company–friendly policy of providing a percentage to the government for allowing the oil company to drill, became a percentage split that went heavily in the favor of the NOC and Libyan government. The NOC became a 51 percent owner of all sites; the oil companies became the service providers.

Initially, this would be met, business force against business force. The major oil companies, such as Shell, Exxon, and British Petroleum, tried to fight the skyrocketing rate hikes and deal changers that the NOC imposed. They balked at the 30 percent price increase. The tax rate against production soared, from 15 percent or less to over 50 percent. They railed against losing "ownership" of what they saw as their fields, because they had provided the equity, labor, materiel, transportation, engineering, and markets. They saw Libya as just being an ungrateful child who needed to be reminded of the privileges gained by these oil giants paying them even pennies on the dollar, for a liquid that could do no good just sitting in the ground (Sampson, 6).

What they hadn't banked on was a young upstart who demonstrated his infrequent, yet periodic, mastery of timing: Muammar Gaddafi. The old way of meeting a problem with force was no longer viable. With Gaddafi in power; the quality of crude oil held in Libya; the expanding markets, therefore expanding demand; and the aftershocks of the 1967 Arab-Israeli War, the rules of the game had changed.

OIL AS A PLOUGHSHARE

While so much has been made of the negative side to oil, within Libya as well as the rest of the world powers, the discovery and consequent extraction of oil, and to a lesser extent natural gas, wasn't all bad for either Libya or the rest of the world. As mentioned earlier, what lay beneath Libya's soil was an estimated 47 billion barrels of oil. Statistically that placed them as number one on the continent of Africa, with Nigeria running second at 37 billion, Algeria in third at just over 12 billion, Angola at number four with 9.5 billion, and the government of Southern Sudan finishing fifth at about 6.7 billion barrels (*Petroleum Insights*).

Libya's take is just about 3.4 percent of the world's supply. For a nation of just under six million people, owning 3 percent of a strategic commodity has allowed them to establish a financial standard of living that is on par with many first-world nations, at about $13,300 in per capita earnings ("Libyan Economic Profile").

Because of the accessibility to the oil, in the lower 2,000-foot range; the availability of secure, relatively stable, and expansive ports; the ability to run pipelines through undisputed territory (the same can't be said for The Sudan and Southern Sudan), and the lack of any strategic choke points (the above-referenced Arab-Israeli War that closed off the Suez Canal), Libya is not only highly sought after by commercial companies, but the relative cost of producing a barrel of oil, taking into effect extraction, processing, shipping, etc., is significantly lower than the more established Middle Eastern nations within the Persian Gulf Region.

The relative lack of infrastructure also served to assist in establishing drilling sites, pipelines, refineries, and the ports. Libya had yet to emerge from a predominantly tribal based, agrarian-driven economy that relied on small communities, nonmotorized equipment, and limited consumption of natural resources.

Three significant oil basins, Sirte, Murzuk, and Ghadames, the former in east central Libya, the latter two in the southwestern and western regions, account for the known deposits of oil. While they are vast fields, they are in exceptionally remote population centers; thus workers had to be imported from the coastal region of Libya, as well as expatriate and contract workers supporting the oil companies. This did infuse those regions and create more of a blended sense of community than had previously been known.

The Sirte Basin, encompassing approximately 43,500 square kilometers of territory (Rusk, 433), has reflected to geologists a capacity of approximately 45 billion barrels of recoverable oil. This basin alone accounts for two-thirds of all Libyan production and ranks as the 13th-largest oil repository in the world. To put the Sirte Basin into perspective, the area of the basin exceeds the size of Denmark, Estonia, or the total size of the five smallest United States, with room to spare in all cases.

At just over 30,000 square kilometers, the Murzuq Basin in southwestern Libya has an approximate volume of two billion barrels of oil and could fit either Belgium or Lesotho within its boundaries, with room left over. About one-quarter of the extracted oil starts its journey from this area (Rusk, 441).

The Ghadames Basin, smallest of the established oil reserves in land area, coming in at about 20,000 square kilometers, could snugly fit El Salvador or just barely be too small to incorporate Israel. Beneath this land surface is reputed to be approximately three billion barrels of light sweet crude (Rusk, 439).

The statistics are readily available to the diligent researcher. The "so what" of these comparisons is to portray the vast scope of one nation's natural resource advantage, and thus its strategic value as a key player in foreign policy and world economics. More to follow on how Gaddafi turned oil from ploughshare to weapon, and then rather grudgingly, or astutely, depending on one's perspective, how he chose to dull the edges of the blade and return it to a productive tool.

Work in the fields was incredibly challenging and daunting as the companies and employees had to fight not only bureaucratic hurdles but Mother Nature, in the form of sand storms and a complete lack of readily available water sources. Despite these conditions, all three fields turned into thoroughly profitable ventures. Profitability in pulling the oil from the ground is only as great as the ability to send the oil to market. Without oil terminals located in a manner in which the security of them can't be held hostage, as occurs in the Sudan with product in the south and terminals in the north. These make for contentious bedfellows as the frequent threats and strikes, by both sides, have demonstrated. Libya has been able to avoid this problem, once they had nationalized the industry. They became owner, producer, transporter, refiner, distributor, and even financier, in a few cases.

Complementing the production sites were the refineries. Four were established to handle the product flow. Ras Lanuf, near the Gulf of Sidra, is the largest refinery, capable of processing 220,000 barrels of oil a day. A relative newcomer, it was constructed during the height of the oil downturn; ironic, yet prescient, given the future need and desire for Libyan oil, once the sanctions era had subsided.

The Az-Zawia refinery, on the outskirts of Tripoli, and a bit older, having been built in 1974, stands second in daily capacity, processing upwards of 120,000 barrels per day, an increase of 100 percent from its original ability to handle 60,000 barrels, when first constructed.

In Tobruk, the number three refinery was built, also in 1985, and possessing a capacity of processing 20,000 barrels of oil per day. Unlike Zawia, which is limited to fuel production, the Tobruk facility is able to handle many other distilled types of chemical products, thus making up in range of product what it loses in capacity of oil.

The Sarir topping facility, several hundred kilometers south of Brega, can process 10,000 barrels a day. Its lack of news play is reflected in its central desert location, away from large population centers, and its single product focus, namely only in refining oil and nothing else.

The oldest and smallest refinery, Brega, was constructed in 1970. At a capacity of about 8,400 barrels a day, it by no means is the economic engine to oil production in Libya. However, it rivaled Ras Lanuf as one of the two most heavily contested sites during the recently concluded 2011 Libyan Civil War and did in fact sustain pretty significant damage from the hands of both rebel and government forces. Brega has diversified to become the largest liquefied natural gas refinery in Libya and was the second such plant to come on line in the world. This adds significant potential to Libya's economic stable given the environmental benefits of natural gas, compared to oil.

Extraction and refinement aren't the only areas in which a once solely agrarian, oft-invaded, and occupied nation has become an economic powerhouse. Oil requires transportation. While the ports during the Barbary Era certainly produced their fair share of trade, pirate haven, and local fishing or recreation spots, the advent of oil production and distribution has turned the northern coast of Libya into a vital hub of import/export activity—import for 75 percent or more of their food; export for 90 percent of their economic gross domestic product, oil and natural gas.

Dotting the northern landscape, Libya has constructed six major terminals with a capacity of just under 12 million barrels of oil, equating to about $31 billion in revenues (Libya Oil Almanac, 56). Leading the way is Es Sidra, at 447,000 barrels per day and about 200 ships a year. Just behind is Zueitina, south of Benghazi, handing about 270 ships a year but only capable of uploading around 214,000 barrels per day. Es Zawiya, just west of Tripoli, can process about 480 ships a year and around 199,000 barrels a day. Ras Lanuf, the largest refinery, can muster 300 ships a year through the terminal and 195,000 barrels a day of black gold. Marsa El Brega, the heavily contested site during the civil war, and once it's back on line, could load 51,000 barrels per day via about 380 ships in a given year. Last of the oil-centric terminals is Marsa El Hariga. While small, given about 80 ships arrive annually, and pumping 51,000 barrels a day, this is the farthest eastern port and does offer both strategic advantage and vulnerability, given its depth and location in approximation to Egypt.

All of the technical dimensions aside, what in fact did all of this oil money buy? Certainly a lot of anguish for the families and communities impacted by actions funded by Gaddafi's regime. But that's later. For now, the positive developments that Libyan oil money purchased.

While the American Congressional quote of "millions for defense, not one cent for tribute" held sway in 1798, by the late 1960s, American capital had been pouring into Libya as an offshoot of the oil and gas industry. King Idris maintained status quo, behaving as a debtor nation grateful for the assistance of outside entities. Muammar Gaddafi's approach to use of revenue was completely contrary to this earlier policy. In line with his *Green Book* on equality, he believed all Libyans deserved a share of their spoils; thus a percentage of oil revenues entered every citizen's bank account. When the population was just under two million, this was nothing more than pencil dust to any first-world government's accounting. As the population exploded and reached north to six million, this did have a statistical impact on the budget but ultimately only a few percent-age points.

What Gaddafi did with the billions that flowed in can be seen through-out the nation, and even spilling over into the balance of the African con-tinent. Education was declared a right for all, thus no tuition for students up through the university system, including paid tuition if the student required overseas education. He enacted salary matching whereby gradu-ates of trade schools and universities who were unable to obtain employ-ment would receive a compensatory salary that reflected the average of that occupation. The expectation was that the graduate continued to seek work in order to remove him- or herself, from this government assistance.

Health care, while not necessarily to the level of the Mayo Clinic in Minnesota, was nonetheless provided to all citizens. For a population of 1.8 million, and using 2013 dollars of approximately $1,200 in premiums per month, that amounted to $32 billion—roughly one year's gross domestic product. The focus of medical care was on preventive care, thus they had one of the lowest rates of infant mortality in Africa. From the time Gaddafi took office in 1969, infant mortality dropped from 147 in 1,000 to 16 in 1,000 in 2011 ("Libya—Mortality Rate").

Housing projects were initiated to provide every family with a resi-dence. The dearth of contractors and skilled craftsman would derail this ambitious project; however, the concept of providing every family with a residence was another direct benefit he saw of the oil boom Libya was party to throughout his tenure. One rather quirky statistic is that through-out the 1970s, Libya was the world's number one consumer of cement, a fact that is quickly confirmed when one views photos of contemporary Libya (Ngab, 202).

The ultimate in either delusion or innovation lay in his creation of "The Great Manmade River." This $25 billion-plus project was going to tap into the aquifers lying deep beneath the Saharan sands of southern Libya and travel over 2,800 kilometers to the many coastal towns that held the pro-pensity of Libya's population. For one of the "new money" wealthy nations was also one of the most water starved. While the project had not, to date, met the $25 billion price tag, it has leapt north of $9 billion and counting, with no end in sight and myriad challenges awaiting the new government. Trying to produce order from chaos, they seek to deter-mine value added projects amidst the ongoing disputes over territorial governance, return to civil order without militia involvement, and a resumption of their economic lifeblood in oil and natural gas, despite repeated strikes and shutdowns at the plants.

Monuments throughout the nation speak to Gaddafi's largesse: the roads, office buildings, housing projects, museums, stadiums, ports, and airfields, not all completed, but all started. Despite his well-publicized and oft-repeated changes in mood, behavior, and loyalties, he can be considered one of the most determined leaders in advancing the stature of his people. The cost was steep; strict adherence to the principles in *The Green Book* and association with a leader who frequently courted pariah status. To a nation living on a starvation diet and existing on technology and economics more relevant to the mid-nineteenth century, this was a price worth paying.

Muammar Gaddafi's financial infusions weren't limited to internal projects for the direct benefit of Libyans. He sought to spread the wealth, and his influence, throughout the continent and, as we'll talk about shortly, to those groups who would aim to bring down Western influence, regardless of the cost in human lives.

It would be fair to say that under the Gaddafi regime, it wasn't as important to make friends as to be able to buy friends. When the African Union was established, Gaddafi bankrolled, and continued to do so through the time of his death, 15 percent of the total operating costs of the Union. The $277 million operating budget had many generous "non-African" benefactors. For the approximately $123 million balance, Libya contributed $40 million, covering not only their own $15 million share but an additional $25 million to cover the membership of several smaller countries in western Africa (Omojuwa).

For every good, someone out there can find a way to turn a resource into a bad. In this case, Gaddafi saw the power of oil as a weapon, for both economic and political purposes. He wasted no time in wielding this mighty stick to astonishingly international effect. No one, whether the OPEC nations or the economic powerhouses of the United States and the Union of Soviet Socialist Republics (USSR), would have envisioned that Libya could bring the world economy to its knees. Yet, for a brief moment in time, that occurred. The world has never been the same.

OIL AS A SWORD

Oil's early and somewhat anemic beginning has already been covered. So low on the totem pole was oil that even when natural gas, an oil derivative, and small pockets of near surface oil were discovered, they were dismissed. For the commodity of choice to Libyans was water. They were a nation with the largest continuous coastline in northern Africa, yet not a drop to be had for safe consumption. They sat atop the Saharan Desert, known throughout the millennial as the final resting place for man, animal, and machine. Water, that chemically simple, yet biologically crucial element for humanity to survive. Oil? Not as much. The sky had provided both light and shade. Animals, transportation. Strong backs, power.

The world had changed, however, chiefly thanks to the innovations of dreamers who believed there were better ways to produce, travel, live, and yes, kill. Machines replaced hands, bows and arrows, plows, carts, mud, and timber walls. Oil drove those machines. Oil became an end unto itself. Those who possessed it, possessed power in ways never before imagined. Every nation had turned want into need. Oil became a commodity hotter than steel, for without oil, steel couldn't erect buildings; manufacture cars and airplanes; build bombs; or create museums. No oil, no paved roads without using gravel, which wasn't available worldwide. But oil by-products, tar namely, were part and parcel of every barrel.

Muammar Gaddafi lived in an era of natural light and total darkness. Farming by hand and bathing by bucket. Indoor utilities were not prevalent in his childhood. Food was what the family could grow. Transportation was how far they could walk, or if lucky, ride on a camel. He watched the world engage in armed struggle using the machinery of the twenty-first century to effectively annihilate the opposition and turn towns to rubble. He knew of the power of atomic bombs, television, and automobiles. He observed airplanes crisscross the sky as they flew from liberated fields now run by the U.S. Air Force.

For all of the trappings of the town jester that Gaddafi may have displayed as a student of military affairs and academia, his astute observations of the addictive nature of oil were decades ahead of his firmly entrenched allied oil producers further east. He also watched his predecessor, King Idris, allow the nation to be low balled in economic remunerations, compared to other oil producing nations, as the King sought to receive "enough" money for the oil.

Gaddafi saw oil as another tool in his ideological arsenal to invert the Islamic and North African mind-set. He saw oil as a weapon that could compel others to behave according to his dictates as he set out to forge what some might consider an ideal "democratic" institution. Sadly, the reality didn't match the fantasy. But, economically, he made a name for himself that will be without equal.

The "weaponization" of oil began in 1968 when the Libyan Petroleum Company (LIPETCO), was founded (Libya Oil Almanac, 16). While initially it was a privately held organization, it became the foundation upon which Gaddafi would build his economic empire via the nationalization of this company; its resultant authority to impose taxation and royalty hikes, and the transition from Libya serving as a carpet upon which other oil companies walked, to the door through which oil companies, now labeled "contractors," must seek permission to enter.

By 1970, Gaddafi had observed enough of the runnings in his new government, the world order, and the pecking order of supplier and supplied, and had decided it was time to turn the tables on the big dogs. One constant was that he always felt like the underdog, always believed his nation was the scorned and deserved a place at the adult's table.

An ace up his sleeve was that the first Prime Minister was a Western-trained lawyer who had worked for Exxon for several years as a corporate lawyer, Dr. Suleiman Maghrabi. Nationalizing all industries was the first step toward his all-inclusive *Green Book* world. The oil piece was just one of the most prominent (Sampson, 3). Using insider knowledge of the American oil industry, Dr. Maghrabi was able to advise Gaddafi on effective methods for bringing the oil giants to their knees. First, they changed the name of the organization to the Libyan National Oil Company (NOC). Next, they moved that the NOC would own 51 percent of all participation agreements, revising the naming of concessions to better reflect in the Libyan mind that outside agencies were participants in what had become a Libyan-owned entity.

Price negotiations became the next arrow in the quiver. In 1969, the price of a barrel of oil was about $1.80. By 1971, with Libya in the forefront, the price had elevated to $2.24; by 1973, $3.29 ("Historical Crude Oil Prices"). Seemingly small increases in retrospect, but given that the American minimum wage sat at $1.60 and a gallon of gas was 36 cents, these increases weren't insignificant ("Federal Minimum Wage Rates, 1955–2013"). Concurrently, in Great Britain, they too were seeing a marked rise in prices. While theirs had been comparable to those of the United States, through 1973, they began to see prices rise by 25 percent a year until by 1979, they were paying almost a dollar a gallon equivalent ("Petrol Prices, 1896 to Present").

Aside from raising the amount paid to Libya for each barrel of oil extracted, taxes on the oil were increased. Royalties on every barrel began to creep up from just over 12 percent to 16.67 percent. Taxes on profits, which had been near an industry standard of about 50 percent, began to rise until they hit 65 percent or more. In real terms, this meant that for every dollar of gain the international oil companies were able to collect from a barrel of oil, they retained from 38 cents in the early days, down to 18 cents by the time of the major oil shocks hit in the mid-1970s.

Remember that these fees were only the beginning, for the oil companies still required transportation by oil tanker to their refineries, unless using one of the refineries in Libya. Then there was the cost of land transportation once the fuel arrived at the distribution site. The lines at the gas pumps were real. One man economically induced highly industrialized nations to call for gas rationing, and he even compelled the only other nation on the planet with the capability to reduce the world to a nuclear wasteland in under an hour, to impose gas station access days according to whether the last digit in a families address ended with an even or odd number.

Muammar Gaddafi had ulterior motives for these actions. Power, certainly. Establishing his mark in the international scene, by all means.

What he didn't let on to was the philosophical bent he was applying, namely the embarrassment he felt the Arab World had suffered at the hands of the Israelis in the 1967 war. This was a means of retribution, cut and dried. His political agenda had to be placed on the table, and what better way of accomplishing this than to hold a precious resource hostage. The world had to listen. And most of them did. The oil companies? Well, not completely. Conventional wisdom would dictate that the oil companies held the bargaining power; i.e., they had the intellectual capital of decades in the oil business. They had the technology and financing to manufacture the machinery. They had the money to expend for prospecting potentially unsuccessful fields.

So why didn't they gather and overpower the Libyan government? Several reasons. First, they weren't united. Independent oil companies, such as Occidental, were less inclined to engage in an economic staring contest with the Libyan government, especially since Libya was their only source for oil. Libya, seizing on this fracture in oil consensus, began negotiating with each of the companies independently. Next, the larger companies initially felt that Gaddafi was bluffing and ultimately there would be a modest increase but nothing significant. As time dragged on and he didn't cave in, they began to worry that his discussions with the Soviet Union might turn into new contracts for Eastern Bloc oil companies, with the West being completely shut out.

Third, the attentions of the larger companies weren't as heavily focused on Libya. The Exxons, British Petroleums, and Texacos of the group had oil holdings in other parts of the world, namely the Saudi Arabia region and down in Venezuela. To them, Libya was an important, but not the most important, site. What they failed to recognize was that a loss in one could well have a ripple effect on their other holdings. That is precisely what happened. OPEC had seen the impact of Libya's actions and, to an extent, they were embarrassed by the ability of this neophyte to the oil industry to be able to flip the giants on their backs. Thus, they had to find some way to reestablish their own dominance. The oil crises of 1974, 1976, and 1979 would be those times.

However, we're still in 1973. Libya, now a trendsetter in oil politics, established the first of a series of Exploration and Production Sharing Agreements (EPSA). These agreements were intended to level the playing field for all companies wishing to do business with Libya. EPSA I, initiated in 1973, served a couple of purposes. First, it simplified the contractual agreements between Libya and the oil companies. The oil companies received a share of the oil, tax and royalty free, about 15 percent. They were expected to pay all exploration and overseas costs; thus they lost what had previously been considered a "recovery fee." Yet after three years, they were also required to pay the NOC a share of those previous development costs. In effect, they paid discovery fees twice. Exploration periods ran about five years, and they could extract for a period of 30 years. Ultimately, with "taxes, tags, and fees," the oil companies were receiving about 19 percent of the value of oil raised from underground (Oxford Institute, 6).

The EPSA II series came online in 1980 and imposed harsher fees on the oil companies. They were now being assessed according to the location of the field and its productive capacity. Thus, the more they made, or were likely to make, the higher their taxes. This was counterintuitive for the student of economics who believed that profit was the catalyst to reinvestment and improving standards of living. This worked only to temper the interest by outside oil companies, or at least the better established, and introduced many smaller companies who were willing to put up with near paralyzing rates. Additionally, sites not having prospected or established oil rigs on portions of their allotted blocks were automatically returned to the NOC for rebidding to other companies, in effect forcing the oil companies to sink wells in every site, regardless of the cost, or give up those sites.

This series of agreements was concluded as the oil glut and the international economic recession were blanketing the globe. Demand was dropping as prices had soared to yet new all-time highs, streaking past the $1.10 mark per gallon, when labor was hovering at $3.35 an hour. Fuel efficiency hadn't thoroughly caught on yet, so cars making 10 to 12 miles to the gallon were still very common. Average citizens were paying half a day's wages for a tank of gas that would last them a week. Yet, in Libya, customers were paying about $0.14 per litre ("Pump Price for Diesel Fuel").

Then the sanctions hit. Why? A little matter of Gaddafi paying the bill for others to terrorize, destroy, topple, and causer overall mayhem. For 20 years, he would live under a shadow of shame as the chief financier of death. Not until 2004, with attentions focused elsewhere in the world, and some seemingly sincere apologizing, was he allowed back into the international market.

Despite his status of pariah nation and sanctions being imposed by the major Western powers, his petroleum ministry executed the EPSA III series. Unlike EPSA I and II, the third series was a bit more oil company–friendly. The chief benefit to the oil companies who were willing to disregard Western-imposed sanctions, more frequently the smaller oil companies from lesser-developed nations, who did not have years of experience, manpower, financial resources, and oil rig equipment, was that they were able to claim a percentage of their extracted oil for use as a "credit" against expenses. This was a lucrative carrot, but it happened to occur during an era in which fuel consumption had dramatically fallen off due to the actions of the oil holders over the previous 15 years. Thus, with little demand, there was little use in expanding the field of oil wells.

The current series of agreements by which Libya controls the deck of economic cards lies in EPSA IV. Libya opened up a significantly larger portion of land to development than they had previously allowed. Under this EPSA, all bids are sealed. There were prequalification procedures (a lesson learned from EPSA III by unequipped oil speculators), minimum commitments, and percentages of gross production that would be paid to the NOC, and then there was the "bonus" (Oxford Institute, 7).

Each bidding company offered a bonus to the NOC as a means of sweetening the pot. The bonus was offered as part of the package and was nonrefundable. These ranged from $1 million to $25 million. Much like a sealed bid art auction, except the artwork they sought to go home with was a place in the sand that the winner hoped would produce sufficient oil to substantiate their gamble that the "Mona Lisa" of Libyan oil contracts was not in fact a "grumpy grezel" of losing the bid to a rival oil company. Such were the costs of doing business that the winning oil company would be lucky to earn 12 percent of the value of each barrel coming out of the ground. To date, post–2011 civil war, this latest round of agreements remained in place. There was discussion of the Petroleum Ministry looking into revised agreements that would reduce the cost of outside agencies doing business in Libya, for the sake of reinvesting capital and providing opportunities for skilled labor to grow.

Muammar Gaddafi had demonstrated that he was a superb student of one-upmanship. While his lines of death had failed to deter the United States, throughout the 1980s, he demonstrated brilliant chess skills in managing the oil table. To that end, while he invested billions in upgrading the infrastructure of his homeland, he devoted equal billions to the cause of destabilization. He wrote many a check that terror groups and anti-incumbent parties were more than willing to cash. His span ran worldwide as well. He didn't limit himself to Africa. He was in the Middle East, Europe, Cuba, Central America, and South America. He also funded groups in Japan. His reach spanned the globe.

OIL AND THE TERRORIST GAME

The very mention of terrorism evokes ice in the veins and a sharp stabbing pain to the heart. It's insidious; dark, seemingly without purpose whatsoever, yet used for surgical matters in the lands in which it appears. There is no single textbook on terrorism or asymmetric warfare. It takes many forms, from intellectual threats via blackmail, to faceless phone calls extolling the virtues of the bomb hidden in some yet to be named, yet very public, location. It may be a blatant assassination or as subtle as the removal of a wealthy patron's life savings. We have seen Israeli athletes gunned down, because they were Jewish. We have watched airline pilots calmly try to strike bargains or speak on behalf of the terrorists, from the cockpit of their aircraft. We have witnessed aircraft blown up in the sky, and we have seen cruise ships taken over and passengers expecting a calm Mediterranean cruise to be witness to murder on the high seas.

The methods have varied from the dawn of time. The weapons have changed to adapt to the technology and skills of the times. What has never fluctuated is the need for a sponsor. Typically, such a sponsor has access to power, technology, and currency. Frequently, that sponsor has ties to politics, organized crime, or even the forces of peace and defense, who are empowered to protect the citizenry.

Muammar Gaddafi had such resources. He had a thriving economy and complete control over his political machine and armed forces. Access to millions of dollars that were not readily accounted for made his job of helping "the enemy of my enemy is my friend." Unfortunately, he had too many "friends." While minor league terrorist supporters may start small, exploding the odd café bomb or striking at a local official, Gaddafi was anything but minor. Like his construction projects and dramatic displays of power, enrobed in beautiful silks and satin of every color, so too were his aspirations on helping the Arab cause, the anti-British cause, the anti–anything Western or democratic.

While research may never completely capture every group to which he had ties, his lineup of recipients reads like a who's who of international terrorism. The first on his list was the Irish Republican Army (IRA). Starting as early as 1972, Gaddafi began by funneling weapons, providing training grounds in his countless miles of desert, and providing funding for the IRA to extend its reach throughout the United Kingdom (Dervan).

Until just months before his death, Gaddafi would be the benevolent uncle to the IRA, providing them with weapons, explosives, and cash with which to further their agenda. For, you see, he cared very little about the IRA's goals. But he cared very much that they were terrorizing Britain. Britain had removed their garrisons from three relatively insignificant islands, Abu Musa, Greater and Lesser Tunb, in the middle of the Persian Gulf, to Iran. This upset Gaddafi as he believed the Arab community had been taken for a ride by the Iranians, given the newly emergent Arab state of the United Arab Emirates. Thus, the war was on, and the IRA could carry it to the home front while Gaddafi and Libya continued to pump the oil and cash the checks ("Abu Musa and the Tunbs").

Libyan SEMTEX, a wicked nasty plastic explosive in its day, was sold and used to tremendous effect in residential bombings over a 20-year period, leaving hundreds dead and thousands without a loved one (Chompsky). Surface-to-air missiles were on the plate, although fortunately, none were ever successfully fired at aircraft. The thought, however, was anything but comforting, even though other Libyan bombs did bring down planes.

The Irish Republican Army wasn't Libya's only proxy. Throughout the 1970s and 1980s, Libya could count no less than eight additional terrorist organizations among his benefactors. These weren't minor league, either. He funded the popular Front for Liberation of Palestine (PFLP) and its splinter group, the PFLP-GC (PFLP-General Command). Both had different viewpoints toward a resurgence in Arabism throughout the Middle East. The former balanced action with politics; the latter was all business. They were exceptionally militant and conducted repeated attacks on Israel and sympathetic partners of the Jewish state.

The Palestinian Liberation Front (PLF), yet another splinter group from the PLFP-GC, caught the eye of Gaddafi and he provided a steady stream of support, mostly with logistical and military aid, to further this most radical of Palestinian organizations. As referenced above, they were the masterminds behind the attack on the Italian cruise liner *Achille Lauro*. They were also frequent contributors to attacks on Israel ("Terrorism: Major Terrorist Groups").

Closer to home, Gaddafi had a hand in supplying weapons and cash to the Revolutionary United Front (RUF), Foday Sankoh's organization in Sierra Leone. Given the close proximity and rather porous landscape that separated Libya from Sierra Leone, movement of arms, equipment, and money was an easy proposition.

The Basque Fatherland and Liberty organization, fighting for the independence of the Basque Territories in Spain, maintained a training ground in Libya, where they could hone their craft in safety and take terror back to Spain. Until their recent renouncement of militant action, they were a heavy user of Libyan space for practicing the art of killing.

Demonstrating his penchant for being bold, Gaddafi invited the headquarters of the Abu Nidal, the chief splinter group from Yasser Arafat's Palestinian Liberation Organization (PLO), to be located within Libya's borders. They took him up on the offer and trained and maintained from Libya throughout their reign of terror.

To demonstrate Gaddafi's willingness to share his nation's spoils with the rest of the world, his millions were traced to Sandinista camps in Nicaragua in the mid-1980s; weapons for M19, a Colombian terrorist group; the Red Brigade in Italy, and organizations operating out of Japan, Turkey, Thailand, and elsewhere (Ganor, 1). Not to be outdone, Libya engaged in some high-profile activities of its own. Aside from assassinations of Libyan expatriates, mostly in Europe, two events were pivotal in the ascension of Libya to terrorism's elite, as well as the collapse of Libya's leading role in advocating terrorism as a legitimate tool of political change.

Pan American Flight 103, departing Heathrow for JFK in New York City and carrying 259 passengers and crew, was blown out of the sky by Libyan associates affiliated with the airline industry. Eleven citizens on the ground in Lockerbie, Scotland, would also be killed by the weight and fire of the debris as the fully fueled and heavily laden Boeing 747 disintegrated just after reaching its cruising altitude of 31,000 feet. This event would require almost 15 years of investigating, negotiating, and politicking before Libya would hand over the suspect, 'Abd al-Basset 'Ali Al-Maghrahi, a former director of security with the Libyan national airline, and his associate, Laman Khalifa Fhimah, the director of Libyan Airlines in Malta (Ganor, 3). Ironically, Al-Maghrahi, after several years of imprisonment, would be released by a Scottish court due to his impending death from disease. His "impending death" would take almost three years to occur. Why did Libya feel the need to engage in this matter? While there are some questions lingering as to true Libyan responsibility, evidence seems to indicate it was retaliation for the U.S. sanctions and the military strikes on Libya on several occasions in the 1980s.

The other high-profile event for Libya involved the blowing up of Union de Transports Aeriennes 772 (UTA 772) over Niger in September 1989. Just minutes after takeoff from N'Djamena International Airport in Chad, en route to Paris, Flight 772 was victimized by a high-altitude bomb that scattered the wreckage and 170 dead passengers and crew in the Saharan Desert. Like the previous December bomb blast that claimed Pan Am Flight 103, this incident was ultimately attributed to Libyan masterminds. Chief among them was Abdullah Senussi, the brother-in-law of Muammar Gaddafi and the deputy chief of Gaddafi's intelligence service.

But why destroy an airliner with no passengers or crew on board who might have been associated with the rationale? Very sadly, they were the victims of revenge. Revenge by the Gaddafi regime over Libya's recent defeat in the Libyan-Chadian war. Revenge over the realization that with this loss, Libya was no longer in a position to become the lead sled dog in the Arabization of Africa, and Gaddafi's span of control was to remain narrowly focused. Revenge because he felt the French and Americans had been responsible for his defeat (Reynolds).

These two highly publicized incidents removed any hope of relaxing or eliminating sanctions previously imposed due to Libya's well-documented attacks on a discotheque in Germany, El Al airline counters in Vienna and Rome, and various U.S. locations in Italy and Germany (Ganor, 3).

The United States took a gamble on both the sanctions and the 1986 military strike at targets in and around Tripoli. Realizing that action may be met with action, and a savvy enemy never fights force on force, the United States chose to run the risk of tangential responses. Over 300 people paid for that risk, however necessary, given the political situation of the time.

Gaddafi also ran a significant risk by engaging in terrorist actions, either directly or through proxies. By funding and participating in such events, he opened the door to retaliation of all forms. Military was the easiest, political next. But economic retaliation wasn't something he expected to actually impact Libya. Oil had been flowing for decades. He was awash in billions of oil dollars for which he was erecting museums, schools, office buildings, housing, and water projects. He was paying his citizens to be families and to own cars. He was propping up "allied" nations throughout Africa, Central America, and South America. He could afford to buy his way out of trouble and he was comfortable with the nations who remained his ally.

Then Gaddafi was hit by the recession. While it had been occurring for years in the balance of the developed world, his relatively small population of just under four million people was insulated from the economic turbulence of the world economy. But several years of sanctions, military actions, external wars, grandiose dreams of water flowing through sand, and becoming the big man on the international political campus, had finally taken their toll. The persistent economic pressures on the other nations had resulted in dramatic innovations in automobiles, carving out extra miles per gallon, which resulted in less gasoline being consumed, therefore less oil required to fuel the world's economy. His single source of wealth began to sludge in the international oil pipe of relations.

The 1990s would prove to be a sluggish time for the Libyan economy, equating to estimates of an $18 billion to $33 billion dollar loss in revenue. Coupled with isolation from nations regarding travel and engaging in other types of business, Libya truly earned "pariah" status (Libya Oil Almanac, 36). Any nation, no matter how tightly controlled, will begin to see cracks within their economic and social walls. Such was Libya, and thus he began to throttle back on external support to agendas that weren't directly tied to Libyan aims.

By 1999, whether out of desperation, maturity, or exhaustion, Libya began to admit culpability in many of the actions of the previous generation, for which they were blamed, but had not been confirmed. Starting with their admission of the Pan Am Flight 103 bomb, Libya was punished monetarily, but nations slowly began to resume relations with Libya. Not hurting Libya's cause was the international military scene in Iraq and Afghanistan. While Afghanistan was all about fighting al-Qa'eda, Iraq held several cards. One was economic. They had, and still have, one of the largest repositories of oil in the world. That's an addiction that has yet to be beaten. Additionally, there was lingering history between the warring powers. Libya, rather astutely, once again, recognized that they had a role to play in the new world order, and thus they wisely humbled themselves so they could return to relations with the West, including transfers of oil, to those nations from whom they had been cut off for about 17 years (Vanderbruck).

LIBYA RESUMES PLAYING IN THE INTERNATIONAL MARKET

The year 2004 began a new era, albeit relatively short-lived, for Libyan oil politics. With the United States and the other international heavy hitters discovering, or deluding themselves as to, Gaddafi's sincerity in atoning for the past, he was admitted back into the community of nations. Economically, this arrived at an ideal time, as the Western powers were engaged in a war with a voracious oil appetite. Ever the shrewd businessman, Gaddafi's oil ministers resurrected agreements that had been in existence prior to the sanctions, marginally maintained during the sanctions period, and then reinvigorated after the sanctions were lifted. Despite EPSA IV's rather stiff new "bonus" schedule, oil companies left and right were ecstatic to get back in the game.

Libya over the final seven years of Gaddafi's rule began to take on a different character. Where corruption with oil had been an established fact, it was well hidden. Emerging from the sanctions era, even Gaddafi himself became a direct player in the game as he began reviewing all contracts exceeding $200 million and trying to squeeze "incentives" from the companies wanting to do business in Libya. Not that Libya needed to extract any extra dollars from the oil companies. When they had entered the sanctions era, oil was running at around $18 a barrel, which raked in a cool $23.4 million per day. As they emerged from sanctions, and were pumping roughly 1.3 million barrels a day, this equated to over $188 million at $145 per barrel. While that peak lasted but six months in 2008, oil at approximately $107 per barrel cost allowed Libya to pull in about $117.7 million per day. Not bad for a nation of 5.6 million people.

Oil has been the topic de jour. It's limited, so it garners all the attention. Yet another ace in the pocket of Libya, and one that may bear exploring sooner than later, is natural gas.

OIL'S "ALIAS"

Natural gas is a derivative of oil. Based on the depth of the fields, and temperatures at such depths, the same commodity that emerges as crude oil can also come blasting out of the ground as natural gas. While they carry only 0.8 percent of the world's supply, that equates to 1.5 trillion cubic feet of fuel that burns cleaner than oil and coal; requires little to no refinement; while volatile in its natural form, has been safely used for

decades; and has an established pattern of reliability and ease of trans-
portability (Libyan Oil Almanac, 36). That adds another $41 million a
year, using 2013 figures of $4 averaged, per million cubic meters ("One
Year Natural Gas Prices").

Not astronomical figures by any means. Yet, raw dollar value per measure doesn't equate to the jobs created, both primary in the production,
extraction, shipment, loading, inspecting, and maintaining of the supplies
and the infrastructure. The diversification created by introducing another
fuel source, like oil in 1969 that sold for less than $2 a barrel, provides
Libya with an opportunity to establish precedent and, more significantly,
the expertise to be a world supplier of an environmentally friendly, suitable alternative to crude oil. This provides a safety valve at the very least,
for the new government to explore as they continue to seek ways in which
to be "not like Gaddafi" but yet remain a vibrant international provider of
energy.

SEALING THE BARREL

As seen in previous chapters, Libya is truly a land of contrasts. They are
one of the more recent entries to the modern technological age; they
emerged from being a stomping ground for nations at war, to becoming
the international leader in hate and violence. They have demonstrated a
level of resiliency and business acumen that could make Wall Street analysts take note. They capitalized on their natural resources and attempted
to functionally share their wealth with their citizens.

Yet, for all of the potential that oil has held for the people and leadership of Libya, it came with a price. One man, Muammar Gaddafi, with
the power of life and death, wielded this strategic asset as if it were his
own toy. While he demonstrated benevolence in providing for the basic
needs of his people, and sprinkled billions throughout the African continent and far-flung corners of the globe, he demonstrated a willingness to
strangle the supply to serve his own despotic purposes. An upstart from
the day he took office, he displayed a level of courage, or foolishness, that
made the OPEC nations and the world take notice; yet he failed to mobilize the oil masses to accept his agenda and pursue his goals for reorient-
ing the world view.

A man of demonstrably good instincts, at times, and yet horrible
judgment and coldhearted violence, was handed the keys to the economic
kingdom. He knew it and so did the world. His ultimate demise in October 2011 brought to an end an era of oil as a weapon. What remains to be
seen is whether the succeeding governmental body of Libya will recognize the potential for good that having so much of what the world needs,

readily available, and managing their exploitation of this resource, to prolong its availability, and turn a commodity into a true lifeblood.

SOURCES

"Abu Musa and the Tunbs: Sovereignty Dispute Between the UAE and the Islamic Republic of Iran." MOFA.gov.ae. Accessed September 11, 2013. http://www.mofa.gov.ae/mofa_english/Uploads/Banners/9_pdf.pdf.

Chompsky. "Gaddafi and the IRA." Broadsheet. Accessed June 29, 2013. http://www.broadsheet.ie/2011/08/23/gadaffi-and-the-ira/.

Dervan, Cathal. "Colonel Gaddafi Sent Millions of Dollars in Cash to Real IRA Last June." IrishCentral.com. Accessed September 11, 2013. http://www.irishcentral.com/news/Colonel-Gaddafi-sent-millions-of-dollars-in-cash-to-Real-IRA-last-June-130553498.html.

Fattouh, Bassam. "North African Oil and Foreign Investments in Changing Market Conditions." Oxford Institute for Energy Studies. Accessed September 4, 2013. http://www.oxfordenergy.org/wpcms/wp-content/uploads/2010/11/WPM37-NorthAfricanOilandForeignInvestmentinChangingMarketConditions-BassamFattouh-2008.pdf.

"Federal Minimum Wage Rates, 1955–2013." Infoplease.com. Accessed September 9, 2013. http://www.infoplease.com/ipa/A0774473.html.

Ganor, Boaz. "Libya and Terrorism." International Institute for Counter-Terrorism. Accessed August 25, 2013. http://www.ict.org.il/Articles/tabid/66/Articlsid/699/currentpage/40/Default.aspx.

"Historical Crude Oil Prices, 1861 to Present." ChartsBin.com. Accessed September 9, 2013.

"Historical Events for Year 1959." HistoryOrb.com. Accessed September 3, 2013. http://www.historyorb.com/events/date/1959.

"Libya—Mortality Rate: Mortality Rate, Under-5 (per 1,000 Live Births)." Index Mundi. Accessed September 8, 2013. http://www.indexmundi.com/facts/libya/mortality-rate.

"Libyan Economy Profile 2013." Index Mundi. Accessed September 23, 2013. http://www.indexmundi.com/libya/economy_profile.html.

"Libya Oil Almanac: An Open Oil Reference Guide." Accessed September 3, 2013. http://openoil.net/wp/wp-content/uploads/2012/08/Libya-PDF-v-2.0.pdf.

Ngab, Ali S. "Libya—The Construction Industry—An Overview." Enpub.fulton.asu.edu. Accessed September 4, 2013. http://enpub.fulton.asu.edu/cement/cbm_CI/CBMI_Separate_Articles/Article%2021.pdf.

Omojuwa, Japeth J. "African Union: A Stream Cannot Rise above Its Source." African Liberty.org. Accessed September 8, 2013. http://www.africanliberty.org/content/african-union-stream-cannot-rise-above-its-source.

Pace, Eric. "Armand Hammer Dies at 92; Industrialist and Philanthropist Forged Soviet Links." New York Times, December 11, 1990. Accessed September 7, 2013. http://www.nytimes.com/1990/12/12/obituaries/armand-hammer-dies-at-92-industrialist-and-philanthropist-forged-soviet-links.html?pagewanted=all&src=pm.

"Petrol Prices, 1896 to Present." The AA Motoring Trust. Accessed September 9, 2013. http://www.theaa.com/public_affairs/reports/Petrol_Prices_1896_todate_gallons.pdf.

"Pump Price for Diesel Fuel (US$ per Litre)." The World Bank. Accessed September 4, 2013. http://data.worldbank.org/indicator/EP.PMP.DESL.CD.

Rachovich, David. "World's Top 23 Proven Oil Reserves Holders, Jan. 1, 2012—OGJ." *Petroleum Insights*. Accessed September 3, 2013. http://petroleum insights.blogspot.jp/2012/01/worlds-top-23-proven-oil-reserves.html#.UkFnFWWmrIV.

Reynolds, Paul. "UTA 772: The Forgotten Flight." BBC News. Accessed June 29, 2013. http://news.bbc.co.uk/2/hi/uk_news/3163621.stm.

Rusk, Donald C. "Libya: Petroleum Potential of the Underexplored Basin Centers—Twenty-First-Century Challenge." *GeoExPro*, Chapter 22. Accessed September 4, 2013. http://www.searchanddiscovery.com/documents/rusk/images/Rusk.pdf.

Sampson, Anthony. "The Seven Sisters: The Great Oil Companies and the World They Made." Biofuel Library. Accessed September 4, 2013. http://www.journeytoforever.org/biofuel_library/sevensisters/7sisters10.html.

"Terrorism: Major Terrorist Groups." Towson University. Accessed September 11, 2013. http://www.towson.edu/polsci/ppp/sp97/terror/groups.html#PFLP-GC.

Vanderbruck, Tobias. "Gaddafi's Legacy of Libyan Oil Deals." Oil-Price.net. Accessed August 24, 2013. http://www.oil-price.net/en/articles/gaddafi-legacy-of-libya-oil-deals.php.

Vandewalle, Dirk. "Libya since 1969." Accessed September 4, 2013. http://www.commandposts.com/2011/03/libya-since-1969/.

Whaley, Jane. "Libya—The Next Chapter." *GeoExPro*. Accessed September 4, 2013. http://www.geoexpro.com/article/Libya_The_Next_Chapter/366a0f99.aspx.

"The World War II Study: North Africa: Supplies." Topedge.com. Accessed July 2, 2012. http://www.topedge.com/panels/ww2/na/frame.html.

CHAPTER 6

The Spark and Fire of the 2011 Libyan "Arab Spring"

This chapter reviews and implicitly examines the similarities and differences of the region's "Arab Springs" of Tunisia, Egypt, and Libya in 2011. How was Libya the same and how was it different? This detailed and comparative case study of the evolution of the protest and revolt, and the war for Libya, is analyzed from various perspectives for these three "Arab Spring" countries. Why and where did they happen, where did they *not* happen, and why were they so different? What was the synergistic interaction between them all and foreign powers? How could the Libyans, so used to 40 years of dictatorship, manage to overthrow a well-armed and financed ruler in a matter of months? What was the nature of Gaddafi's power, and why did he fail?

The spark of the "Arab Spring" that rejected the three or more decades of the dark Arab Winter is a process that is still very much underway. The nations that were ignited by this movement had various social and political contextual fuels. Likewise, the transformational "sparks" varied. There are some cases where governments were rather quickly toppled, such as Tunisia (following the "martyrdom"/suicide of Muhammad Bouazizi on December 17, 2010) and Egypt (following the brutal police murder of "martyr" Khalid Muhammad Sa'ed on June 6, 2010). Some of these movements were by popular mass protest; some took a protracted armed struggle (Libya, Yemen, and Syria); some could meet the challenges by reform (Bahrain and Morocco); and others managed to have various combinations of repression and reform to stay intact (Algeria and Sudan). Other nations failed to be blown by these winds of change. Most importantly, the changes intended by the revolts may be been diverted, or are incomplete, or are at a stage that is too early to judge the final results.

With such diversity and complexity, it will be hard to find a general model that fits all circumstances. Books by Brynen et al., Noueihed and Warren, and Owen in 2012 have attempted this task of comparative analysis and give us a good starting point to view the few years since the Arab revolutions of 2011. According to Owen, the contextual "fuel" generally included a mixture of corruption, repression, frustration, fear, authoritarianism, cronyism, extreme centralization, indifference to widespread youth unemployment, phony elections, poor governance, arrogance, patronizing attitudes, lack of due process, little accountability or transparency, partisan judicial procedures, bribes, and nepotism. Such fuel of collective and widespread grievances was just simmering beneath the surface, and the regular application of repression managed to keep the lid on protests, not to mention serious antistate movements.

One approach to looking at this question follows American military doctrine that the universal sources or levers of power can be subsumed by the acronym "DIME" that stands for Diplomacy, Information, Military, and Economics. Using this as a key to dissect the prerevolutionary period, the Gaddafi years, may help to identity the context as well as the precipitating sparks of specific incidents, demands, and social media that paralleled the *Girifna* ("We're Fed Up") movement in Sudan and the *Kifaya* ("Enough") movement in Egypt.

In the world of Libyan *diplomacy*, one asset that he had was certainly vast unchecked wealth to do as he wished. The troublesome indulgences of his reckless sons certainly did not help his reputation, nor did his idiosyncratic ways, such as meeting people in the middle of the night and in his tent. In order to strengthen his ties with the Arab World, Gaddafi made endless errors that insulted or outright attacked others and thereby isolated him. His unique radical positions on a variety of topics never reached the Arab mainstream or the Arab League. His monopoly on his interpretations of Islam was typically at variance with orthodoxy and even with extremism. His effort to ingratiate himself with sub-Saharan nations meant that he could, or would, buy off the weaker and poorer states to have a larger voice at the African Union, but these weaker states, even when grouped together, still lacked a large and effective voice. His flamboyant clothing styles, especially later in life, became a silly caricature of a Hollywood "dictator" or "King of Kings" that was not to be taken seriously. Strong reliance on the Soviet Union, which collapsed, and friendship with rogue regimes such as Uganda, Zimbabwe, and North Korea did not help much, either. Whimsical and mercurial relations with France, Great Britain, and Italy, tempted by Libyan oil and ability to purchase arms, only added to Gaddafi's unpredictable nature. When UN Security Council resolutions stacked up, Libya's isolation seemed almost complete.

For *information*, Gaddafi's *Green Book* was something of a knock-off of Chairman Mao's *Red Book*. Anything one needed to know was found there, and if it was not there, you didn't need to know it. Gaddafi's insistence on Arabic for all transactions added to this isolation. The Gaddafi stranglehold on mass media, press, radio and television, education, and public relations, foreign or domestic, was so strong and under direct control from Tripoli that all creative or independent-minded citizens spoke publicly or even privately at great risk. Tourism in Libya had great potential that was never fully realized.

For *military* power, Gaddafi was also "generous" with providing arms to a wide variety of insurgent and rebel groups; but then, as well as now, once these weapons left his control, it was hard to know or control where they might end up. It is easy to find recipients of this largesse, but, much, much harder to find cases of where they lead to something lasting or constructive. He also invested heavily in conventional and expensive military systems that, in the end, did him no good. Many were old-time Soviet-era army and naval assets that steadily became obsolete over his decades in power. Indeed, the expansive number of small arms and light weapons (SALW) helped to arm the TNC rebels, Libyan Islamists, and the extensive smuggling of SALW across the Sahara, North Africa, and now into Syria. Gaddafi's experience with weapons of mass destruction (WMD) was also, happily, never used. Once again, this represented yet another major expenditure without any return.

For *economics*, one might say that the standard of living, social and health services, housing, and education generally had broad improvement during the Gaddafi epoch, but virtually all of this was financed by oil production, as seen in Chapter 5. It is well known that undiversified economies are structurally unsound. The "curse of oil" in particular is highly fungible, volatile, nontransparent, and unaccountable, so this gave a strong foundation for the infamous corruption and abuse by the Gaddafi dynasty. The prodigious wealth of Libya attracted all manner of foreign and domestic sycophants hungry to acquire a piece of the economic action. Gaddafi initiated a host of ambitious showcase projects, such as the "Great Man-Made River"; many were ill advised, others delayed or never completed or properly maintained.

With this analysis, Gaddafi's utilization of the "DIME" "levers of power" meant that he was notoriously poor in his political judgments, in which only fear, repression, and domestic intelligence were the first and last lines of defense against the enemies that he steadily created.

PREREVOLUTIONARY CONTEXT

The *Boston Globe* (August 18, 2009) reported on discussions in Washington between Secretary of State Hillary Clinton and Hosni Mubarak on potential peace talks between Israel and Palestine. All was "normal" gridlock on this topic, and no apparent ripples on the political surface in Egypt. The war in Afghanistan plodded along and bombs went off in Ingushetia. The Dow Jones index was limping at 9,135.34. The following day, the *Globe* headlined a story from the Boston FBI saying (ominously) it was "lacking firepower" and "vulnerable to terrorist attack." Presidents Mubarak and Obama met at the White House as Taliban bombs rocked Kabul. Everything was "normal."

By September 29, 2009, "normal" continued for the *Boston Globe* writing about 13 civilians being killed in Somalia, and the day before, 10 al-Shabab fighters executed two Somalis in the Mogadishu livestock market for being "spies for foreign organizations"; a trial was missing. More bombing in Iraq and NATO troops killed 30 Taliban in Afghanistan. The *Boston Globe* for October 6, 2009, noted a suicide bombing against a UN target in Islamabad, Pakistan, as well as "no exit" for Afghanistan and sanctions against Iran, and Al-Azhar University officials in Cairo banning face veils. No news from Libya.

The *Boston Sunday Globe* (October 11, 2009) reported on Hamas resilience, "militants" attacking the Pakistan Army; Turkey and Armenia signing an accord; wildlife returning to South Sudan; and Taliban chief Mullah Muhammad Omer making a "come back." No news about Libya; one presumes that such "normal stuff" was also being followed there, but from different perspectives.

Even a year later, the *Boston Sunday Globe* (November 7, 2010) reported more of the same: the Taliban attacked NATO troops in Afghanistan, while the United States was handing over some bases there; escaped al-Qa'eda leader Qassim al-Raini vowed to strike the United States; and Harvard vowed to address neglected diversity issues. Nothing about Libya, but the perception that NATO and the United States were fighting against Islam was circulating.

But in one more year, for example, in the *Boston Sunday Globe* (May 1, 2011), the situation was very different, and a full story headlined: "Khadafy Survives NATO Missile Strike: Youngest Son and 3 Grandchildren Killed in Attack." Meanwhile, the Taliban launched a new offensive, Syrians stormed a mosque, and the Yemeni President, Ali Abdullah Saleh, declined to resign. By May 5, 2011, the *Globe* reported that "Khadafy's Forces Kill Four after Aid Ship Docks in Port" (at Misrata); while faked pictures of a dead Osama bin Laden circulated in Washington after a U.S. SEAL team killed him in Abbottabad, Pakistan; 20 were killed in north-south border clashes in Sudan; and in Palestine, Fatah and Hamas "agree[d] to reconcile." On May 8, 2011, with the war in Libya going at full tilt, the *Boston Sunday Globe* was still much focused on the death of bin Laden and the war in Syria; but there was still a major article on "Khadafy Forces Bomb Fuel Depot in Rebel-Held City under Siege" (i.e., Misrata).

As May came to a close, the *New York Times* (May 31, 2011) carries the front-page article "Egypt's Christians Fear Violence as Changes Embolden Islamists," while no progress is reported on page 10 on talks with South Africa President Jacob Zuma and Colonel Muammar Gaddafi to bring the Libyan war to an end. So, in short, how can the Middle East in general, and Libya in particular, transition from quiet obscurity to a flaming and murderous war, in such a short period.

2011 STARTS OFF

This chronology is compiled from many electronic and print media, especially the daily *New York Times* (2011–2013) and the weekly *Economist* (2012–2013).

From the "Jasmin Revolution" to the west in Tunisia that promptly deposed President Zein al-Abdin Ben 'Ali on January 14, 2011, to the east where the "6th of April" Social Media movement in Egypt managed to topple President Hosni Mubarak on February 11, 2011, it was likely inevitable that the glowing spark of the "Arab Spring" revolt would strike Libya as well as Syria, Sudan, Yemen, Bahrain, Algeria, and the monarchies in Morocco, Bahrain, and Jordan. But Muammar Gaddafi in Libya would not go so easily. It would take a full-scale civil war with major foreign intervention.

Unlike protests in capitol squares in Tunis and Cairo, the uprising in Libya began in its second-largest city, far from the capitol (Rogan, 505). The protests in Benghazi were founded on a very long history of heroic anticolonial revolt by Omar al-Mukhtar, who was hanged by the Italians; and anti-Tripoli tension, rivalry, and marginalization by Gaddafi, which also has roots in colonialism, oil politics, history, and culture. The Libyan spark quickly ignited this dry tinder to the shock and surprise of the local citizens of Cyrenaica as well as the Gaddafi leadership far away in Tripoli. Probably both camps had thought they might escape the Arab Spring. However, in January, a few small protests took place in Benghazi, nominally over economic issues, but partly inspired by events in Cairo and Tunis. That was that.

On February 3, 2011, the *Wall Street Journal* reported that: "Col Muammar Gadhafi [*sic*] has been in power since 1969. Although he hasn't announced a successor, some analysts suspect his son, Saif al-Islam Gaddafi [*sic*], is being groomed. So far only minor protests have been reported against Col Gadhafi's [*sic*] dictatorship."

Then, by February 15, just after the fall of Mubarak in Egypt, the small demonstrations grew in Benghazi, and by February 17, the protests had spread to the historic town of Tobruk and the Islamist center in Derne; this got the attention of the authorities in Tripoli. Fearing a greater spread of revolt, Gaddafi sent two military jets to bomb Benghazi on February 21. The following day, in a classic long-winded Gaddafi oratory in Tripoli's Green Square, the President spoke of ridding Benghazi of the "rats and cockroaches"—frighteningly parallel to the words used in the Rwanda genocide (Rogan, 505).

The embers of revolt were now glowing hot, and by late February, the Transitional National Congress (TNC) was formed in Benghazi and adopted the flag of the former monarch. Thus was thrown down a brazen challenge to the four decades of Gaddafi rule. Far to the west, fear, propaganda, police action, and quite a few foreign mercenaries were still able to keep "order" in Tripoli in this east-west standoff. Enough was enough. Undefended military garrisons were promptly looted and arms seized by the civilians who were, in many cases, already familiar with military life and technology. The towns of Tobruk and Bayda fell to the rebels, and Benghazi would follow suit a week later. The war was now engaged, and far to the west, the long battle and punishing siege of Misrata, a city of 300,000, was underway.

Gaddafi angrily proclaimed that "inch by inch, room by room, house by house, alley by alley" he would clean out the "rats" with "no mercy." Instead, this furious warning was to turn against him when this humanitarian threat was perceived and marketed by rich French philosopher Bernard-Henri Levy to encourage French military action by French President Nicolas Sarkozy under the Responsibility to Protect (R2P). The temporary stalemate was radically broken on March 10 when Sarkozy recognized the TNC as the legitimate government of Libya. Following this lead, on March 12, the Arab League voted for a no-fly zone over Libya, and on March 18, the first French planes attacked Gaddafi's military forces, camped outside of Benghazi, to block his aggressive threats. British, American, Jordanian, UAE, and Qatari military planes soon joined in to bomb Gaddafi's supply lines and military depots to enforce no-fly and put a naval blockade on Libya (Rogan, 506). Any perceived threat to civilians was attacked.

Also in March, Libyan TV journalist and blogger, the "martyr," Mohammed Nabous set up *Libya Hurra* ("Free Libya"), a parallel to the Egyptian blogger, Khalid Muhammad Sa'ed; both challenged authority and paid the highest price. Nabous was killed by Gaddafi's snipers on March 19. But the more they repressed, the more that Gaddafi's soldiers began to revolt and defect.

A week later, Egyptian leader 'Amr Mousa of the Arab League said this was more than he had approved. Russia and China also protested, but the war was now on, and there was no going back in this fight to the finish. And there was more controversy on April 30, 2011, when a NATO strike killed Gaddafi's 29-year old son, Saif al-Arab, and his three children, but narrowly missing Muammar Gaddafi and his wife Safia, who had just been in the same dwelling hours before (*Boston Sunday Globe*, May 1). Perhaps this meeting was to meet his key aide Moussa Koussa (Noueihed and Warren, 182). NATO said it was going after command-and-control centers; others said this was a badly failed assassination attempt. Nevertheless, this was only followed by more night raids by NATO planes throughout the month of May as well as trying to clear sea mines from the channels into Misrata. Calls for negotiations and cease-fires by Gaddafi and the TNC fell on deaf ears as long as civilians were in danger.

When a relief ferry, the *Red Star One*, tried for days to dock in Misrata to provide for humanitarian evacuation and deliver supplies, Gaddafi's forces shelled the port, causing panic and the death of four stranded civilians. The United Sates provided $6.5 million for this relief mission, while Gaddafi's navy was laying sea mines to block such aid. The TNC in Benghazi protested that this was a crime against humanity. Fighting was also reported in Kufra, far to the southeast and known as a historic Sanusi stronghold. The International Criminal Court prosecutor said it would seek arrest warrants for the leaders responsible for the systematic arrests and attacks on civilians in such places as Misrata, Tripoli, Al-Zariya, Zintan, and elsewhere in the Nafusa Mountains after the UN Security Council asked, on February 26, for a report in two months (*Boston Globe*, May 5, 2011).

With the war now full blown, Gaddafi's army again fired heavy Grad rockets at Misrata that had been under siege by land and sea already for two months. His rockets hit three tanks at the main fuel depot, cutting supplies, food, water, telephones, and power for the city. Hundreds of residents in the city had already been killed by this time (*Boston Sunday Globe*, May 7, 2011). By mid-May, Gaddafi's siege of Misrata was finally broken by steadfast resistance in this strategic coastal center of Libya that essentially broke Gaddafi's supply lines to the east. Misrata's buildings and infrastructure, especially the fought over Tripoli Street, was heavily damaged and finally its civilians were killed in the thousands.

By this time, African Union hope for exile for Colonel Gaddafi, a negotiated settlement, or even a cease-fire to halt the NATO bombing campaign was rapidly diminishing. South African President Jacob Zuma and Gaddafi tried again to seek a breakthrough in the violent conflict in a six-hour meeting in Tripoli, but failed in an ongoing stalemate. Eight more senior Libyan military officers, including five generals, defected in Rome, adding to the list of 120 top officials including five cabinet members who had broken with Gaddafi (*New York Times*, May 31, 2011). This was not yet the tipping point in this conflict, but Gaddafi's options were now much narrower, and the trends for his collapse were growing stronger by the day.

THE TRAMPLING PLACE

As with the arrival of Phoenicians and Arabs that was resisted by Berbers, or the German-British clashes of World War II, the 2011 war in Libya had few strategic defensive points such as rivers or mountains; thus there was a great deal of movement and flux as military supplies arrived and were consumed by opposing forces. For the 2011 war, the more stable anchor points, or rear areas, were Gaddafi forces from Tripoli and the TNC forces of Benghazi, both making for the intermediate towns of Ajdabiya, Brega, and Ras Lanuf, were heavily contested by Gaddafi's armor and artillery and the improvised weapons of the TNC, especially after the no-fly zone was dominated by NATO aircraft and attrition of Gaddafi's military assets accelerated. In the west, Jebel Nafusa rebels struggled along with arms arriving from Tunisia to the town of Nalut and Zintan to move out of the mountains and on toward Tripoli and finally taking Zawiyah, its refinery, a key road to the west, and more arms.

Meanwhile, in neighboring Tunisia, a nation a fraction of the size of Libya, events were moving at a faster but less bloody pace than Gaddafi's Libya. The Tunisian leadership had found that exiled President Ben Ali and his wife Leila Trabelsi were guilty of taking state funds and sentenced them *in absentia* to 35 years in prison and a fine of $566 million (*New York Times*, June 21, 2011).

Among other contentious issues, an incident at the Rixos Hotel that served as the base for foreign journalists in Tripoli took place when a Libyan minder was allegedly shot by a rebel sniper from the jihadist group Libyan Islamic Fighting Group (LIFG). This was all in the context of increasing rebel pressure on the capital, such as the deadly NATO attack at the luxurious estate of Khoweildi al-Hamidi, a long and close ally of Gaddafi. Killing of civilians on both sides of the conflict was certainly taking place (*New York Times*, June 21, 2011). LIFG despised Gaddafi for his dictatorship as well as his unorthodox applications of Islam. The long-standing oppression and substantial experience in other jihadist theaters added to their resolve and sacrifice.

THE TIPPING POINT

As an American political sidebar to the war in Libya, the White House was reminded that any hostilities involving U.S. forces that lasted more than 60 days required either an ending date or request for declaration of hostilities, and a report to Congress, under the 1973 War Powers

Resolution. One might start that clock on about March 20, meaning that a report was due on May 20; but it was closer to June 20 that Congress was informed. The Obama White House claimed that these were not really "hostilities" but much more of an enforcement, defense suppression, intelligence, and "non-kinetic" supporting role for NATO allies. There were officially no boots on the ground for Americans, and the main combat role was handed over to NATO in early April. Congress was rather skeptical and wanted more information than was forthcoming as there were about 60 American attacks on Libyan air defenses, and 30 Predator drone attacks on Libyan forces. The information eventually provided seemed to appease Congress, and as the war was going rather well, there was little more word at the time from Capitol Hill (*New York Times*, June 21, 2011).

Although China had abstained in the UN Security Council, balked at the expansion of the no-fly zone, and criticized the bombing campaign, by mid-June it was becoming more clear that Libya under Gaddafi was heading for its end. Chairman of the TNC Executive Board Mahmoud Jibril was invited to visit Beijing in hopes for a settlement. Earlier in June, Chinese diplomats in Qatar met with TNC Chairman Mustafa 'Abd al-Jalil. These were additional diplomatic failures for the Colonel, even though Libyan Foreign Minister 'Abd al-Atti al-Obeidi had traveled to Beijing earlier to head off these developments. China sent military planes to Libya as the fighting began to evacuate the 30,000 Chinese workers in Libya (*New York Times*, June 21, 2011).

With negotiations ended, and options limited, one can say that by the end of June 2011 or in the first weeks of July, Gaddafi's forces were at the tipping point of no return. He was on the verge of finally losing Misrata and beginning to intellectually sense inevitable defeat, even though many more lives would still be lost. War is always about politics and perception, and Gaddafi charged that NATO bombs had killed 15 civilians at a bakery and restaurant in an attack on Brega by its warplanes. Five were also alleged to have been killed on the previous Friday (*Boston Sunday Globe*, June 26, 2011).

THE ENDGAME

With increasing diplomatic isolation, defections, military setbacks, supplies not arriving, and his oil revenue cut, the position for Colonel Gaddafi was increasingly bleak after six months of war. One journalist reported that the military base at the town of El-Ga'a south of the Nafusa Mountains had been seized by rebels in their quest for arms and ammunition. There were no rifles, but tons of rounds and parts for manpad missiles that would later spread across the Sahara and other parts of the Middle East. The rebels thought this would help in future offensives to take Zintan and Zawiya and a probing attack on Bir al-Ghanem on the road to Tripoli. Gaddafi's forces never returned, and the military noose on Tripoli only tightened (*New York Times,* June 29, 2011).

With Gaddafi's many past and horrendous abuses (Lockerbie, for example) and the present military campaign so well covered in global media, it was surprising to read that prominent Harvard and London School of Economics professors were recruited by "Monitor Group" in Cambridge and highly paid and supported to visit Libya from 2006 to 2008 under the assumption that this was a public relations mission of "reform." With fees, costs, expenses, and reimbursements reaching $6.7 million, it certainly raises serious ethical and legal (Foreign Agents Registration Unit of the American government) questions and demonstrates how Muammar and Saif Gaddafi could use the great oil wealth of Libya to try to manipulate public opinion (*Boston Globe,* July 2, 2011).

Juxtaposed to that story was the headline "Khadafy Threatens Attacks on Europe: Warns NATO to End Airstrikes." Despite this defiant statement, broadcast to a rally of his remaining supporters in Tripoli, and while NATO responded with more bombs, his remarks were not taken seriously, given the fact he had been directly responsible for attacks throughout Europe in years prior to this conflict. Four days earlier, the ICC had issued an arrest warrant for Gaddafi and his son Saif (*Boston Globe,* July 2, 2011). Fearing European prejudice through the ICC, the African Union opposed the arrest warrant, stating that it "complicates" a political solution for the crisis (*New York Times,* July 3, 2011). By this late time, the political solution wished for by AU Chairman Jean Ping was probably not very realistic.

Others were not willing, or able, to see the trends on the battlefield. Colonel Muhammad 'Ali Etish, a defector from Gaddafi who was now commanding a force of rebels in the mountainous west, believed they were not in a strong enough logistic position to take the capitol and needed to coordinate with an internal uprising. This cautious view was partially addressed with increasing links to urban rebel cells, but the end was closer than he thought (*Boston Globe,* July 8, 2011).

The American House of Representatives, noted for its ideological gridlock divisions, voted (225–201) on that Thursday to block aid to Libyan rebels, but they did allow continuing U.S. nonlethal support of $25 million as well as $53 million for humanitarian aid for the mission there. This mixed message was founded on reluctance to support a third war, in addition to those in Iraq and Afghanistan that Americans are gradually exiting. On the other hand, the vote to continue the U.S. role in Libya was approved 229–199 (*Boston Globe,* July 8, 2011).

Thus, gradually, another existential piece of the "Obama Doctrine" fell into place, which, according to David Sanger, is a cautious blend of collaborative, smarter, leaner, and meaner military engagements, such as in

Libya and with the "Arab Spring" in general, in this challenging and volatile region (*New York Times Book Review,* July 15, 2011).

One glitch in this revolutionary process was the defection of Gaddafi's former Minister of Interior, Maj. Gen. 'Abd al-Fattah Younis al-Obeidi (1944–2011). While his defection was heartily welcomed as a serious blow to Gaddafi, he came with onerous political baggage (and lots of practical military experience) since he had been closely involved with a number of Gaddafi's brutal and violent acts against foreigners and against fellow Libyans. He was quickly placed in the General Command of the Free Libyan Army of the TNC, but with substantial anxiety by the rebels. While the precise circumstances of his suspicious death are still disputed, there is reason to believe that out of revenge for some of his past acts he was killed by a member of the 17th of February Martyr's Brigade on July 28, 2011.

Despite his ever expanding setbacks, Gaddafi should be credited with tenacity. Even when the war slogged on with NATO warplanes striking three television broadcast dishes, Gaddafi got them running again and broadcasted from an unknown location. This pushed at the credibility of the mandate to only protect citizens as defensive measures, not in flying offensive missions to support the rebels, although the focus of the mission steadily slipped in this direction (*New York Times,* July 31, 2011).

With TNC rebel momentum growing incrementally and Gaddafi's regular and mercenary forces defecting, dying, retreating, and escaping, this was already on the downside of the proverbial tipping point. At the same time, with victory now on the horizon and with critical NATO backup, the rebels were faced with their own issues. First among them was the killing of 'Abd al-Fattah Younis in July and the 'investigation' that followed. This also led to other leaders in the judiciary and law enforcement whose allegiance to the national revolution was questioned. Other thorny issues about who joined the revolution and when were raised, as well as the big and enduring problem of loyalty to local militias instead to the new national army. Meanwhile, NATO bombs continued to fall as the "right to protect" clearly became "regime change" (*New York Times,* August 5, 2011).

Despite the fact that Gaddafi was a political maverick and radical, he was never a supporter of Islamic extremism; and when his son Saif said that he would join with some Islamists, within the rebel movement, his father promptly rejected that move even though Saif was often projected as his successor. One presumes that the death of 'Abd al-Fattah was seen as a division among the rebels that Saif thought he might exploit. In short, the brief incident raised more questions than it answered (*New York Times,* August 6, 2011).

Another sad incident along the road to revolution was that hundreds or perhaps thousands of Libyans tried to reach Mediterranean islands or

Italy to escape the fighting. Very many drowned on the way. One group of
370 survivors complained that a NATO ship did not assist them with food
or water, and some 30 or more had perished for this reason on their hard
battle to reach the Italian island of Lampedusa (*New York Times*, August 6,
2011).

As Chinese Chairman Mao Tse-Tung was famously quoted, "a revolution is not a tea-party." Clearly, the Libyan revolution was proving this
adage correct for both sides, but the TNC rebels had their eyes on the
prize to seize Tripoli and rid it of Colonel Gaddafi, who was desperately
holding on to less and less. Since the eastern regions of Cyrenaica were
rather secure by this time, the no-fly protocol was still in effect, and with
Misrata freed, the towns and region of Tripolitania next commanded
NATO attention. The rebels in the mountains needed to secure their rear
areas and advance on the capitol. With NATO air strikes opening the
way, and with more and better arms and some armor, the rebels began
to move and open a new front after weeks of essential stalemate in July.
Leaving the comparative security of the Nafusa Mountains the rebels set
their sights on the important towns of Sabratha and Zawiya that were still
under regime control. If these would fall, then it would be on to Tripoli.
Zawiya still had many rebel sympathizers, but who were badly crushed
when they rose early in the war. The ebb and flow of the battle involved
trading tank fire on occasion but mostly remained a small arms clash.
Casualties on both sides were taken to local hospitals, and some more
Gaddafi soldiers were captured (*Boston Sunday Globe*, August 7, 2011).

Such was the pattern of small gains and some setbacks for the next two
weeks of slow but steady advance, and Gaddafi supporters were finally
driven out of Zawiya on Saturday, August 20, 2011, making only a 30-mile
distance left to travel to reach Tripoli. Fragmentary reports from the
capital suggested that the uprising had also begun there and some rebels
had entered from the east as well as that arms caches had accumulated
in the city from deliveries by sea. Some civilians fled from the imagined
urban targets.

GAME OVER—MORE OR LESS

On the night of Sunday August 21, 2011, Operation Mermaid Dawn
activated all of the rebel units from the west, from Zawiya (backed by crucial NATO strikes, that blocked a Gaddafi countermove), from the south
from Gharyan, from the east from Zlitan and badly beaten Misrata (where
they could advance on Mitiga International Airport), as well as by boats
coming from Misrata and urban revolutionary cells (the Tripoli Brigade)
for the final assault on Tripoli that was now fully encircled. Strategic
Brega that had been swapped several times was under rebel control.
Mustafa 'Abd al-Jalil of the TNC said that "all evidence is that the end is

very near, with God's grace." Sirte on the coast and Sabha further south were still in the hands of Gaddafi supporters. And no one really knew where Gaddafi was at this point, but more of his senior officials were now fleeing for their lives, even while snipers were taking positions to "save" the city, while an amazed gentleman said "I swear to God, freedom is beautiful" (*New York Times*, August 21, 2011).

By noon on Monday, August 22, 2011, rebels had poured into the symbolic stronghold city from all directions in its final major offensive. Some skirmishes had taken place on Sunday night and early Monday morning at the Rixos Hotel (just southeast of the Bab al-Aziziya complex that was still not taken) and a few other locations between government and rebel forces, but by afternoon much of the city was under rebel control in the first day of Tripoli's freedom from Gaddafi, who had likely fled some days earlier. The central "Green" (now Martyr's) Square of Tripoli that had been the scene of so many "encouraged demonstrations" of support for Gaddafi was now filled with his opponents. Critical to this victory was NATO and American aerial surveillance with drones to provide the intelligence coordination to the rebel forces. With withering attacks on Gaddafi's command and control, he finally ran out of assets to mobilize after 7,459 strike missions. On the previous Saturday, only 39 sorties had been flown and 22 of them were in Tripoli, to accelerate the precipitous decline of Gaddafi's forces.

The TNC declared from jubilant Benghazi: "We congratulate the Libyan people for the fall of Muammar Gaddafi and call on the Libyan people to go into the street to protect the public property. Long live free Libya." The military base of the notorious and essential Khamis 32nd Brigade, headed by Gaddafi's son, was quickly taken. The rebels claimed that they had also captured Gaddafi's sons, Saif al-Islam (at the Rixos Hotel) and Muhammad, but this awaited independent confirmation as rumors rapidly flew about. As it turned out, Saif al-Islam was not seized, nor was his father Muammar. Other senior officials, such as Omran Abukraa (Oil Minister); 'Abd al-Salam Jalloud (former deputy) and Nasser al-Mabrouk (security official) had rapidly escaped abroad. With the location of Gaddafi himself not being known, there was also a substantial fear of a counteroffensive or renewed insurgency against the rebels.

More worrying at this exciting and tumultuous time was that there were few thoughts about governance and creating a new administration. Especially concerning was to establish control of Gaddafi's considerable stores of weapons and ammunition, most notably his "manpads" (SAM-7, heat-seeking antiaircraft missiles). Equally alarming were concerns that revenge killing might unfold and that the rebels' loose command would not know or observe the "international rules of war" (*New York Times*, August 22, 2011).

Until Gaddafi was killed, or in custody, this was not over, and even the penetrating assault on Gaddafi's residential office complex at

Bab al-Azizyah on August 23 along with looting, souvenir hunting, and acquiring weapons and ammunition did not resolve these many serious concerns and move new Libya toward a stable, secure, and democratic transition. In Chapter 7, we will see that this would be a bumpy and twisted road to tread.

At the personal and local level, celebratory gunfire continued in Tripoli for several days as the rebels and their leaders began to contemplate their next steps and sort out their complex swirling emotions of vengeance, anger, fatigue, loss, and confusion, while burying the bodies of their friends, family, enemies, and mercenary recruits. Other citizens were still overwhelmed with newfound freedom, the end of violence and insecurity, and executions that dominated for that last half a year. Mature Muslim leaders recalled the primordial values in Islam of mercy, compassion, and forgiveness to help to sort this out. Rebel leaders had to try to put Libya back together again and recover sequestered assets in order to rebuild. At the international level, Africans and Arabs had to determine whether to offer condolences or congratulations, or have hopes or fears for their own nations. The allied NATO nations had to figure out the military, economic, and political costs, benefits, and lessons learned from this experience (*New York Times*, August 27, 2011).

Some 30,000–50,000 died by early September (Nouiehed and Warren, 185) after about six months of war. While foreigners were not "supposed" to be in Libyan territory, Western "spotters" were on the ground to help coordinate and identify targets, and Qatar was training Libyan soldiers. The TNC officials in Benghazi pieced things together and gradually made local organizations of local militias, but at first they hesitated to leave Benghazi without the elusive Gaddafi being captured or killed. Was he still hiding in Tripoli? Had he headed south to Sabha? Did he go to his hometown at Sirte?

Meanwhile, American General Carter Ham, commander of the U.S. Africa Command (USAFRICOM), who had just started his new position, plunged professionally into this military mission and now had to reflect on the tactics and strategies employed. What happened in Libya might be a useful model in other NATO conflicts elsewhere (such as in way more complicated Syria) as this would be added to the evolution of the "Obama Doctrine" (*New York Times*, August 29, 2011).

In September, the UN began a three-month political support transition. The looming questions were how new and how fast the new Libya could be built. Oh yes—by the way where are Mutassim, Muammar and Saif-al-Islam Gaddafi? It was hard enough to build the new Libya with these persons still at large.

Even three weeks after the victory in Tripoli, there were still important Gaddafi holdouts in Bani Waled to the southeast of the capital and Sirte on the central coast, prompting strategists to imagine that the former

President might be in either place or one or two other towns that were not under rebel government control. The call for Gaddafi supporters to surrender was aborted on Friday, September 9, when they received incoming fire from these locations.

Now it was going to be a back-and-forth war and street-to-street fighting once again to root out pro-Gaddafi snipers by the TNC rebels. A legal offensive was also underway with Interpol warrants for the arrests of Saif al-Islam and Abdullah Senussi who, rumor had it, were fleeing toward Niger. At least Gaddafi's Tuareg General 'Ali Kana and Libyan Air Force General 'Ali Sharif al-Rifi had made it to the Nigeriene capitol of Agadez to stay under uncertain terms in the Gaddafi-owned Etoile du Ténéré Hotel. Back in Libya, the TNC and ICC's search for Colonel Gaddafi continued on without result. The TNC rebel rank and file was not impressed by late "side-switchers" as the Gaddafi "ship of state" was already in a fatal list. This would be an ongoing problem in trying to construct the new post-Gaddafi state, where previous administrative experience might be useful if the former office holders were not too tainted with Gaddafi's bloodshed (*New York Times*, September 10, 2011). The future Libya would also have to deal with issues of institutional corruption that was rampant in the Gaddafi era, as well as the means to address international standards of accountability and transparency for the new economic life.

As much as this unfinished business was still underway, other steps to normalize Libya's domestic and international life were also taking place. This included reopening the American Embassy in Tripoli that had been closed and looted during the 2011 revolt. Ambassador Gene A. Cretz could now return to his post to speak about some 150 American firms that could be interested in future business opportunities in resurrected Libya that needed to rebuild war-damaged buildings and infrastructure and had the oil resources with which this would be possible (*New York Times*, September 23, 2011). Concerns about heavily armed Islamist militias were also raised by Ambassador Cretz.

Yet, the search against Gaddafi holdouts was still incomplete. Former Gaddafi Prime Minister Al-Baghdadi 'Ali al-Mahmoudi had been arrested in Tunisia in late September, but TNC fighters were still being shelled and resisted in Sabha, Beni Walid, and Sirte, which they could just not manage to bring under their control. At the same time, the places for the Gaddafis to hide were steadily diminishing (*New York Times*, September 23, 2011).

The impressive international Ouagadougou Conference Center and the Ibn Sina Hospital in Sirte were taken on Sunday, October 9. Before the war, it was in Sirte that Gaddafi sought to be at the center stage in African politics; now this was a battleground in which 30 Gaddafi soldiers were killed and some 400 were wounded. Perhaps Muammar and Mutassim Gaddafi were still in this city—or in Beni Walid? Back-and-forth advance and retreat from Gaddafi snipers would keep this question unanswered for now, but the price, so far in this Sirte offensive, on the rebel side, was 17 TNC rebels dead and 250 wounded. Highly motivated anti-Gaddafi fighters from Misrata attacked Sirte from the west with tanks, mortars, Kalashnikovs, and RPGs. The tenacity of this fight added to the enthusiastic belief that that Gaddafi leaders were possibly in this city (*New York Times*, October 10, 2011).

The following week, the American Secretary of State, Hillary Clinton, arrived in Tripoli to celebrate the many military and political accomplishments to date (October 18, 2011). But it was two days later, on October 20, when Muammar and Mutassim Gaddafi were captured and ignominiously killed in a culvert in Sirte. Their bodies were displayed in a cold storage building and then buried anonymously in the desert. The option for a trial and symbolic new start for the "rule of law" would never be realized. This part of the struggle was definitively over.

A month later, Saif al-Islam was finally captured at Ubari and, as of this writing, was still being held by rebel militias in Zintan, who were reluctant to hand him over to the weak Tripolitanian government. Another week later, interim Prime Minister 'Abd al-Rahim al-Keeb announced a temporary cabinet including a Zintan rebel as the Minister of Defense.

On November 23, 2011, the President of Yemen, 'Ali 'Abdullah Saleh, also joined the ranks of fallen Arab dictators who had remained in power for too long (Rogan, 507).

POSTREVOLUTIONARY CONTEXT

While this chapter has been centered on the military side of the 2011 Libyan revolution, it has also revealed tremendous new, and formerly repressed, aspects of Libyan society. Not the least of these is the explosion in the social, electronic, and print media. MCT (66–69) provides a long list of such new and "liberated" media, as outlined in Table 6.1.

Table 6.1

Libyan Media Outlets as of February 2011

Location	Source	Medium
Tripoli	*Al-Asesema* (The Capital)	Television
Tripoli	*Libya Al-Arddia* (Libyan Land)	Television
Tripoli	*Libya Al-Watan* (Libyan Homeland)	Television
Tripoli	Libya Radio and Television (LRT)	Television
Tripoli	Libya One	Television
Tripoli	Libya Satellite Television	Television
Tripoli	Libya TV	Television

Table 6.1 (*continued*)

Location	Source	Medium
Tripoli	Tripoli TV	Television
Tripoli	2020 TV	Television
Tripoli	*Akhbar Tripoli* (Tripoli News)	Print
Tripoli	*Al-Assema* (The Capital) ⁻	Print
Tripoli	*Al-Bilad* (The Country)	Daily Print
Tripoli	*Al-Nahar* (The Day)	Weekly Print
Tripoli	*Al-Medina* (The City)	Weekly Print
Tripoli	*Al-Ra'ed Al-Jadid* (The New Guide)	Print
Tripoli	*Al-Ra'i Al-Aham* (The Important Opinion)	Twice Weekly
Tripoli	*Al-Umma* (The [Muslim] Nation)	Weekly Print
Tripoli	*'Arus Al-Bahr* (Bride of the Sea)	Print
Tripoli	*Trablus* (Tripoli)	Print
Tripoli	Tripoli Post	Weekly Print
Tripoli	*Sawt Trablus* (Voice of Tripoli)	Radio
Tripoli	Radio Libya	Radio
Tripoli/Benghazi	*Libya Awalan* (Libya First)	Television
Tripoli/Benghazi	*A'alam al-A'amal* (Business World)	Monthly Print
Tripoli/Benghazi	*Al-Zahabia* (Golden)	Monthly Print
Benghazi	*Libya Al-Hurra* (Free Libya)	Television
Benghazi	*Libya Al-Ahrar* (Liberal Libya)	Television
Benghazi	*Al-Kalima* (The Word)	Weekly Print
Benghazi	*Al-Qurna* (The Peak)	Print
Benghazi	*Akhbar Benghazi* (Benghazi News)	Print
Benghazi	*Al-Taghyer* (The Change)	Print
Benghazi	*Berniq* ("Cyrenaicia")	Print
Benghazi	*Intefadat Al-Ahrar* (Liberal Uprising)	Print
Benghazi	Radio Sawa	Radio
Benghazi	Libya	Radio
Benghazi	Tribute FM	Radio
Benghazi	*Libya Al-Hurra* (Free Libya)	Radio
Benghazi	Radio Shabab (Youth Radio)	Radio
Benghazi	Libyana Hits	Radio
Misrata	*Al-Menbar* (The Pulpit)	Weekly Print

(*continued*)

Table 6.1 (*continued*)

Location	Source	Medium
Misrata	*Al-Risala* (The Message)	Print
Misrata	*Al-Shari'a al-Libya* (The Libyan Way)	Print
Misrata	*Al-E'tlaf* (Coalition)	Weekly Print
Misrata	*Al-Jebha* (The Front)	Biweekly
Misrata	*Al-Watan* (The Nation)	Bimonthly
Misrata	*Al-Wataniya* (Nationhood)	Biweekly
Misrata	*Jamiat al Sabatashar Febraier*	Monthly
Misrata	*Al-Kilimat al-Haq* (True Word)	Biweekly
Misrata	*Libya Al-Watan* (Libyan Homeland)	Print
Misrata	*Misrata Al-Hurra* (Misrata, the Free)	Print
Misrata	*Sada Al-Thawra* (Revolutionary Echo)	Monthly
Misrata	*Radio Tobacts FM*	Radio
Misrata	*Radio Hurra Misrata*	Radio
Garian	*Saidat al-Garian* (Ladies of Garian)	Monthly
Jadou	*Radio Nafousa*	Radio
Murzuq	*Sada* (Echo)	Weekly
Nalut	Radio Free Nalut	Radio
Tobruk	Radio Free Tobruk	Radio
Zuwarah	Radio Zuwarah	Radio

Media Summary

City	Television	Radio	Print
Tripoli	9	2	20
Benghazi	2	7	6
Tripoli/Benghazi	1	0	2
Misrata	0	2	12
Others	0	4	1
Total	**12**	**15**	**41**

Notes: The media for Sirte are missing, and Gaddafi's home area remains an unhappy region. Reasonably, Tripoli, the capital, dominates the national mass media; but Benghazi has more local radio stations than even the capital. Misrata also has a remarkable proportion of local print media, and its bloody struggles in 2011 made for special fervor. It remains to be seen how many of these can be sustained by the domestic market in subsequent years. Large distances and remote populations in Libya mean it is especially appropriate for telecommunications.

Analysis

The protests, revolt, and military contests to protect civilians, which finally evolved to regime change in Libya, were humbly fanned in Benghazi by the sparks from the Arab Spring in Tunisia and Egypt. Why did one spark go out in Algeria and in the Arab monarchies, but ignited a firestorm elsewhere as in Libya or Syria?

This 2011 chronology started as another "calm" year under the Gaddafi dictatorship. Then a local, then international, revolutionary war, with its fluctuations, its victories and defeats, and finally its military tipping point, endgame, and mopping up. Now Libya was on its way to rebuild and remake a new Libya, but the road ahead would not be easy.

The collapse of the Libyan *jamahuriya* was accelerated by the regional upsurge in the Arab Spring, serious economic problems, and political alienation that was advanced further by foreign air invention. At the same time, it was slowed by the climate of fear, the power of great oil wealth that had ruled Libya and had made it difficult to get organized politically and militarily. These factors of speeding up and simultaneously slowing down the fall of Gaddafi represented the strategic ebb and flow as well as the military back and forth that typically characterized the long history of domestic and foreign uprisings and interventions in Libya. As Gaddafi's supply lines were broken up by foreign air and protracted insurgency, he could not deploy or resupply his forces even when he turned to heavy artillery, coercion, and mercenary recruitment. On the rebel side, improvised weapons grew better, morale was high and buoyed by popular support, and practical experience was gained despite the "fog of war" and vicissitudes of combat. Slowly but steadily, the available options narrowed for Gaddafi. His charisma, terror, hubris, and purchased "loyalties and friendships" could only take him so far, and the cumulative defections persistently eroded these "strengths."

As the Transitional National Congress movement quickly evolved into a united front insurgency against the Gaddafi regime, their tactics also evolved. Initially unarmed, the simple goal was to protect the revolting populations in Cyrenaica in general and Benghazi in particular. The military tactics of the insurgency were initially built around defense of this vulnerable population. As world, NATO, and USAFRICOM forces joined this equation, the political forces of the TNC rather rapidly coalesced. And as local militias, already knowledgeable in the use of firearms, were joined by collapsing and defecting units of the Gaddafi regime, eastern Libya became the rear area of the anti-Gaddafi insurgency.

As this insurgency evolved, it was matched by parallel revolts in the Berber areas south of Tripoli, some border towns, and especially in Misrata. Other areas were brutally suppressed by Gaddafi security and military forces. As a consequence, the insurgency morphed into a civil war, and the offensive counterinsurgency forces of Gaddafi were put on the defensive by the no-fly zone that curbed his air forces and air defense as well as degraded his armor. Meanwhile, the insurgent rebels improvised light armor, gained combat experience, and steadily acquired more small arms (AK 47s, RPGs, mortars, and mines). Given the numerous case studies of historical conflicts in Libya from Arab, Turkish, Italian, and Anglo-German battles, the fight unfolded in a very similar way of give-and-take, back-and-forth skirmishes along the coast with many of these battles taking place along the Gulf of Sidra with pro-Gaddafi elements in Sirte and anti-Gaddafi forces concentrated in Misrata.

By the summer of 2011, Gaddafi was getting desperate and close to the tipping point, and certainly it was clear by then if not before that "regime change," not only "R2P," had become the goal. At the same time, proposals and interventions floated by African and other leaders to create pressure-resolving models whereby President Gaddafi, some family members, and high-ranking officials could seek exile in a welcoming country, continued to surface.

These options, that could have saved many lives on both sides, sadly did not reach fruition as the tipping points moved on to the endgame against steadily degraded Gaddafi forces, and broke the siege of Misrata, while tightening the military noose on the capital. Even the tactics of degrading Gaddafi's command-and-control centers with drone intelligence and sophisticated telemetry of guided missiles was only a slightly veiled strategic call to topple Gaddafi. While Muammar Gaddafi's humiliating death in Sirte on October 20, 2011, thwarted both his exile and judgment in a Libyan or Hague court, it did bring these four decades of dictatorial rule to a decisive close.

Clearly, this epoch was over, but the route ahead was not so clear on the road to building a new Libya. In the world of *diplomacy*, one may legitimately expand this to include domestic and international diplomacy as well as creating, *de novo*, a new legal foundation for the new state's constitution and parliament. Relations with Algeria remained testy because of the Gaddafi exiles then there, and relations with Egypt also had volatility because their own "Arab Spring" kept unfolding in new and violent ways. In addition, Tunisia was facing a variety of post-conflict issues that paralleled those in Libya.

The new Libyan lever of power in *information* was working well as seen in the proliferation of print and electronic media listed above—at least it was working well from the grassroots up—but the common voice of the fledging government was shaky and not always trusted with confidence. The role of the television company al-Jazeera played a strong role in furthering the rebellion in Libya, and both Gaddafi and al-Sisi in Egypt wanted to stop this by any means possible (Brynen et al., 235).

The word did get out for the elections and debates that were widely considered fair, free, and successful in process, if not in content, to create a functional parliament. In terms of elections, there were some forms, half-hearted perhaps, in Egypt and Tunisia; while in Libya, the quixotic nature of Gaddafi rule meant only electoral frustration (Brynen, et al., 160). On the other hand, in the post-conflict period, *En-Nahda* kept a strong minority position; while Egypt's Muslim Brothers (Freedom and Justice Party) had a weak majority position being opposed only by a Mubarak holdover, Ahmed Shafik, in second-round elections. Naturally, this overlooks the reimposition of military rule by 'Abd al-Fatah at-Sisi in 2013 when the Muslim Brothers were severely repressed. For Libya, the Muslim Brothers did not have much time to get organized electorally and were kept in a minority presence in the new Libyan parliament. Yet armed Salafists (*Ansar al-Shari'a*) fought hard in the 2011 war and, tragically, continued their approach in their murderous attack on the American diplomatic mission in Benghazi.

Comparing internet usage in 2010 (Brynen et al., 237) notes that Tunisia had 36.8 users per 100 inhabitants; Egypt had 26.7; while more repressive Libya had only 14.0 users. Gulf States generally had far more users (United Arab Emirates at 78.0 per 100; Oman, 62.0 per 100; and Bahrain, 55.0 per 100). Yet Yemen had only 12.4, and the lowest number of users was in Iraq at just 2.5/100. Clearly Gaddafi used Internet control and filtering as a major factor in political limitation, and presumably this number will rise in coming years in a freer Libya.

The *military* lever of power was, however, not at full strength. The armed forces of Gaddafi were broken, dispersed, and defeated, true enough; but as seen in the Iraq invasion and occupation, this can be as much a problem as an asset. Militaries and police are needed for public stability and security. Into this vacuum came the local militias who cobbled together some sort of order, but without much law to back it up.

In the case of Libya, there was some history of armed Islamists with the LIFG, while the Muslim Brothers in Egypt and *An Nahda* in Tunisia were not so involved. Perhaps *Jama'a Islamiya* and its franchise relationship with Al-Qa'eda should be included for Egypt, but the mass action of the generic April 6 movement kept those types out of the main centers of struggle in 2011. With this as background, only recently did a small armed insurgency erupt in Tunisia, and the electoral transition to the Muslim Brothers in Egypt was more or less peaceful. The overthrow of Ben Ali in Tunisia was very speedy and of Mubarak in Egypt was mainly by mass action, and those killed in Egypt were largely carried out by his security forces. Libya (and later bloodied Syria) stands out with previously experienced armed Islamist insurgents ready for long-term protracted battle with an imploded and defecting military of Gaddafi being replaced by harshly recruited mercenaries and guns to the back for the remaining regulars who had left to deploy. Gaddafi's navy and air force were rather quickly degraded by NATO air strikes.

Decentralized and transferable guerilla forces made a difficult target for Gaddafi's repression, but without a focused command and control and proper discipline, the militias did not appear when and where needed or, worse yet, pursue assassinations and bombings. In some cases, this took on an Islamist agenda that was inimical to the interests of the new state. The weak state faced many problems in reasserting the state monopoly of the use of force. As of this writing, this was a glaring and unresolved present issue even though one may forecast a brighter outcome for the Libyan future.

The post-conflict lever of power in the realm of *economics* has also been problematic. Libya is the richest in oil in these Arab Spring nations and the relatively smallest of the populations. So, one could be most optimistic about the future for Libya, even though oil and gas production was substantially restored once the war stopped because the facilities were broadly protected. But, as seen in previous chapters, this oil production was not sustained and has seriously declined because of oil workers' protests, cautious investors, some damaged infrastructure, and especially security problems. The future of oil in Libya will certainly receive more scrutiny and, one hopes, more economic diversification, transparency, accountability and less of a foreign rentier presence.

These matters will all be pursued in Chapter 7, which explores the years of 2012–2013 after the revolution, as the new Libya is being constructed with challenges even greater than the defeat of the dictatorship.

SOURCES

Aftandilian, Gregory. *Egypt's New Regime and the Future of the US-Egyptian Strategic Relationship.* Carlisle, PA: Strategic Studies Institute, U.S. Army War College, 2013.

Brynen, Rex, Peter W. Moore, Bassel F. Salloukh, and Marie-Joëlle Zahar. *Beyond the Arab Spring: Authoritarianism and Democratization in the Arab World.* Boulder, CO: Lynne Reinner, 2012.

MCT (Media in Cooperation and Transition). *Reinventing the Public Sphere in Libya: Observations, Portraits and Commentary in a MCT Newly Emerging Media Landscape.* Berlin: German Federal Foreign Office, 2012.

Noueihed, Lin, and Alex Warren. *The Battle for the Arab Spring: Revolution, Counter-Revolution and the Making of a New Era.* New Haven, CT: Yale University Press, 2012.

Owen, Roger. *The Rise and Fall of Arab Presidents for Life.* Cambridge, MA: Harvard University Press, 2012.

Rogan, Eugene. *The Arabs: A History.* New York: Basic Books, 2011.

Sanger, David. *Confront and Conceal: Obama's Secret Wars and Surprising Use of American Power.* New York: Crown Publishers, 2012.

CHAPTER 7

Bumpy and Twisted Roads to the New Libya: 2012–2013

INTRODUCTION

The previous chapters have detailed the historical, economic, and geographical foundations of modern Libya, as well as the context, strategies, and conduct of the 2011 war. This pioneering work also described and analyzed the "new type" of UN, NATO, and U.S. Africa Command roles supporting the war. How could air power be so important in coordinating with the TNC? The military victory of the TNC over Gaddafi's forces is very clear, but now two years later, was this a political success? How do we know and measure? Are two post-conflict years enough time for us to judge? What are the issues and trends that still confront this massive rebuilding project for a nation with such a rich history? The two most recent years in the modern, post-Gaddafi period have brought an end to high-intensity armed insurrection and major foreign intervention, but the judicial, economic, political, and infrastructural issues faced by the new authorities have kept the agenda very full. With this chapter, we are at the end of this unfinished story.

If there were not enough contentious political issues in Libya, two British journalists, Gareth Montgomery-Johnston and Nicholas Davies, were charged with illegal entrance into Libya and possible espionage as they were evidently trying to contact other Britons held by the Faraj Sweheli–led Misurata militia (*New York Times*, March 15, 2012).

Writing a survey on democracy in Africa and the Middle East, the question was raised about which way Africa was headed. Plenty of changes were taking place across the continent, but according to this source,

Somalia was the only failed state and Mali had a revolution and coup. Without considering all the cases, Tunisia had moved from an "authoritarian regime" to a "flawed democracy," while Egypt and Libya had moved from an "authoritarian regime" to a "hybrid regime" (*The Economist*, March 31, 2012). This is not a strong trend, but it is at least some motion in the right direction. Legal and security issues, rounding up stray arms, reining in the militias, Islamists' agendas, assassinations, a new constitution, cabinet shifts, and a murderous raid on the US diplomatic mission in Benghazi, were all in the mix for 2012–2013.

In a chilling interview with Marwan Gdoura, torturer and executioner of Gaddafi, journalist Robert F. Worth wrote an article trying to understand this individual who was "just following orders" and who is now a prisoner himself, being guarded by the brother of one of the men he killed. Will Libya's future include mercy or revenge to resolve these deeply emotional and legal issues? (*New York Times Magazine*, May 13, 2012).

So many normal processes in Libya were distorted or suspended during the Gaddafi years. Among them was the confiscation of private property in the name of the socialist republic of Libya. With memories long, records confused or nonexistent, and the Gaddafi dynasty utterly toppled, thousands of Libyans have begun to try to recover lost real estate and lands. Lost land registries and a hobbled court system will not make this an easy or fast process (*New York Times*, May 14, 2012).

Another international issue that could now be reexamined more openly after Gaddafi's death is that of 'Abd al- Basset 'Ali al-Megrahi (April 1, 1952–May 2012), the former Libyan intelligence officer and convicted 1988 Lockerbie bomber who was released from a Scottish prison on the grounds of his "impending" death from cancer. He was welcomed back to Libya by Saif al-Islam, Gaddafi's heir-apparent son. Allegations swirled that Gaddafi turned to "good behavior" from his 20 counts of murder, and the British wanted to consummate significant arms or oil and gas sales. It didn't hurt that this relationship was sweetened by $2.7 billion paid to the victims' relatives by Gaddafi and the early release by the British of al-Megrahi. Of course, to add to the emotional complexity of this man and case, he failed to pass away as fast as had been forecasted. Finally, al-Megrahi did die, three years later, at age 60, in May 2012. Perhaps hidden files will get discovered that will add additional clarity to this long-running, and foggy, case (*New York Times*, May 21, 2012).

Meanwhile, across the Sahara in Mali, the Tuareg Mouvement National de Liberation de L'Azawad (MNLA) separatists were overtaken by the Ansar ed-Din extremists in their revolt, fueled in part by weapons trafficking from Libya via Algeria and Niger and by elections in neighboring Egypt that brought a Muslim Brother to power in May 2012. Libya's unguarded stocks of weapons are also feared to have been part of this volatile mixture (*The Economist*, June 2, 2012). Other articles also portrayed a Libyan connection when the press reported that the number two in al-Qa'eda, Abu Yahya al-Libi ("the Libyan") was killed in Pakistan's Tribal Belt by an American drone strike (*New York Times*, June 5 and 6, 2012). Al-Libi's real name was Muhammad Hassan Qaid and he was the brother of 'Abd al-Wahab Muhammad Qaid, now a moderate member of the new Libyan Parliament (*New York Times*, October 7, 2012). While such people were consistently opposed by Gaddafi they had recruitment roles in the well-armed anti-Gaddafi militias that were now frustrating the creation of a new military in Libya. Amidst all of these foreign events, back in Libya the trial began for Gaddafi former intelligence chief, Bouzid Dorda (*New York Times*, June 6, 2012). Over the border in Egypt the court case against former President Hosni Mubarak was still unfolding and the ever bloodier Syrian war continued in this troubled region (*The Economist*, June 9, 2012). This al-Libi ("the Libyan") is not to be confused with Abu Anas al-Libi (seized in Tripoli in early October 2013).

Orderly justice was also hitting snags in Libya, where the militias holding Saif al- Islam Gaddafi refused to hand him over to the new Tripoli authorities, and when a legal team from the ICC went to check on the situation they also found themselves not free to leave (*New York Times*, June 10, 2012). If this were not enough, Libyan preparations for the much anticipated election were slowed to the point that the elections had to be postponed from June 19 until July 7 (*New York Times*, June 11, 2012). A week later, the ICC legal staff from The Hague was still being held against their will (*New York Times*, June 15, 2012).

Building the new Libyan nation was hitting more "speed bumps," not only with these sorts of practical and judicial issues, but even the very model of the new state was being heavily contested between jihadist militias seeking Islamic law and more democratically plural forces. Hopefully this would be sorted out in the elections (*New York Times*, June 24, 2012). Events in neighboring "Arab Spring" Tunisia also interfaced with Libya when the Tunis authorities agreed to extradite Gaddafi's former Prime Minister back to Libya, or at least it appeared to be the case until the top leaders of Tunisia seemed to be reverse themselves and not be in full agreement about this decision.

Eager to have some good news, several investigators concluded that the list of unexploded arms in Libya was seen as limited; this is not to say that the huge flow of trafficked arms was alleviated, but at least it was considered reduced (*New York Times*, June 25 and 26, 2012).

Upset at the allocation of National Assembly seats, protestors in the Cyrenaican enclaves of Tobruk and Benghazi sacked and looted the offices and ballot boxes of the High National Election Commission on Sunday, July 1, 2012, in a violent act of resistance prior to the intended vote taking place on July 7, under the now weak authority of the TNC. Fearing historical marginalization, this action adds to the rising of the political temperature in this eastern region of Libya that had already faced violence and protests toward the diplomats of the United States, Britain, and Tunisia, and fighting down south in Kufra, as well as assassinations and lawlessness of the local and Islamist militias that provided "security" for the TNC (*New York Times*, July 2, 2012).

At last, following a month of diplomatic and legal skirmishes, a Libyan militia group in Zintan freed a four-person International Criminal Court team that was trying to consult with prisoner Saif al-Islam Gaddafi. After being freed, they immediately returned to Tripoli and the international airport to head back to The Hague. Thoughts of prosecuting them were also halted, but confidence in Libyans to hold a fair and free trial also collapsed (*New York Times*, July 3, 2012).

With the elections postponed, there was not only more time for campaigning, but also more time to stir up contentious issues among the parties. Four decades without elections certainly generated many volatile and unresolved issues. Militia threats, shooting down a helicopter carrying ballots, local ethnicity, regional polarities, marginalization, struggles over oil revenue, a weak TNC, no constitution, and vows to disrupt the procedures were among the serious problems all serving to tarnish the hopes for a peaceful transition to a broad democracy.

Perhaps the gravest incidents involved trashing the electoral offices in Tobruk and Benghazi, in already suspicious Cyrenaica, burning down a ballot warehouse in Ajdabiya, and shutting off three oil pipelines, also in the east. Deeply dividing issues of *Shari'a* versus civil society models of governance, as well as the position of women, remained problematic among the 85 percent of registered voters planning to cast 2.8 million ballots. Until, or unless, this became more settled, the election of a new representative parliament and the constitution that needed to be written were both suspended (*New York Times*, July 7, 2012).

THE ELECTION FINALLY HAPPENS

Despite this pre-election violence, the ongoing protests, and the complexities of this first election after four decades of political repression, the event finally took place on Saturday, July 7, 2012, with some interesting results. As the partial tallies came in, it appeared that the former Islamist militant and torture victim 'Abd al-Hikim Belhaj and 'Ali al-Sallabi of the Al-Watan Party and the Muslim Brothers ("Justice and Construction Party") did not fare so well. The biggest victor was former interim "liberal" Prime Minister Mahmoud Jabril (who earned his PhD at the University of Pittsburgh) of the majority Warfala ethnicity from tension-laden Beni Walid. This was well received in the West after Islamists in Tunisia and Egypt had generally done well in the post 'Arab Spring elections in those nations. Of course, virtually all Libyans are Muslims, so the centrists like devout Jabril, his ally judge Suleiman Zoubi, and former minister 'Ali Tarhouni, protested the allegations that they were not. It was estimated that the Muslim Brother party captured less than 25 percent of the allocated 200 seats. Bel Haj kept his position on the Tripoli Military Council. The fact that neither Belhaj nor his ally 'Abd al-Hikim al-Hasadi won in the Islamist historic stronghold of Derne was also remarkable. Relative to the Warfala majority, 'Abd al-Rahman Sewehli held a minority position in a Misrata contingent. This first step to forming a democratic government was congratulated by UN Secretary General Ban Ki-moon and U.S. President Obama (*New York Times*, July 9, 2012; *Providence Journal*, July 9, 2012). The official results of the High National Election Commission, as published by the *Libya Herald*, appear in Table 7.1.

An editorial in the influential *New York Times* considered this election as "an important step forward" and "a heartening outcome" after 3,000 candidates competed for the 200 seats, thus countering some recent trends in other Arab states. Major work was still ahead to write a constitution, appoint a Prime Minister, resolve the role of Islam in the state, allocate oil revenues, create new armed and police forces, and build an inclusive coalition (*New York Times*, July 10, 2012).

Table 7.1

Libyan National Assembly Election Results, 2012

Party	%	Seats
The National Forces Alliance[1]	48.14	39
Justice and Construction Party[2]	10.27	17
National Front Party[3]	4.08	2?
Union for the Homeland[4]	4.50	3?
National Centrist Party[5]	4.00	2
Wadi al-Hayah Party	0.47	2
Al-Watan[6]		0
Other Parties 1 seat or none		

[1] Of Mahmoud Jibril
[2] Of Islamist, Muhammad Sowan
[3] Of Muhammad al-Magarief
[4] Of 'Abd al-Rahman Sewehli of Misrata
[5] Of 'Ali 'Abd al-SalamTarhouni
[6] Of Islamists 'Ali al-Sallabi and 'Abd al Hakim Belhaj (formerly of LIFG).

Meanwhile, Syria continued to get bloodier and bloodier (*The Economist*, July 21, 2012) and arms trafficked from Libya (and Qatar and Sudan) were reaching the Free Syrian Army as this battle expanded and spilled over the border—more worries about what to do regarding Islamists and the Egyptian President as he tried to curb the powers of the military (*The Economist*, August 4, 2012).

On Wednesday, August 8, 2012, the interim 200-member new Libyan National Assembly elected Muhammad Magarief as its new President from the National Front Party that took over from the now dissolved Transitional National Council (NTC). Margarief was credentialed as a long-time Gaddafi opponent as well as an opponent to Islamist extremists and local militias. It is the National Assembly that elected the Prime Minister, passed legislation, and drafted a Constitution in 2013. These acts were considered to be a major step forward to a peaceful, legitimate, democratic society in the new Libya (*New York Times*, August 10, 2012).

THE CHRONIC CRISIS CONTINUES

Any hope that the elections would bring a sudden turnaround in the contested Libyan political terrain was to be dashed in a series of car bomb explosions. At the Ministry of Interior, one bomb went off; two more bombs went off at a former police headquarters used by the Ministry of Defense, killing two; and a fourth failed to explode near the Ministry of Interior in Tripoli. It was unclear if these bombings were the work of pro-Gaddafi loyalists, militia members, or others who had been responsible for recent assassinations and bombings (*New York Times*, August 20, 2012).

Two obituaries made for interesting sidebar footnotes in the Libyan saga. The death of the independent-minded Maltese Prime Minister (1955–1958; 1971–1984), Dom Mintoff (1916–2012), a devout socialist and labor leader, was announced. His political maverick status meant courting a long relationship with his symbiotic ally, President Muammar Gaddafi (at least until a dispute over oil territory), and evoking allegations of Western coup plots to topple him, as he played major powers against each other over the geographically tiny, but politically and militarily strategic, Malta (*New York Times*, August 22, 2012).

The other death was that of Edwin P. Wilson, age 84, who was a former "invisible" CIA operative, wealthy tycoon, and convicted arms dealer who sold explosives to Libya. Claiming that a 1982 shipment of 20 tons in explosives was delivered to Libya as part of a sanctioned CIA mission to cull favor and build credibility with Muammar Gaddafi, Wilson had been sentenced to 52 years in federal prison. The stake in his judicial heart was testimony by the number three official in the CIA, who denied Wilson was acting on CIA instruction. Some 20-plus years later, Wilson produced records proving that he had been set up, and he was released. On par with his strange series of assignments to become an insider in various illicit drug and arms deals, on behalf of the CIA's quest to root out enemy espionage activities, he was assigned earlier in his career to go to Libya and watch for the Venezuelan terrorist Ilich Ramírez Sánchez, aka "Carlos the Jackal," who occasionally lived in Libya. In an intriguing conspiracy, on August 14, 1994, "Carlos" was arrested in Khartoum, Sudan, and smuggled back to France where, after his trial, he was to spend the rest of his life in prison.

In such odd contexts, Wilson was also somehow involved in getting pistols to Libyan embassies, one of which was used to kill a Gaddafi dissident in Bonn. In 2004, Wilson said "he felt bad about that," but this might not have been the only instance. His unusual connections to Libya included getting former Green Berets to train Libyan troops and to get airplane and helicopter pilots to work for Libya. Other parts of Wilson's life are equally convoluted, mysterious and contentious (*New York Times*, September 23, 2012). But among the living, the Libyan government, especially the Interior Minister Fawzi 'Abd al-A'al, appeared to be helpless in curbing the extremists vandalizing of popular UNESCO-endorsed Sufi shrines, mosques, and graves (*New York Times*, August 29, 2012).

Another important development in bringing the Gaddafi era to a conclusion took place when an ICC arrest warrant was served on Abdullah Senussi, the former intelligence chief and brother-in-law of Muammar Gaddafi. He was brought back to Libya on Wednesday September 5, 2012, from Nouakchott, Mauritania, which he had "illegally" entered. There is speculation that substantial funds moved from Tripoli to the Mauritanian capital to encourage this development. Senussi was believed responsible for many acts of international terrorism and domestic assassinations, as well as for ordering the infamous prison massacre. This diplomatic achievement was very popular in Libya but did not make The Hague too pleased, since it just added more alleged criminals to those already held in Libya rather than being sent to The Hague for an impartial and free trial. Deputy Prime Minister Abu Shagour indicated that the full charge list was not yet drawn up; however, witnesses abounded for the prosecution. France also has a significant emotional and legal interest in prosecuting Senussi, as he was linked to the 1989 bombing of the French UTA Flight 772 airliner that exploded over Niger. There was ongoing worry that the untested and overwhelmed Libya judiciary of the still weak government was not up to the task (*Wall Street Journal*, September 6, 2012).

THE ATTACK ON THE AMERICAN CONSULATE IN BENGHAZI

On the night of September 11–12, 2012, another major diplomatic incident occurred in Libya in the wake of widespread protests against a provocative anti-Muslim film "The Innocence of Muslims." The film had been produced by an Egyptian Copt named Nakoula Basseley Nakoula, age 55, who was residing, and arrested without bail, in the United States. In convergence with the anniversary of the infamous airplane attack on the World Trade Center, opportunistic terrorists in Benghazi used this as their chance to attack the American consulate in Benghazi as a significant American target. Meanwhile the man linked to making the film was being questioned in the United States (*New York Times*, September 16, 2012, and September 28, 2012).

SEPTEMBER 11, 2012: WHAT HAPPENED?

During the day of Monday, September 11, 2012, widespread protests were taking place regionally and in Benghazi, which had been struggling with the anti-Gaddafi militias in general, such as the 17th of February Brigade led by Fawzi Bukatef and the Muslim Brother leaders 'Ali and Isma'il Salabi, or one of the "Libyan Shield" militias such as the Benghazi leader Wissam bin Hamad. In particular the local *Ansar al-Shari'a*, an essential franchise of Al-Qa'eda in the Islamic Maghreb (AQIM) that itself is a branch of al-Qa'eda was centrally involved and trucks with their logo were reported on the scene, despite denial by its spokesperson Hani al-Mansouri or its local commanders Muhammad 'Ali al-Zahawi and Ahmed Abu Khattala. Their logo holds up the singular Salafi finger, an open Quran, two Kalashnikovs, and the Muslim *shahada*, profession of Islamic faith. Its opposition to political democracy as not being part of "God's law" was broadly rejected by other Libyans (*New York Times*, September 16, 2012).

Precisely when the *Ansar* group decided to use the general protest as a cover for their attack is not clear, but with the widespread presence of arms in the wake of the 2011 revolution, and with the anti-Gaddafi and Islamist Libyan Islamic Fighting Group (LIFG) and Ansar's practical military experience, a complex, advanced plan was not necessary. If there are future prosecutions, then perhaps more facts will emerge. The street protests took a sharp turn at 9:30 or 9:40 p.m., when gunfire was heard by the 20 Americans inside. Then explosions followed, aimed at breaching the main gate into a part of the extensive diplomatic mission compound. A dozen or more terrorist attackers broke through the burned gateway and onto a barracks building, burning three cars on the way, and then headed toward the Ambassador's residence. Still stunned by this fast-moving quasi-military assault that broke through this outer perimeter, the broadly appreciated and admired U.S. Ambassador J. Christopher Stevens, age 52, and his aide Sean Smith ran to the stout safe room for additional safety at about 10:00 p.m., while two additional buildings were torched by the attackers. Stevens was a long-experienced Arabist diplomat from California who preferred openness and conversation but was well aware of the risks of his current assignment, having been an early supporter of the anti-Gaddafi movement (*New York Times*, September 16, 2012).

Mr. Smith may have been dead by about 10:15; Ambassador Stevens had not yet been located. An amateur video shot by Fahd al-Bakkosh shows Libyans helping to retrieve the envoy's unconscious body from a window (*New York Times*, September 17, 2012). In a separate facility, about half a mile away to the south southeast, a CIA security team was alerted to try to retake the breached facility around 10:45 p.m. At about the same time, Deputy Chief of Mission (DCM) Gregory Hicks, away in Tripoli, was alerted that the consulate was "under attack." Stevens may have been in the safe house, but there was not sufficient protection against fire and smoke generated by diesel fuel, which was ignited on that structure to smoke them out. Instead, Smith and Stevens tried to brave the smoke and were most likely asphyxiated from inhaling these fatal fumes. At about the same time, at least six CIA and 16 Libyan security people had left the annex and headed to regain the main compound to search for Stevens and Smith, who were likely dead by this point. By 11:00 p.m., a surveillance drone arrived in the airspace over the compound to acquire better intelligence, and by about 11:20 p.m., a joint American-Libyan force evacuated the remaining personnel to the second compound.

SEPTEMBER 12, 2012

One report, later denied, claimed that *Ansar al-Shari'a* sent a 12:07 e-mail to American authorities claimed "credit" for this attack. Some unknown Libyans, maybe looters, civilians, or attackers, found Stevens and took him to a local hospital where he was found to be dead. Sometime between 1:15 and 1:30 a.m. on September 12, a rescue team arrived at the Benghazi airport from Tripoli to rescue some 30 Americans from the annex, but the team came under five minutes of mortar fire and retreated, without taking casualties. By about 2:00 a.m., Deputy Chief of Mission (DCM) Hicks, still in Tripoli, had reported to Secretary of State Clinton of the need to evacuate all Americans from Benghazi. The bodies of Stevens and Smith had been located and removed for this evacuation. By about 2:30 a.m., both buildings appeared to be back under American control with the attackers driven out.

However, the assault did not end with this, and at about 4:00 a.m., the extremists mounted a heavier attack with well-placed mortar rounds falling on the Embassy roof. Former U.S. Navy SEALS Glen A. Doherty and

Tyrone S. Woods were killed in this attack. Around 6:30 a.m., most of the surviving staff members flew out of Benghazi back to Tripoli. Between 9:00 and 10:00 a.m., the last rescue plane flew out of Benghazi with the bodies of Smith, Doherty, Woods, and Stevens all aboard. Mopping up found damaged and burned buildings, along with Islamic graffiti on the main gate professing that "God is Great" and the holy *shahada* "that there is no god but god and that Muhammad is his prophet." The political storm in Washington and the reverberations in Libya were just starting. The conditions for criminal forensics were terrible for a proper investigation. Chain of control was lost in this unsecure crime site. Cooperation with the local and national authorities was not ideal, and likely some evidence was destroyed. Amidst all of this the "blame game" of highly partisan Washington went into overdrive. Despite setbacks and major challenges with the local militias in Misurata and Zintan, Salafist militias, and the death of Ambassador Stevens and his aides in Benghazi, Libya, there was still progress in rebuilding Libya's civilian administration and infrastructure.

For a few days, the Department of Justice (DoJ) was hot on the trail of 'Ali Harzi, a Tunisian arrested in Turkey as a possible suspect. But this lead seemed to wither away. Then DoJ filed charges against Ahmed Abu Khattala as the alleged leader of the attack, and it was seeking more information on him as "a person of interest." He admitted that he was on the scene but was not involved. Four other images were circulated in Libya and in the world press, but with no known result. Meanwhile, Salafists and other extremists attacked shrines, the British Ambassador's convoy, and offices of the Red Cross and United Nations. Libyan Congress President Muhammad Yussef Magariaf indicated that there were about 50 arrests, and many were seen not even to be Libyans. Susan Rice, U.S. Ambassador to the United Nations, speaking from a CIA-approved memo, indicated that this attack started as a spontaneous assault; but as more facts became known, it was clear that there was certainly a pre-organized dimension to it. This quickly evolved to be a partisan electoral issue in the United States about when and what was known, when this shifted from "protest" to "terrorism," and who should be "blamed" for security not being adequate to prevent the "Arab Spring" attack in the first place (*New York Times*, October 22, 2012).

Beyond these serious problems, there was generally hopeful and nonviolent progress with the election of the General National Congress (quasi-parliament) and the election of Mustafa Abu Shagur as Prime Minister. On this list, in these fair and free elections, the Islamist Justice and Construction Party won only 17 of 80 seats. In particular, 'Abd al-Hakim Belhaj, the longtime prisoner of Gaddafi then assisted by the British who was strong financed by Qatar, won no seats at all. A very strong, perhaps even intolerant, spirit of Libyan nationalism also prevailed, for better or worse. The "rule of law" was still the goal, even though it still had a long way to go, especially with some 7,000 persons still held in custody by the new government. If oil production gets restored, this would also help to rebuild stability (*The Economist*, September 15, 2012).

The attack on the American mission by this fringe group highlights the problems of Libya's militias whereby the government is still so weak that they are needed for some local security roles, like guarding the Al-Jala Hospital, but they are so autonomous that they undermine the very security they are expected to provide. Also, the most extreme, like *Ansar al-Shari'a*, are beholden to foreign interests and do not even agree that exclusive *Shari'a* is compatible with plural inclusive democracy (*New York Times*, September 16 and 21, 2012).

As a result of the attack in Libya, the United States prepared for a long siege of Arab unrest, not even realizing how much worse things could get in the coming weeks (*New York Times*, September 16, 2012). Nonetheless, Prime Minister Mustafa Abu Shagur of Libya was reluctant to tackle the Islamists head on with his nascent security forces. Other high-ranking officers were divided about who was responsible for the Benghazi consulate attack and what to do about it. The clearest statements came from Muhammad Magarief, the speaker of the new Parliament, who said that the *Ansar al-Shari'a* group was responsible and should be arrested and shut down since they also had ties to the other Islamist extremist group AQIM. Magarief also viewed another anti-Gaddafi Islamist group, "the National Shield," in the same light. The new Army Chief of Staff, Yousef Mangoush, also had the same strong perspectives of no compromise with extremism in building the New Libya. General Hamid Belkhair, new commander of the Benghazi forces, said that he was ready to move against them as well if *Ansar al-Shari'a* refused to lay down its weapons. Anti-extremist forces were planning to march against the offices of *Ansar* on September 21 to put more pressure on the military for action. This action was critical to preserve and protect the fragile democracy of Libya. Tunisia's Muslim government was also facing serious challenges from armed extremists, and Mali was facing such jihadists as *Ansar al-Din* in more than half of their nation (*The Economist*, September 22, 2012). This came to another crisis point in Benghazi on September 21, 2012, a Friday (a popular day for protest marches) when two protestors died and many were injured while angrily storming militia bases (*Ansar al-Shari'a* and the "mainstream" *Rafallah al-Sehati*, headed by Isma'il al-Salabi) to seize their weapons and capture militia men, some of whom were later discovered outside the city with gunshots to their heads. This popular violent reaction took place in the wake of the September 11–12 U.S. mission attack and the Libyan government's inability to reign in, or crush, such militia groups (*New York Times*, September 23, 2012).

Turbulent security in Benghazi was such that the new authorities could not restrain the militias, the (informal police) militias had no experience or capacity for governance and blame for all was battered about like a sports contest. True enough, in Benghazi, the *Ansar al-Shari'a* had overplayed its hand; but there were still the Islamist February 17th Martyr's Brigade and the *Rifala al-Sahati* militias despite the government effort to disband them all by Mustafa Abu Shagur. Militias also functioned in Misrata and Zintan, where very bloody battles took place against the Gaddafi military in 2011 (*The Economist*, September 29, 2012). In these towns the militias are not necessarily Islamist and they bring some security, but are not under central government control unlike the Supreme Security Council (SSC) that tries to be subordinate to the Ministry of Interior; yet this is not a perfect situation since some number of Islamists and Salafists work with the SSC to be closer to power and influence since the vetting process is deficient. Thus the nub of this strategic problem was that the new government needed security and stability to avoid chaos, but the groups that they were working with tactically (or can't work with) were sometimes providing the opposite with an undemocratic and unpopular model of state government.

Political debates from the U.S. mission attack still echoed across Libya and around the globe, and one news report considered this as a major blow to covert CIA monitoring efforts about the local Salafi militias, groups opposed to them, and pro-Gaddafi loyalists. Another setback was restrained monitoring of local arms trafficking (including "manpads") and perhaps the shipping of Libyan arms to the FSA in Syria. The notable number of Americans evacuated from Benghazi alerted Deputy Prime Minister Mustafa Abu Shagur that more was going on in Benghazi than he had known. The destruction or capture of American files was a problem, and poor security meant that the FBI investigators were stranded in Tripoli and delayed and hampered in their efforts to reach the crime scene in Benghazi, to piece together a more precise timeline, and to determine possible persons of interest to address the growing controversies in Washington and Tripoli (*New York Times* September 24 and 28, 2012).

If there was any good news from the attack, it was the increased resolve and necessity to rebuild the Libyan military and police forces while curbing the growth, and power, of the militias (*New York Times*, September 29, 2012). On the American side there was revised training for special FAST (Fleet Anti-Terrorism Security Team) Marine security units, given the well-rehearsed orchestration of the Embassy attack, as one of their responsibilities is to protect diplomatic missions from becoming victim to just such riots and attacks (*New York Times*, September 29, 2012). Prepositioning of USAFRICOM military assets to mobilize more quickly was also addressed as the closest units at the time were located at bases in Rota, Spain, and Bahrain.

Since this event occurred deep into the 2012 American presidential campaign, there were a multitude of interpretations and accusations about whether the Libyan killings might cost President Obama reelection, or at least provide an opening for his Republican opponent Mitt Romney, himself viewed as weak on foreign policy, to exploit as a strategic foreign policy failure by the incumbent. On the other hand, it is rare that a single foreign policy issue gains much traction among the American public. In the October debate in Las Vegas, the discussion about Susan Rice and the Benghazi mission security did not get much attention from the Republican camp, especially when it was discovered that repeated requests for additional security had been rejected by the Republicans on the House committee in charge. With this in mind, the Republicans focused their criticism on Ambassador Rice, and the Democrats defended by looking at the bigger picture of Libya and trying to track the killers. After the election, won by President Obama, Libya appeared from time to time on the American political agenda, but other matters such as Egypt, Syria, Iran, China, and the economy usually trumped Libya.

With armed attacks by *Boko Haram* insurgents in northeastern Nigeria, uncertainty about Iranian nuclear intentions, and complex relations between Egypt, Israel, and Palestine, the problems in Libya would not get the attention they deserved. In particular, still more questions were raised about how effective the Tripoli government could be in controlling the independent Libyan militias. Nonetheless, progress was made slowly, and with fits and starts by the government and especially by public opposition to extremist militias. Ten days later, angered Benghazi opponents attacked the building housing the *Ansar al-Shari'a* folks who fled, but 11 were killed in this action. Yet Prime Minister Mustafa Abu Shagur, who came into office on the day after the death of Ambassador Christopher Stevens, had not shown enough political strength to tackle this serious problem. And *Ansar al-Shari'a* was not the only such group in Benghazi where the ardently Islamist and Qatari-backed "17 February Martyr's Group," and *Rifala al-Sahati*, also represented challenges to the fledging government. Qatar is also the home of the influential al-Jazeera television network. In Tripoli, Misurata, Zintan, the Nafousa mountains, and elsewhere, there were similar semiautonomous militias who did not accept the central authority of the Supreme Security Council (SSC), which had its own sympathies with Salafists and extremists. Complicating this situation, these groups provided some needed local security in the absence of a rebuilt police force. Whether such groups were absorbed or must be crushed remained the looming political dilemma (*The Economist*, September 29 and October 6, 2012).

The United States' top-secret Joint Special Operations Command was trying to track the killers and was apparently planning a secret mission to kill or capture them but had been thwarted in the local investigation, although various names did emerge for persons the FBI would like to interview. Libyan officials also warned the United States of backlash if they attempted to violate Libyan sovereignty (*New York Times*, October 3, 2012). Ironically, on October 9, 2013, the Prime Minister was briefly abducted by a Libyan anticrime unit, just two days after the capture of Abu Anas al-Libi by U.S. forces and the announcement by the Libyan government of the need for outside intervention to assist in quelling the rise in militant actions throughout Libya (Bloomberg, October 10, 2013).

Fallout from the Ambassador Stevens incident still unfolded in the American political arena as Republicans sought to charge Ambassador Susan Rice with misrepresenting the nature of the murderous Benghazi attack even though she had only been following an edited script from the CIA. Evidently, the GOP strategized that this might be a good way to test the mettle of Secretary of State Hillary Clinton, the anticipated Democratic rival in the 2016 presidential elections (*Newsweek*, October 15, 2012). These political "deck chairs" would soon be reshuffled with Ambassador Rice's transfer to a higher national security position and Secretary Clinton being replaced by Senator John Kerry and new political issues on the horizon. The controversy about where Saif al-Islam should be tried for crimes against humanity was a much greater issue in Libya than the political dust-up about Ambassador Rice. If the Libyan judiciary could be judged to be fair and free, the trial could be held there, but the ICC in The Hague was not convinced. Moreover the rebel militia had still not turned him over to Tripoli. Similarly, the case of Abdullah Senussi, brought back from Mauritania, was also in suspended animation. In the balance was justice versus revenge, and military rule versus the new government (*New York Times*, October 10, 2012; *Newsweek*, October 22, 2012).

Reports in late October identified some persons of interest in the Benghazi attack. These included Faraj al-Shibli (age 46) from Sidi Arhuma al-Marj, Libya as well as Egyptian Al Alwan Faraj Mikhail 'Abd al-Fadil Jibril (age 43) and Al Warfali Faez Abu Zeid Muftah. Al-Shibli was formerly a LIFG member opposed to Gaddafi. Two Tunisian men, including 'Ali Harzi, were arrested in Turkey earlier in October but it was not clear if they were witnesses or suspects. Another militant, "Hazem," blew himself up in Cairo. The Tunisians were later freed in Tunisia. All were suspected of having ties to AQIM or *Ansar al-Shari'a* in Libya (*New York Times*, October 6, 2012; CBS News, October 24, 2012). Amidst these developments the Libyan human rights lawyer, 'Ali Zeidan, was named as interim Prime Minister. His principle tasks were to curb the sometimes feuding local militias and replace them with a new police and military force; rebuild damaged infrastructure, specifically water, power, and garbage removal; and build a diverse cabinet having a broad consensus. The former Prime Minister Mustafa Abu Shagur had the same tasks but was replaced 25 days later when he was deemed to be making too slow progress (*New York Times*, October 8, 2012; *Boston Globe*, October 15, 2012). Equally slow progress was being made with the electoral and partisan parsing of the words of UN Ambassador Susan Rice, as some Republicans charged her with lying while Democrats said she was speaking straight from a CIA-approved script that was continuously modified as the rapidly evolving Benghazi affair became clearer (*Newsweek*, October 15, 2012).

These delicate and challenging tasks were assisted by $8 million from the US Department of State and Pentagon Special Operations, as all were concerned with bringing justice (human rights), stability, and security to Libya (rooting out AQIM and *Ansar al-Shari'a*, border control, and tracing the small arms trafficking that had swept Libya) as well as tracking those responsible for the Benghazi attack. Part of this plan involves creating a 500-man elite Libyan security force, capable of deploying on a moment's notice. This force is considered even more critical in the absence of any elected or appointed Minister of Interior or Defense (*New York Times*, October 16, 2012).

Angry protests by citizens from Bani Walid on Sunday, October 21 filled the Tripoli parliament complaining about ongoing violence. Their pro-Gaddafi stance in the 2011 war slowed reconciliation (*New York Times*, October 22, 2012). Equally contentious was who should have custody of Seif al-Islam, and where he should be tried for his role in the 2011 revolution. Would a trial be reduced to revenge or could authentic, impartial justice, by the International Criminal Court, be meted out, wondered this popular magazine? (*Newsweek*, October 22, 2012).

By November it was also clear the American CIA played a major role in trying to fight back the Benghazi attackers. Their role was fourfold: bringing a rescue party from a secret base in that city; sending backup forces, including two commandos, from Tripoli; flying a military reconnaissance Predator drone over the area, which occurred at 11:11 p.m.; and creating a 50-truck, heavily armed Libyan convoy to evacuate the survivors to the Benghazi airport and onto a military transport plane, in order to evacuate from Libya. All of this was initiated 25 minutes after the attack was first reported to them at 9:40 p.m. At first, there was reluctance to describe these actions in order to minimize their very low-profile presence to the media, such as Fox News, who claimed the CIA had blocked a response to help. Indeed, after the first violent outbreak, there was a four-hour pause that made it seem the crisis was under control (*New York Times*, November 2, 2012). Mustafa 'Abd al-Jalil was questioned about the death of General A/Fattah Younis (he was KIA in July 2011) (*New York Times*, November 2012).

Trying to be optimistic about the near future of Libya and its tourist potential for Roman antiquities, one must also be realistic about the crushing top-down dictatorship of the Gaddafi decades. Along with the daunting task by relatively inexperienced civil servants in running civil society, with a constitution and popularly elected legislative officials, from the bottom up, and in the context of weak security and Islamist challenges to this political project, rising from the battlefields of 2011 represents a work in progress and a story that is only just beginning. Rebuilding damaged infrastructure; getting electricity and water flowing in all communities; removing the thousands of mines Gaddafi's forces planted throughout the country; reopening schools, hotels, and the health care system; keeping cafes and restaurants opened; recovering oil production and revenue; trash pickup and removal; and restoring air and road networks are all competing on the overflowing agenda. There is hope, but lots of hard work and job creation lay ahead (*The Economist*, November 17, 2012).

The Benghazi attack remained in the news as a controversial partisan issue, while actually much bigger security matters raged in Libya. Senator Dianne Feinstein (D-CA), Chair of the Senate Intelligence Committee, held hearings on the topic and found that the White House only changed the words from "consulate" to "mission" to more accurately reflect its diplomatic status, and that the CIA, then headed by General David Petraeus, clearly stated it was a terrorist attack when it was clear what was happening. No one misrepresented this, she said. Nonetheless Senator John McCain (R-AZ) and Senator Lindsey Graham (R-SC) continued to blame UN Ambassador Rice as misrepresenting the nature of the attack for still unclear political reasons (*New York Times*, November 19, 2012).

On the other hand, it was clear that the probe into the Benghazi attackers was stalled. No suspects were named, detailed, arrested, or being prosecuted more than two months after the event. Some individuals believed to be on the scene of the mission attack were walking freely about in Benghazi. At least one Libyan security officer, Colonel Farag al-Dersi, was assassinated in Benghazi, and the FBI and diplomatic security people were doing their best, under very frustrating circumstances, and wanted to interview Ahmed Abu Khattala, the local leader of *Ansar al-Shari'a*, as a person of interest with knowledge of the attack (*Providence Journal*, AP, November 23, 2012). Trying to move on from this controversy, the White House proposed Ambassador Susan Rice as Secretary of State to replace the retiring Hillary Clinton; however, this was promptly blocked by Republican opponents (*Providence Journal*, AP, November 27, 2012).

SUMMARY FOR LIBYA IN 2012

After the turbulence and violence on all sides of the 2011 revolution, the task in 2012 was to figure out what the pieces were in the historic

Figure 7.1

Summary of Three Phases of Libyan Political and Economic Contradictions

GADDAFI ERA:	POST-GADDAFI ERA:
Autocratic	Weak central authority
Whimsical governance	Institutional weakness
Too much centralization	Too little centralization
Oil-centric economy	Slowed oil production
Terrorist sponsor/advocate	Terrorist free spaces
Inter-state focused	Intra-state struggling
No democracy	Weak democratic authority

A BRIGHTER FUTURE?
Economic diversification
Politically inclusive
Restored security and stability
Rebuilt police and military
Expanded tourism
Restored health and education infrastructure
Shared national culture and identity

wreckage of Libya from the Gaddafi years and from the months of warfare. There were ironic survivors, refugees, and victims. There was severe infrastructural damage and other sites hardly scratched. There were political forces that were synthesized in the struggle and those that appeared after hiding within the shifting political sands of Libya. There were old domestic interests and new foreign interests. There was broad consensus to bring stability, security and development to Libya, but not so much agreement on the models and means to achieve it (see Figure 7.1).

The historic "Arab Spring" tossed the entire region into considerable confusion with the old guard institutions trying to hold on and political newcomers trying to seize innovative opportunities with new parties, media, followers, and leaders. Important elections in Tunisia and Egypt brought Islamists to power and elections in Libya kept them more or less out of power. Libyan arms, looted from Gaddafi warehouses, percolated into Algeria and across the Sahel to Niger, Mali, Nigeria, and who knows where else, fomenting insurgencies and asymmetric warfare in a broad swath. Desperately needed police and paramilitary forces were sought but not found, and self-guided militias swept in to play this role and perhaps cause more chaos than they thwarted for the embryonic central government. Ethnicity, regional origin, and political organization were often matters of serious division. Clearly for Libya, these were absolutely the most important matters at hand in 2012.

On the domestic front, there were also important contests waged in the legislature about who could, or should, serve as the lawmakers for the

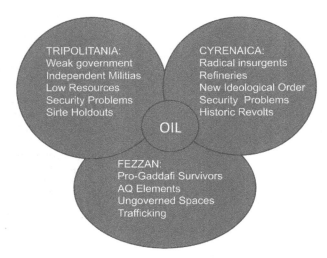

Figure 7.2

Geostrategic Issues for the Libyan Future

new Libya. Settling disputes via revenge or mercy over land and past grievances generated emotions and sometimes bloodshed. International issues of Libyan terrorism simmered, and The Hague pressed on with its concerns over transparency, accountability, war crimes, and crimes against humanity, with notable friction and paralysis on the Libyan side (see Figure 7.2).

The investigation into the American Embassy mission attack in Benghazi was thwarted and stalled with no arrests or prosecutions. Electioneering and highly divisive partisan politics of the blame game, in the United States, kept Benghazi and murdered Ambassador Stevens in the news, while Libyan officials were being assassinated in far greater numbers. So, for 2012, these were the benchmarks to reference the passage of the year and to offer some metrics to have in mind for examining trends in 2013.

JANUARY 2013

Founded only in March 2012, the Libyan Muslim Brothers, aka the Justice and Construction Party (JCP), received about a fifth of the votes in the first national election, winning 17 seats out of 80. But half of the 120 independent seats are sympathetic, much less than their counterparts in Egypt. But the JCP is trying to rapidly change this situation with offices in all major towns, including a seven-story tower in Benghazi. JCP leaders were drawn heavily from businesspeople and academics who officially advocate a "moderate" view of Islamism. Others were not so convinced (*The Economist*, January 12, 2013).

Also related to Libya is the, literally, postmortem investigation of the bloody hostage situation (38 hostages killed along with 29 kidnappers) at the In Amenas gas production facility in Algeria. Just 30 miles away, in neighboring Libya, the logistics planning took place, and they were armed by weapons trafficked from the collapsed authority in Libya. The attackers included those extremists from Egypt, Algeria (like the escaped leader, Mukhtar Belmukhtar), and other North African nations. Algeria, sadly, leads in North African terrorist attacks, with over 160 in 2011, not to mention Libya also being a major source of arms in the *Ansar el-Din* insurgency in Mali when the French have intervened militarily to block the fall of Bamako (*New York Times*, January 21–23, 2013). Although Mali does not have a contiguous border with Libya, arms trafficking across the Sahara had no trouble in reaching the well-armed *Ansar ed-din* and the Salafist Movement for Unity and Jihad in West Africa (MUJAO) insurgent groups there. These groups are also affiliated loosely with AQIM (*The Economist*, January 26, 2013).

The judicial and political future of 'Abdullah al-Senussi, Gaddafi's former intelligence chief, was described by his British lawyer, Ben Emmerson, as heading to a fast military trial and execution, by February 15. He called on the ICC in The Hague to redouble its effort to have him tried in Europe for crimes against humanity (*New York Times*, January 25, 2013). In fact this judicial tug-of-war continued on into the fall and no execution or resolution took place.

A bigger threat to Europeans was by terrorists operating through Libya, especially in Benghazi. The British claimed that some of the attackers at In Amenas, Algeria, were also present in the Benghazi attack that killed the American ambassador and three other Americans in September 2011 (*New York Times*, January 25, 2013).

FEBRUARY 2013

Elsewhere in northeast Africa, Egypt was in crisis with broad public and military suspicions and opposition to the Egyptian Muslim Brothers headed by steadily less inclusive President al-Morsi. It was hard to imagine how much worse this could get, until it did (*The Economist*, February 2, 2013).

The ICC was still struggling with Libya to get Abdullah Senussi transferred to their custody in The Hague, but this judicial battle continued without resolution (*New York Times*, February 8, 2013). Major weapons trafficking reported from Libya to Syria, Egypt, Gaza, Chad, Lebanon, and Mali. These included AK-47 Kalashnikov assault rifles, NR-160 recoilless rifles (armor-penetrating with finned projectiles), M-40 antitank munitions, rocket-propelled grenade launchers (RPGs), other machine guns, and large quantities of assorted ammunition (*New York Times*, February 8, 2013). In the quest for "justice," formerly repressed local militias and Islamists continued an informal campaign of assassinations of Gaddafi-era officials such as Colonel Faraj al-Dersi, who was shot to death in Benghazi in 2012. He was just one of about 40 other killings. The Tunisian assassination of Chokri Belaid, on February 6; the French invasion into Mali and military operations there; the serious security concerns for Algeria; and rising tension in the Central African Republic were all tense reminders that much was at stake for the entire region (*The Economist*, February 9, 2013).

If the logjams in Libya were not enough, the political gridlock in Washington only added to the complexity when GOP Senator Lindsay Graham said he would hold up Defense (Senator Chuck Hagel) and CIA (John Brennan) nominations if he did not receive more answers (that he liked) about the Benghazi mission attack (*Boston Globe*, February 11, 2013). General Carter F. Ham, Commander of U.S. Africa Command (AFRICOM), testified that the sequestering of the Pentagon was only complicating the "leaner and meaner" "soft power" fights required against Islamic extremism (AQIM franchises), arms and drug trafficking, serious security problems in Nigeria, DR Congo, and Mali without getting sucked into major Middle Eastern or African wars (*New York Times*, February 12, 2013).

The capturer, or killer, of Gaddafi, Omran Shaaban from Misurata, was himself tortured for two months by pro-Gaddafi militias in restive Bani Walid; Shaaban later died in France. Such an atmosphere is pushing legislation to exclude these tainted former officials from new government positions (*Providence Journal*, AP, February 18, 2013). On the second anniversary of the 2011 revolution, the pace had slowed, complications had mounted, the progress on the constitution was limping, and holdover laws from the Gaddafi era were discouraging social, economic, and political reform. Jihadist militias such as the Libya Shield groups in Benghazi, Misrata, Zintan, and Derne were still active threats and trafficking of all sorts was a problem in the south and west. Arrests for the Benghazi mission attack had not yet taken place. The National Congress building was hardly under the control of the legitimate authorities (*The Economist*, February 23, 2013).

MARCH 2013

For the Muslim Brothers, out of power in Tunisia, Libya, Egypt, and elsewhere, they could market their program as moderate and reformist. But, for Tunisia and Egypt, with such Islamists in power, they seemed incapable of being inclusive, tolerant, and reigning in their police forces; they are so eager to institute their programs that they show little self-control and lack the critical managerial skills to run a real government (*The Economist*, March 9 and 23, 2013). Perhaps the lessons seen in these two cases will alert the Libyans that they might be playing with fire.

Speaking of fire, homemade methanol alcohol killed 51 and sickened or blinded 330, according to Libyan Heath Minister Nouri Doghman (*New York Times*, March 12, 2013). President Barack Obama and Prime Minister 'Ali Zeidan met in Washington. While there was still no progress in finding the Benghazi attackers, President Obama vowed to bring them to justice. The new American ambassador was the highly experienced Deborah K. Jones, former ambassador to Kuwait and many other Middle Eastern diplomatic posts. The new Charge d'Affairs was Lawrence Pope. While in Washington, Prime Minister Zeidan also met with Secretary of State John Kerry and Tom Donilon, National Security Advisor (*New York Times*, March 14, 2013).

Probably the most significant event for Libya in March was the announcement by Prime Minister 'Ali Zeidan of a $2 billion grant to the ailing Egyptian economy a few days after Egypt agreed to return 40 to 80 Gaddafi loyalists back to Tripoli. Egyptian reserves had been $36 billion before their 2011 revolution and then fell precipitously to less than $14 billion and continued to dissipate up to the latest Egyptian power struggle. Those arrested include: Ahmed Qaddaf al-Dam, a cousin of Muammar Gaddafi; 'Ali Maria, former Libyan ambassador to Egypt; and Muhammad Ibrahim, brother of Gaddafi's spokesman Moussa Ibrahim. Their fates remained unknown (*New York Times*, March 25, 2013). Meanwhile, back in Egypt, the economy, political administration and human rights were in virtual freefall with the Al-Morsi government just digging in further rather than reaching out to make more friends than enemies (*The Economist*, March 30, 2013).

APRIL 2013

A Gaddafi footnote popped up in the press when the government of François Bozizé of the Central African Republic, situated on the southern border of Chad, was toppled in March by coup leader Michel Djotodia. On his arrival in Bangui, the capital, Djotodia got his troops to pry open the doors of the five-star Ledge Plaza Hotel, that had been one of many such "good will projects" financed by Muammar Gaddafi (*New York Times*, April 14, 2013). One small stretch of Cameroon is all that separates Central Africa from Nigeria, and there the horribly violent *Boko Haram* insurgency in the northeast is tearing that region apart and threatening the Abuja government. *Boko Haram* is a local Hausa knockoff of Salafism (*The Economist*, April 27, 2013).

MAY 2013

Other important debates in Libya focused on a new proposed law backed by Islamist militias that would ban former Gaddafi-era officials from public office. Ironically, this could include President Muhammad Magariaf, Mahmoud Jibril, opponent to the Islamists and Prime Minister 'Ali Zeidan, all of whom briefly served in the Gaddafi government but were more often his stalwart opponents (*New York Times*, May 6, 2013).

After endless debates, the law was rapidly passed. No one with senior connections to Gaddafi could function in the new state, but could the new state function without people with these skills and experience? While this law may compel Muhammad Magarief and Mahmoud Jibril to resign, Prime Minister 'Ali Zeidan was expected to retain his post since he was not high ranking under Gaddafi. As much as the Libyan Muslim Brothers did not fare well in the elections, this legislative move put them in a stronger position to exclude their political rivals—at least until the August 2013 events unfolded in Egypt that were trying to crush the Muslim Brothers there. Certainly Wesam Ahmedia of the Supreme Revolutionary Committee appeared to be content, while human rights groups worried about laws based on "guilt by association" rather than specific criminal convictions (*The Economist*, May 11, 2013).

By the end of the month, this law was in effect and the speaker of the Parliament, Muhammad al-Magariaf, was forced to resign, even though he had not served Gaddafi since 1980 and was an opponent; he could not hold high public office for a decade (*New York Times*, May 29, 2013).

The political disputes over Benghazi, in Washington D.C., continued to swirl, especially when the Republican opponents of the White House received copies of the e-mails that indicated a change in the "talking points" that described the situation as it shifted in Libya. A full-scale Congressional hearing featuring diplomat Gregory Hicks, the Department of State Counterterrorism Bureau's Mark Thompson, and Eric Nordstrom, the Department of State's regional security officer, sought to get to the bottom of the story of when a "protest" became an "attack." This was after Secretary of State Hillary Clinton had already testified in January 2013 (*New York Times*, May 9, 10, 11, and 14, 2013). Editorially, the same paper considered this issue as "The Republican Benghazi Obsession," and while they focused on the September 2012 mission attack, Libya had far greater issues for its stability and security. President Obama, for his part, dismissed the Benghazi debate as a "sideshow" orchestrated by very conservative Representative Jason Chaffetz (R-Utah), who went to Libya to conduct his own controversial and tense "investigation" along with his USAFRICOM "host" General Carter Ham. Instead, President Obama joined with Republicans on a probe of the IRS that was apparently targeting certain partisan groups in violation of IRS regulations (*New York Times*, May 14, 2013).

Meanwhile, in Benghazi, bombs exploded outside two police stations (with casualties) after the British embassy cut its staff in Tripoli. The French Embassy there had been bombed only a few weeks earlier, despite the fact neither London nor Paris had engaged in partisan terminological debates over this matter (*New York Times*, May 11, 2013). Two more police stations were bombed during this period, and three days later, another car bomb exploded on a busy street in Benghazi, killing at least four people and wounding more than a dozen (*New York Times*, May 14, 2013).

JUNE 2013

A well-trod story was repeated in the ICC quest to have Libya hand over Seif al-Islam Gaddafi, but the nascent Ministry of Justice in Libya said it was conducting its own investigations and, moreover, still did not have custody since this son of Muammar Gaddafi was still held by militias in Zintan (*New York Times*, June 1, 2013).

An announcement by the U.S. Department of State said that a $5 million reward was being offered for Yahya Abu al-Hamman and Mukhtar Belmukhtar for their attack on an Algerian oil facility just over the border from Libya in which three Americans were killed, and $7 million reward for Abu Bakr Shekau of the Boko Haram terrorist group in Nigeria (*New York Times*, June 4, 2013). Both were believed to have arms trafficked from Libya. Shekau was later wounded by members of his own group who feared his extremism.

Another development that descended from the Benghazi attack that became a partisan issue in the United States was that Ambassador Susan Rice, age 48, was "promoted" from her United Nations position to become the National Security Advisor. Alongside with her move was to name the Darfur-advocate and strong-willed Samantha Power as the new permanent U.S. Ambassador to the United Nations, and Tom Donilon, the former National Security Advisor, moved on to work with the Council of Foreign Relations (*Providence Journal*, AP, June 6, 2013).

The economic lifeblood of Libya remains its high-quality crude oil and natural gas. It sputtered on and off during the 2011 revolution even though the major facilities were fairly well spared from destruction and then seemed to head back to a robust level of production of 1.5 million barrels per day. By mid-2013, the disruptive role of the militias and a broken bureaucracy had taken its toll on oil production as well. Production, in a nation owning Africa's largest proven reserves at 47 billion barrels, was now heading down to less than 350,000 bpd, with a commensurate decline in badly needed revenues for rebuilding infrastructure and generating jobs. With oil resources and pipelines heavily found in the east and governance in the west, there were also regional tensions that needed to be addressed (*The Economist*, June 8, 2013).

With 31 anti-militia protesters killed in Benghazi in the previous week, there was hope that their deaths would not be in vain and this would motivate the government to reign in these autonomous militia groups or "committees," such as the discredited *Ansar al-Shari'a* and *Libya Shield* (numbers 2, 3, 4, etc.) that have utterly lost any popular support and are scattered. Yousef al-Mangoush, a militia supporter and military chief-of-staff, had lost his position when such militias surrounded the Ministries of Justice and Foreign Affairs in Tripoli to force their positions and compelled the government to bring them to an end (*New York Times*, June 10, 2013).

Frederic Wehrey, former U.S. military attaché in Libya, wrote that Libya did not need more militias; rather, they needed to curb them as soon as possible. Groups such as "Libya Shield," led by Wissam bin Hamed, in particular, did not fall under centralized command and control from Tripoli and were responsible for destabilizing modern Libya and not providing effective security to the new state. Disarming, training and restructuring them was a pressing but delicate concern (Op-Ed, *New York Times*, June 11, 2013).

The shifting tides between diverse militias and the struggling government of new Libya read like a weather report. The June 8 clash with "Libyan Shield Number One" seemed to be over, with the new police force winning that battle. Was this the beginning of the end of semiautonomous rule by militias, random Salafists, pro-Gaddafi holdouts like his former *al-Saiqa* units led by assassinated 'Abd al-Fatah Younis, or former members of LIFG who wandered on into *Ansar al-Shari'a* (AQIM), or just a lull before the next storm? Army chief of staff Salim Gneidy hoped that the resignation of Yusef Mangoush was just such a turning point. More purges of Islamists and Afghanistan veterans could be expected, but with a legislative or violent backlash, too? Normal police cars patrolling the streets of Benghazi are another encouraging sign (*The Economist*, June 15, 2013).

A front-page story in the leading American newspapers highlighted how the Syrian rebels, the "Free Syrian Army" (FSA), had been acquiring major stocks of Libyan weapons. Since the United States and Western Europe were highly concerned about Libyan arms trafficking across the Sahara as well as not getting enough lethal weapons to the FSA this might be considered a tactical contribution to these strategic security issues. There is some evidence that some CIA operatives in Benghazi at the time of the attack were working on such programs. Crates of old Libyan weapons (with the 412 Triangle logo) were photographed in Idlib, Syria, including Belgian-made 106 mm heat-seeking recoilless rounds for M-40 rifles, Russian-made Konkurs-M antitank guided missiles, assault rifles, RPGs, mortars, and assorted other weapons and munitions. It appears that this had been going on for at least one year and some of these collected weapons were shipped on Qatari military vessels or C-17 transport planes from Mitiga airfield in Tripoli or from Benghazi to Turkey. It was not very clear if these Libyan arms were from the militias or from the weak Libyan government; sometimes it is hard to distinguish the two. There was also concern that some weapons may reach extremists in Syria, too (*New York Times*, June 22, 2013).

Following clashes with the militias in Tripoli in which 10 people were killed and 100 were wounded, the Minister of Defense, Muhammad al-Bargathi, was removed from his position by Prime Minister 'Ali Zeidan (*New York Times*, June 28, 2013). Meanwhile, Gaddafi "holdouts" and folks tired of violence continued to undermine Libya's government, while tensions in neighboring Tunisia and Egypt became more violent and frequent (*The Economist*, June 29, 2013).

JULY 2013

On July 3, General 'Abd al-Fattah al-Sissi arrested President Muhammad Al-Morsi of the Muslim Brothers in Egypt and began several days of widespread arrests and a very bloody crackdown in which 1,000 people were killed, in order to break the back of the Muslim Brothers. The implications of this were not realized as of this writing but varied and contradictory perspectives were held in Egypt and in neighboring Libya, where many of the parallel issues and actors are present.

Libyan arms were still in the news as they popped up across the Sahel (in Mali and contiguous Niger) to support Islamist insurgencies there, and it now appears that the rather large Benghazi mission that was attacked in September 2012 had the job of collecting the many weapons drifting about in that city and then sending them on via Turkey to the Free Syrian Army and *Liwa al-Tawheed* rebels (dubious thanks to Qatar) in Syria. Hopefully such weapons would not reach *Jabhat al-Nusra* in Syria, but it is hard to say or control (*The Economist*, July 6, 2013).

The still struggling Libyan government finally regained control of its Interior Ministry, taken over by a militia group on July 2. The siege lasted a week, but was yet another ache in the growing pains of this young and inexperienced government. These militiamen had piled sand in front of the main door of the building and said they would not come out until the more heavily, and better equipped, Supreme Security Committee was disbanded (*New York Times*, July 11, 2013).

A far more serious regional problem, rather than this localized political headache, was the continued search for Mukhtar Belmuktar, the leader of the AQIM franchise "Signers in Blood" and the mastermind behind the violent January 16–19, 2013, attack on the Algerian gas production facility at In Amenas, just over the border from Libya. He was formally charged for this attack, which claimed the lives of several Americans. A $5 million reward as of this writing may help to sweeten the search for him (*New York Times*, July 20, 2013).

Yet another sequel to the regional "Arab Spring" revolutions reverberated in Tunisia when an AQIM follower assassinated Tunisian "Popular Front" liberal leader Muhammad Brahimi, age 58, quite possibly by the same pistol that killed Chokri Belaid in February. An attack on the U.S. Embassy in Tunisia may also be related. Brahimi's funeral brought out thousands of his supporters who blamed the Islamist *Ennahda* government for the security failure, rather parallel to the problems in neighboring Libya (*New York Times*, July 27–28, 2013).

Amidst these political deaths and virtual anarchy, the focus suddenly lurched back to Tripoli with anti-militia protestors attacking offices of Islamist parties who were assumed to be involved with an assassination in Tripoli of 'Abd al-Salam al-Musmari, an activist opposed to the Muslim Brothers. At the same time there was a major jailbreak at the Al-Kweifiya prison in Benghazi of up to 1,200 inmates. Some were recaptured, some wounded in the precarious and deteriorating security situation of this major city in which three security officers were killed on Friday and a colonel was killed on Saturday (*New York Times*, July 28, 2013). The existential crisis for the nascent Libyan government took another turn when Youssef al-Mangoush was replaced by Major General 'Abd al-Salam Jadlaah al-Salihine al-Obeidi, by the new President of the National Congress, Nouri Abu Sahmein, in order to intensify the fight against the Muslim Brothers (*New York Times*, July 30, 2013).

AUGUST 2013

The saga of tracking those responsible for the Benghazi mission attack progressed when Department of Justice officials in the United States filed murder charges against Ahmed Abu Khattala, a Benghazi militia leader, along with two others. Unfortunately, these charges, under seal, are not matched with arrests in Libya. Assuming that those charged are still at large in Libya, the government does not seem able to bring them under their custody. In his own defense Abu Khattala said he was there at the mission but he played no role in the attack and tried to rescue the Libyan guards there and said this was turning into an American election issue (*New York Times*, August 7, 2013). And so this story continues.

SEPTEMBER 2013

Wishful thinking had Libya slowly and patiently putting the nation back together. Searching for Ahmed Khattala, associated with the *Ansar al-Shari'a* attack on the American mission in Benghazi, for questioning, was one part of the unfinished judicial business that was also a political issue in partisan America. Even if brought into custody, where should he be tried or held, and under which civilian or military court? On top of this, Saef al-Islam appeared in a "tribal court" in Zintan, to "progress" on the charges by the International Criminal Court. However, the militia forces that were holding him on lesser charges, for the past two years, refused to pass him on to the Tripoli authorities. Tripoli had also pledged to not hand him over to the ICC. This judicial stalemate, one step forward and two steps backward, did not auger well for building the new Libyan state (*New York Times*, September 20, 2013).

Meanwhile, following a 20 percent wage increase to oil workers, there was hope to get oil flowing, as it represented a massive 95 percent of all foreign export earnings and 75 percent of badly needed government revenues resulting from oil production falling to as few as 80,000 bpd (*New York Times*, September 13, 2013). A week later, the news appeared to be better when an important pipeline in Tobruk, in independent-minded eastern Cyrenaica, far from Tripoli, was reopened. Various strikes and protests had reduced oil production to only 10 percent (at just 150,000 bpd) of its original production capacity. The output at Tobruk was expected to bring production to 700,000 bpd, but still this is far from the usual level of daily production at 1.6 million bpd and way further still from the maximum production in 1970 at 3.3 million bpd of Africa's largest proven reserves of high-quality oil.

So once again, Libya's future is bright while its present is heavily contested. Aside from the great economic impact to Libya, it was also a blow to the weak government of Prime Minister 'Ali Zeidan, including the lack of transparency about how the pipeline was reopened. Also, the efforts to get foreign firms and personnel to return to Libya hang in the balance. This is especially the case in western Libya, where the militias in Zawiya and Mellita are slower to open the valves at the al-Feel and al-Sharara oilfields (*New York Times*, September 21, 2013).

OCTOBER 2013

October opened with a spontaneous assault on the Russian Embassy in Tripoli because of allegations that a Russian citizen, Ekaterina Ustyuzhaninova, was responsible for a murder of a Libyan Air Force pilot. Evidently she had been a supporter of Gaddafi and provocatively wrote a message in blood on the walls. Precisely what happened remained to be seen in a Libyan court, but resorting to violence and the lack of protective security was another blow to the legitimacy and credibility of the government, although this sentiment was rejected by Libyan Foreign Minister Mohammad 'Abd al-Aziz (*New York Times*, October 3, 2013).

But this controversy was quickly dwarfed by an even greater tragedy, when hundreds of desperate freedom-seeking Africans sought to reach the Italian island of Lampedusa. A mere one-fourth mile off shore, the overcrowded boat capsized with at least 111 dead, and more than 200 missing. This is far from the first such tragic, high-risk effort by Libyans and other citizens of impoverished and failing states, to seek asylum. There are thousands of refugees ever year who are trying to reach France, Spain, Italy, or Greece (*New York Times*, October 5, 2013).

In this case, it appears that a crowded trawler set out from Misrata in Libya with some 500 passengers from Eritrea and Somalia, amongst other nations. As the 60-foot vessel was in sight of Lampedusa, some passengers wanted to signal Italian authorities by burning a blanket that, in turn, ignited gasoline and, fleeing this fire, the passengers fled to the other side of the boat and turned it over, with many drowning outright or getting trapped in the overturned vessel. When the sea settled, Italian divers extracted 83 more bodies trapped under 165 feet of water.

The pace of headline-grabbing events centered on Libya did not end. Frustrated by the very slow progress with the Libyan government in their pursuit of international terrorists residing in Libya, American security officers and commandos from the CIA and FBI raided a Tripoli street to snatch up an al-Qa'eda operative Abu Anas al-Libi (age 49, aka Nazih 'Abd al-Hamed al-Ruqai).

Al-Libi had been indicated in 2000 for his part in the August 8, 1998, bombing of U.S. Embassies in Kenya and Tanzania. He was charged with doing surveillance for al-Qa'eda of the embassies in 1993 and 1995 that led to the great destruction (killing 244 people) of those targets as well as other anti-American missions in Yemen, Saudi Arabia, and Somalia. This Tripoli operation took place at the same time as SEALs raided Shabab targets in Somalia. Although al-Libi was not involved with the more recent Benghazi mission attack, he was well versed in bomb-making, sabotage, and disguises. He was also an activist in the anti-Gaddafi group LIFG (Libyan Islamic Fighting Group), and in the 2011 Libyan revolution, he was fighting with the rebels in the Nafusa mountains (*New York Times*, October 8, 2013). He was removed from Tripoli to a U.S. naval amphibious landing ship, the USS *San Antonio*, which was deployed in the Mediterranean. Before heading to New York for likely criminal charges and trial, he was going to be questioned for intelligence analysis under the "law of war."

Americans claimed that some Libyan security officials were aware of the impending attack, but afterward, the popular sentiment was that this "kidnapping" violated hard-won Libyan sovereignty. Other Libyans welcomed the bloodless raid, saying, essentially, good riddance. On top of this, in a neighborhood of al-Libi supporters, Libyan masked militia fighters attacked Libyan regular soldiers in five cars assaulting a checkpoint southeast of Tripoli at Tarhuna in which 15 Libyan soldiers were killed (*New York Times*, October 6–7, 2013).

Topping off the week, Prime Minister Ali Zeidan was briefly "kidnapped" by a Libyan militia group, the Revolutionaries Operations Group, ostensibly on corruption charges that had been leveled by the Ministry of Justice. The ministry vehemently denied that their Prosecutor General had issued such a warrant, while a spokesman for the group stated they were only acting upon the Prosecutor General's orders. Six hours later, the Prime Minister was released. However, what does such wanton enforcement of laws, and the ability of armed groups to capture the highest ranking civilian in the new Libyan government, say about the stability and security of the new Libya? This too is not a story that has seen its last chapter (BBC News, October 10, 2013, Jawad).

Prime Minister 'Ali Zeidan will have much to answer for when he is called to address to General National Congress. Will Libyans be listening, believing, and still patient? Still another tragic death of an American, in this case teacher Ronnie Smith, killed by extremists while jogging in Benghazi on 5 December 2013 raises the stakes even higher (The Guardian, 5 December 2013).

SUMMARY FOR LIBYA IN 2013

With 2013 heading to the end, it is premature to judge the metrics left over from 2011 and 2012, but clearly there has been slow progress in the struggle to disarm the heavily armed militias. The Islamists seem to be making some progress feinting toward the political center, but the political events in Tunisia and Egypt in 2012 and 2013 may give many pauses to reflect beyond these two case studies. More persons of interest appear in the investigation in the Benghazi attack, but it has been exceedingly slow, if not virtually stopped. Arrests have still not happened. Oil production has only slowly regained ground, but such sluggishness undermines reconstruction budgets and plans. Trials in Libya and The Hague are stalled and Washington's interest in Libya has waned as they have shifted to the even bloodier struggles in Egypt and Syria. Progress on the Benghazi attack has also been glacial. Crises of various sorts, like terrorist attacks on security points, and sinking boats, only exacerbate the shaky credibility of the government struggling for accountability, transparency, and effectiveness.

Wael Ghonim, a pivotal figure in the 2011 Egyptian revolution, wrote enthusiastically in 2012 that "the power of the people is greater than the people in power." That was certainly the spirit in Libya and witnessed as well in Egypt in 2011 and 2012. He said "The rejoicing and celebrations in the streets were incredible. Car horns, fireworks, scrams, chants, and applause were heard everywhere. It was a defining moment of Egypt's modern history. The will of the people vanquished the will of the rulers." (Ghonim, 290). Or, as the slogan shouted in Tahrir said: *"Al-Sha'b yurid isqat al-nizam"* [the people want to overthrow the regime]. But *"nizam"* can also mean "discipline" or "order," and this was also toppled and "the people's" plan to rebuild a new *nizam* was lacking after 5,000 years of no democratic transitions. After all, and very sadly, brutal authoritarianism worked to achieve stability.

Certainly the departures of Ben 'Ali, Gaddafi, and Mubarak created such deep emotional sentiments in Tunisia, Libya, and Egypt. It turns out that inspiring a revolution and even toppling dictators is not as difficult as consolidating those gains. But in retrospect, in 2013, with Tunisia facing armed Islamist insurgents and major economic, legal, and social problems; Libya is facing more of the same as the militias do not want to surrender their Islamist and regional goals nor the weapons they used to bring Gaddafi down; Egypt faced an exclusive and polarizing Muslim Brother leadership under President al-Morse that so disappointed and became despised, the Supreme Council of the Armed Forces, led by General 'Abd al-Fatah al-Sisi, declared that "enough was enough" with the Brothers and with "Kifaya"; and so he violently turned back to killing, jailing, punishing, and restoring "emergency rule," which is leading toward uncharted waters. This calls to mind the historically parallel series of events in Algeria, where the military and the Islamic Salvation Front (FIS) clashed bloodily for years in a civil war that cost some 200,000 lives. And this is not to mention ongoing issues with Algerian terrorism, small-arms trafficking, and a perilously disturbed Sahel region. We hope it does not get this horrible, but we already have the civil war in Syria, indicating just how much suffering, violence, conflict, and poison gas can cause. Moreover, hope is not a plan for national salvation and reconstruction.

Long-term perspective and patience are required to monitor the Middle East with any accuracy. A few years are not enough. Free-flowing arms within and beyond Libya's borders slow any gains. Properly trained police and armies are slowly increasing, but is it fast enough? Oil is flowing; rebuilders are rebuilding. Libyans are drinking coffee and tea again, even while ducking car bombs; American raiders and local militias have both continued to disrupt the day-to-day incremental gains in stability. The senior political offices are filled and shuffled, but they don't stay filled. Libya is not a failed state, just really weak. The "roadmap" to rebuilding an accountable and transparent judiciary, police, and military in Libya is neatly packed in the glove compartment, while the engine idles, the clutch is depressed, and debate continues about what speed and direction to take. The state building choices are there. Will human rights and human interests be secured with the rule of law, democracy, and due process, or by local ethnicity, religious affiliations, and orientations? Or will force of arms again be king?

In 2011, Joseph Siegle, Research Director of the Africa Center for Strategic Studies of the National Defense University, wrote that in studying such places as Libya:

Stabilizing fragile states is a central security challenge of the early twenty-first century. While these states may seem marginal on the global landscape, when ignored, the threat to the broader international community is heightened. The problem they pose is seemingly intractable, but there has in fact been a commendable record of stabilizing fragile states over the past two decades. This has required integrated political, security, and development efforts, sustained over time, almost always with hands-on engagement by leading international actors. This recognizes that stabilizing fragile states is, in most cases, a state building (rather than rebuilding) process that must redress a long period of deterioration overseen by illegitimate leadership that has fostered deep inequities in a society. While opportunistic spoilers emerge in such contexts and can cause great devastation, by and large these insurgents are fairly weak. They are a symptom of the state's fragility and not normally the cause. Accordingly, while stabilization efforts must address organized violence, they should keep their focus on the overarching challenge: building legitimate and effective states that can earn and maintain the support of their populations.

Brynen et al. (301) put it this way:

At stake in these on-going struggles throughout the Arab world is ownership of the foundations upon which a new political order is being built. Will it be built on the popular will institutionalized in formal democratic political institutions, or will it be built on alliances between old and new actors aimed as constraining this will? It is these popular struggles and the responses they trigger from local, regional, and international actors that will determine the future of authoritarianism and the potential for democracy in the Arab world.

We hope that we have compiled an integrated record for the past present and future of Libya. Hope for an end to tyranny started the 2011 revolution. Hope for a brighter future in Libya is attainable with seat belts tightly fastened over the bumpy road with sharp turns to keep the drivers of this new vehicle of state formation on course and not crashing off the road. Failing to reap the bounty and growth of the "Arab Spring" can result in a public opinion shifting to a bitter harvest of a regional infection of insecurity.

Our book comes to an end, but the Libyan future is still being written.

SOURCES

Brynen, Rex, Peter W. Moore, Bassel F. Salloukh, and Marie-Joelle Zahar. *Beyond the Arab Spring: Authoritarianism and Democratization in the Arab World*. Boulder, CO: Lynne Rienner, 2012.

Chido, Diane E., *From Chaos to Cohesion: A Regional Approach to Security, Stability, and Development in Sub-Saharan Africa*. Carlisle, PA: Strategic Studies Institute, U.S. Army War College, 2013.

D'Inka, Werner, et al. *Reinventing the Public Sphere in Libya. Observations, Portraits and Commentary on a Newly Emerging Media Landscape*. Berlin: Media in Cooperation and Transition (MICT), 2012.

Ghoneim, Wael. *Revolution 2.0: A Memoir*. New York: Houghton Miflin Harcourt, 2012.

Jawad, Rana. "Libya abduction: Freed PM Ali Zeidan calls for calm." Accessed October 11, 2013. http://www.bbc.co.uk/news/world-africa-24481032.

Siegle, Joseph. "Stabilizing Fragile States." *Global Dialogue*, 13, no. 1 (2011).

Siegle, Joseph, et al. *Africa and the Arab Spring: A New Era of Democratic Expectations*. Africa Center for Strategic Studies, National Defense University, 2011.

Appendix

BASIC FACTS

Nomenclature

Kingdom of Libya	1951–1969
Libyan Arab Republic	1969–1977
Great Socialist Peoples' Libyan Arab Republic	1977–2011
National Transitional Council	2011–2012
General National Council	2012–2013
State of Libya	2012–2013

Heads of State (President/Speaker of General National Congress)

Office Holder	Period
Muhammad al-Magariaf	9 August 2011–25 June 2013
Nouri Abu Sahman	25 June 2013–present

Head of Government (Prime Ministers)

Office Holder	Period
Mahmoud Jibril (Head of TNC)	March 5, 2011–March 23, 2011
Mahmoud Jibril (Interim PM)	March 23, 2011–October 23, 2011

(*continued*)

Head of Government (Prime Ministers) *(continued)*

Office Holder	Period
'Ali Tarhouni (Acting PM)	October 23, 2011–November 24, 2011
'Abd al-Rahim El-Keib (Interim PM, TNC)	November 24, 2011–August 8, 2012
'Abd al Rahim El-Keib (Interim PM, GNC)	August 8, 2012–November 14, 2012
'Ali Zeidan (PM)	November 14, 2012–January 9, 2013
'Ali Zeidan (PM State of Libya)	January 9, 2013–Present

Notes: Al-Magarief is the first Berber to be elected to high position since the revolution. In second-round voting his National Front Party won 113 seats compared to Ali Zeidan's 85 seats. Al-Magariaf (PhD, finance) is from Benghazi and served in the Gaddafi regime in the 1970s before his exile to the United States in 1980, where he founded the armed opposition group, The National Front for the Salvation of Libya (NFSL). He favors a plural (moderate) Islamic outlook. 'Ali Zeidan is from Jufra in the southern Fezzan (MA, International Relations), also worked with the Gaddafi regime as Libya diplomat in India under then Ambassador Muhammad al-Magariaf. Both defected to form the NFSL.

Basic Descriptors

Population:

2007	2009	2011
6.17 million	6.42 million*	6.48 million*

Size: 679,147 sq. mi; 1,759,450 sq. km.

National: 6,597,960; (166,510 nonnationals)
Urban: Tripoli, 1,065,405 (2013)
Urban/Rural Ratio: 22/78

Health:

Annual Growth Rate: 2.064% p.a.
Life Expectancy: 75.34 (males); 80.08 (females); 77.83 (2012)
Infant Mortality: 17.7/1,000 (2000–2005); 15.0/1,000 (2005–2010); 12.7 (2012)
Crude Birth Rate: 24.3/1,000 (2000–2005); 24.0 (2005–2010); 17.5 (2012)
Crude Death Rate: 4.0/1,000 (2000–2005); 4.0 (2005–2010); 12.7 (2012)

GDP	71.70bn	60.40bn	36.90bn*
GDP/capita	11,773usd	9,529usd	5,691 usd*
Inflation	6.2%	2.7%	14.1%*

Oil Output	1,848 bpd	1,652 bpd	479 bpd
Natural Gas Output	15.2 bncum	15.3 bncum	4.1 bncom
Exports (fob)	46,970 musd	37,055 musd	12,986 musd
Imports (fob)	17,701 musd	22,002 musd	11,200 musd
Balance of Trade	29,268 musd	15,053 musd	1,786 musd
Current Account	24,278 musd	9,481 musd	-2,278 musd
Total Reserves (-gold)	79,405 musd	104,026 musd	103,552 musd*
Foreign Exchange	77,897 musd	100,917 musd	100,582 musd
Exchange Rate:	1.22/usd	1.17/usd	0.80/usd

Sources:
Nations of the World: A Political, Economic and Business Handbook, 12th edition, Amenia, NY: Grey House Publishing, 2013. * = estimates; m = million; bn = billion; usd = U.S. dollars; bpd = barrels per day; bncum = billion cubic meters; musd = million U.S. dollars.
Global Studies: Africa. 14th edition, New York: McGraw-Hill, 2011; *CIA FactBook.*

Parliamentary (General National Congress) Elections in Libya, July 2012

Party	Seats Won
National Forces Alliance[1]	39 (led by Mahmoud Jibril)
Justice and Development Party[2]	17 (led by Muhammad Sowan)
National Front Party[3]	3 (led by Muhammad al-Magariaf)
Union for the Homeland[4]	2 (led by Abd al-Rahman Sewehil)
National Centrist Party[5]	2 (led by 'Ali Tarhouni)
Wadi al-Hayah Party	2
Libyan National Democratic Party	1
The Message	1
The Foundation	1
National Party for Development and Welfare	1
Nation and Prosperity	1
Authenticity and Renewal	1
Moderate Ummah Assembly	1
Labaika National Party	1
National Party of Wadi Ash-Shati	1

(continued)

(continued)

Party	Seats Won
Centrist Youth Party	1
Libyan Party for Liberty and Development	1
National Parties Alliance	1
Libya: the Hope	1
Wisdom	1
Independents	120
Total	**200**

Source: HIS Jane's Sentinel, Country Risk Assessments, 2013, issue 32.
[1.]Liberal secular alliance, follows Islamic principles.
[2.]Muslim Brotherhood Party, wants *Shari'a* as national law.
[3.]Gaddafi opponents from the National Front for the Salvation of Libya, led by Al-Magariaf, a Berber.

LIBYAN CIVIL WAR (FEBRUARY–OCTOBER 2011)

United Nations Resolutions

United Nations Security Council Resolution 1970 (UNSCR 1970)
Demand for immediate ceasefire. Sanctions including arms embargo.

United Nations Security Council Resolution 1973 (UNSCR 1973)
Demanded end to violence against Libyan civilians; authorized a no-fly zone; authorized all necessary means to protect civilians and their property threatened by attack, short of foreign occupation.

Operation Odyssey Dawn (March 19–31, 2011)/Operation Unified Protector (March 31–October 31, 2011)

United States	Operation Odyssey Dawn
Canada	Operation Mobile
France	Operation Harmattan
United Kingdom	Operation Ellamy
NATO	Operation Unified Protector

Mission: Enforce provisions of UNSCR 1970/1973; to establish and maintain a no-fly zone. To conduct noncombatant evacuation operations.

Coalition Forces

Commanders (Operation Odyssey Dawn)

United States Africa Command	General Carter Ham
Joint Task Force Odyssey Dawn	Admiral Samuel Locklear III, USN
Joint Force Maritime Component	Commander Vice Admiral Harry Harris, USN
Joint Force Air Component Commander	Major General Margaret Woodward, USAF
Joint Special Operations Task Force Commander	Brigadier General Christopher Haas, USA
Joint Force Land Component Commander	None

Commanders (Operation Unified Protector)

Supreme Headquarters Allied Powers Europe	Admiral James Stavridis (USA)
Allied Joint Command	LGen Charles Bouchard (CAN)
Allied Air Command	Lt. Gen. Ralph Jodice II (USA)
Allied Maritime Command	Vice Admiral Rinaldo Veri (ITA)

Army

No ground forces assigned due to the stipulations and limitations imposed by UNSCR 1970 and 1973, as well as the agreement by providing nations that this was to be a supporting effort to the Libyans fighting for their independence, versus having it turn into a larger conflict with forces from more materially modernized nations.

Navy

Country	Ship Type	Number	Mission
United States	Submarine	3	Cruise Missile Platform*
	Cruiser	1	Missile/Anti-Air Defense*
	Destroyer	4	Anti-Ship/Air Defense*
	Amphibious Assault	5	Multi-Role
	Replenishment	3	Fuel/Stores
Belgium	Mine Hunter	2	Mine Counter Measure
Bulgaria	Frigate	1	Air/Sub Defense*
Canada	Frigate	2	Anti-Air/Sub Defense*
France	Submarine	1	Cruise Missile Platform*
	Aircraft Carrier	1	Aircraft launch platform
	Destroyer	5	Anti-Ship/Air Defense*

(continued)

(continued)

Country	Ship Type	Number	Mission
	Frigate	6	Anti-Air/Sub Defense*
	Corvette	1	Shallow-Water Patrol
	Amphibious Assault	1	Multi-Role
	Replenishment	2	Ammunition/Stores
Greece	Frigate	1	Anti-Air/Sub Defense
Italy	Aircraft Carrier	1	Aircraft Launch Platform
	Amphibious Assault	3	Multi-Role
	Submarine	2	Anti-Ship Defense
	Destroyer	2	Anti-Ship/Air Defense
	Frigate	3	Anti-Air/Sub Defense
	Patrol Combatant	3	Coastal/Long-Range Patrol
	Replenishment	2	Fuel/Ammunition/Store
Netherlands	Mine Hunter	2	Mine Counter Measure
Romania	Frigate	1	Anti-Air/Sub Defense
Spain	Submarine	2	Anti-Ship Defense
Turkey	Submarine	1	Anti-Ship Defense
	Frigate	4	Anti-Air/Sub Defense
	Replenishment	1	Fuel/Stores
UK	Amphibious Assault	1	Multi-Role
	Submarine	1	Anti-Ship Defense
	Destroyer	1	Anti-Ship/Air Defense
	Frigate	1	Anti-Air/Sub Defense
	Mine Hunter	1	Mine Counter Measure

*Cruise missile capable ships

Air Force (Including Navy and Marine Corps Aircraft)

Country	Type	Number	Mission
United States	Fighter	12	Air-Air/Ground Attack
	Bomber	7	Strategic Bombing
	Ground Attack	30	Air-Ground Attack
	Electronic Warfare	7	Radar Jamming
	Signals Intelligence	5	Intel-Surveillance-Recon (ISR)
	Maritime Patrol	1	Maritime/Anti-Submarine

Country	Type	Number	Mission
	Early Warning	2	Airborne Command and Control
	Refueler	22	Air-Air Refueling
	Unmanned Aerial Vehicle	11	Aerial reconnaissance/strike
	Helicopter	8	Air-Ground Attack
	Helicopter	4	Heavy Transport
	Tilt rotor	12	Medium Transport
Belgium	Fighter-Attack	6	Air-Air/Ground Attack
Canada	Fighter-Attack	7	Air-Air/Ground Attack
	Refueler	2	Air-Air Refueling
	Maritime Patrol	2	Maritime/Anti-Submarine
Denmark	Fighter-Attack	6	Air-Air/Ground Attack
France	Fighter-Attack	12	Air-Air/Ground Attack
	Air Reconnaissance	3	Aerial Reconnaissance
	Refueler	7	Air-Air Refueling
	Helicopter	16	Air-Ground Attack
	Unmanned Aerial Vehicle	1	Aerial Reconnaissance
Italy	Fighter	24	Air-Air/Ground Attack
	Ground Attack	6	Air-Ground Attack
	Refueler	2	Air-Air Refueling
	Unmanned Aerial Vehicle	2	Aerial Reconnaissance
Jordan	Fighter	6	Air-Air/Ground Attack
NATO	Early Warning	3	Airborne Command and Control
Netherlands	Fighter	6	Air-Air/Ground Attack
	Refueler	1	Air-Air Refueling
Norway	Fighter	6	Air-Air/Ground Attack
Qatar	Fighter	6	Air-Air/Ground Attack
Spain	Fighter	4	Air-Air/Ground Attack
	Refueler	1	Air-Air Refueling
	Maritime Patrol	1	Maritime/Anti-Submarine
Sweden	Aerial Recon	8	Aerial Reconnaissance
Turkey	Fighter	6	Air-Air/Ground Attack

(*continued*)

(continued)

Country	Type	Number	Mission
	Refueler	1	Air-Air Refueling
UAE	Fighter	11	Air-Air/Ground Attack
UK	Fighter	18	Air-Air/Ground Attack
	Early Warning	3	Airborne Command and Control
	Signals Intelligence	3	Intel-Surveillance-Recon (ISR)
	Refueler	2	Air-Air Refueling
	Helicopter	5	Air-Ground Attack

Airfields

Base	Location	Forces Occupying	Mission
Souda Bay	Crete	Norway	Fighter/Attack
		Qatar	Fighter/Attack
		United States	Radar Jamming/ISR
Akrotiri	Cyprus	UK	Transport/Refueler
		UK	Early Warning/ISR
		United States	ISR
Avord	France	France	Early Warning
		France	Refueler
Dijon	France	France	Fighter/Attack
Istres-Le Tube	France	France	Refueler
Nancy	France	France	Fighter/Attack
Orleans	France	France	Transport
Solenzara	France	France	Fighter/Attack/ISR
St. Dizier	France	France	Fighter/Attack
Araxos	Greece	Belgium	Fighter/Attack
Aviano	Italy	Jordan	Fighter/Attack
		United States	Fighter/Attack
		United States	Radar Jamming
Decimomannu	Italy	Netherlands	Fighter/Attack
		Netherlands	Refueler
		Spain	Fighter/Attack
		Spain	Refueler/Maritime
		UAE	Fighter/Attack

Base	Location	Forces Occupying	Mission
Giola del Colle	Italy	Italy	Fighter/Attack
		Italy	Refueler/UAV
		UK	Fighter/Attack
Pisa	Italy	Italy	Transport
Practica di Mare	Italy	Italy	Refueler
Sigonella	Italy	Canada	Maritime
		Denmark	Fighter/Attack
		Sweden	Reconnaissance
		Sweden	Refueler
		Turkey	Fighter/Attack
		Turkey	Refueler
		United States	Radar Jamming/ISR
		United States	Maritime/UAV
Trapani	Italy	Canada	Fighter/Attack
		Canada	Refueler
		Italy	Fighter/Attack
		Italy	Refueler
		NATO	Early Warning
		UK	Early Warning
		UK	Refueler
Moron	Spain	United States	Refueler
Rota	Spain	United States	Early Warning/ISR
RAF Lakenheath	UK	United States	Fighter/Attack
RAF Marham	UK	UK	Fighter/Attack
RAF Mildenhall	UK	United States	Fighter/Refueler
Ellsworth AFB	United States	United States	Strategic Bomber
Whiteman AFB	United States	United States	Strategic Bomber

Note: All aircraft/helicopter numbers are estimates, based upon multiple sources. Due to security concerns, some nations will not necessarily report exact numbers.

Libyan Loyalist Forces

Ground Forces

Reliable figures don't exist for the number of soldiers outfitting Libyan Loyalist fighting forces. Some estimates place the number at about 50,000 soldiers, half regular army, half draftees.

The most well-known ground fighting force, and considered the most professional and therefore deadly, was the 32nd Brigade, also known as the "Khamis Brigade" after Muammar Gaddafi's youngest son.

Principal Equipment

Type	Country of Origin	Quantity (Approx.)	Age
Main Battle Tank	Soviet Union	500	20–40 years
Armored Vehicle	Soviet Union	2,400	20–40 years
Artillery	Soviet Union	1,250	20–40 years
Rocket Launchers	Soviet Union	750	20–40 years
Surface-Air Missiles	Soviet Union	1,860	20–40 years
Surface-Surface Missiles	Soviet Union	130	20–40 years
Antitank Weapons	Soviet Union	750	10–20 years
Mortars	Soviet Union	490	10–20 years
Antiaircraft Guns	Soviet Union	1,400	20–40 years

Navy

Roughly 8,000 sailors comprised the navy. The chief missions for the navy involved coastal defense and near shore interdiction. While they had several submarines, by the time of the Libyan Civil War, none were operational.

Type	Source	Quantity	Status
Submarine	Soviet Union	1	Unserviceable
Frigate	Soviet Union	2	1 operational
Corvette	Soviet Union	2	1 operational
Fast Attack Boats	Soviet Union	21	11 operational
Mine Hunters	Soviet Union	9	5 operational

Air Force

About 22,000 people served in the air force. They had the full spectrum of aircraft to perform long-range bombing, fighter and ground attack missions, and transport. They didn't have an electronic warfare or intelligence, surveillance, or reconnaissance capability.

Type	Source	Quantity	Status
Fighters	Soviet Union	71	All destroyed/captured
Attack	Soviet Union	80	All destroyed/captured
Bombers	Soviet Union	7	All destroyed

Type	Source	Quantity	Status
Transports	Soviet Union	12	All destroyed/captured
Helicopters	USSR/USA/ ITA/FRA	200	All destroyed/captured

Note: All numbers are estimates, as some aircraft were photographed on the ground but in unknown condition, and reports of possessed versus ordered aircraft could not be deconflicted.

National Liberation Army (affiliated with the National Transitional Council)

Ground Forces

No reliable number can be provided, as initially the war was fought by militias, communities, and mercenaries. As the war progressed and recognition from world powers grew, the ability of the NTC to fund, equip, and train local forces into some semblance of an organized army improved. However, the liberation army was always a blend of former loyalist forces and men and women from the contested towns who joined in the patriotic spirit that often sweeps a nation newly at war. By war's end, they could count roughly 64,000 soldiers, sailors, and airmen in 38 "brigades," which ranged from a few hundred to over 1,000 men and women.

Ground Equipment

The liberation army used whatever they had available: Captured main battle tanks, antiaircraft guns, mortars, machine guns. Much of the training was carried out by the few loyalist soldiers who defected in the early days of the war. As often as not, the rebels had to learn through trial and error, to operate the weapons systems.

As the war progressed, the liberation army began to receive MILAN antitank missiles from France and Qatar; small arms, pistols, rifles, and assault weapons from Egypt, France, Italy, Poland, the Sudan, and the UAE. The UK and United States provided medical and communications equipment, no items for combat actions.

Additionally, technical advisors, mainly special operations–type soldiers, trickled in to provide training and to assist the NATO forces in positively identifying targets, to avoid civilian casualties and fratricide incidents.

Air Force

The National Liberation Army didn't possess any aviation assets throughout the conflict. There were rumors of UAVs being flown, but no substantiating documentation could be found.

Navy

The National Liberation Army had sailors with experience, and they did in fact capture one of the loyalist ships, a fast attack combatant. They didn't possess any regular naval forces, however.

Sources: PRISM, 3, no. 2 (March 2012), Washington, DC: NDU Press; International Institute for Strategic Studies, London, England; Royal Canadian Navy, accessed June 2, 2013, http://www.navy-marine.forces.gc.ca/en/multimedia/gallery-ships.page; ArmyRecognition.com, accessed June 9, 2013, http://www.armyrecognition.com/libya_libyan_army_land_ground_armed_forces_uk/libya_libyan_armed_army_land_ground_forces_military_equipment_armoured_vehicle_intelligence_pictures.html; "Operation Harmattan," *The Aviationist*, accessed June 2, 2013, http://theaviationist.com/?s=OPERATION+HARMATTAN.

Air Strikes and Engagements

February

Generalized protests and small-scale clashes erupted throughout the whole of Libya. Particularly contested sites were Ajdabiya, Benghazi, Brega, Misurata, Ras Lanuf, Sirte, Tripoli, and Zawarah. Bayda and Darnah were captured and retained by the rebels with relatively little challenge. Western border towns of Zawarah and Zawiyah, along with Nalut, and Jadu saw more localized fighting and some of the earliest occurrences of loyalist forces deserting to the rebel cause. Oil production, distribution, and the headquarters of the nascent rebel movement, Brega, Ras Lanuf, and Benghazi, respectively, were primary sources of action.

At this time, no NATO or UN presence was in play, and given the balance of "Arab Spring" events, the world wasn't particularly interested in watching yet another nation implode. However, the scope of violence in Libya had not matched that of surrounding nations, thus the attention hadn't turned to protecting civilians caught in the crossfire.

March

Benghazi, Bayda, and Darnah were considered firmly in rebel hands. Fighting seesawed in Ajdabiya, Brega, Ras Lanuf, and the western towns of Zawarah, Zawiyah, Nalut, and Jadu. Sirte and Tripoli were still pretty firmly in the loyalist grasp, despite some initial probing attacks by rebel forces. Chiefly holding back more extensive rebel assaults were the lack of experience as a fighting force; immature command and control structure, and the lack of supporting fires from long-range artillery or aviation.

By March 19, 2011, following the mandate of UNSCR 1970 and UNSCR 1973, the U.S.-led mission, Operation Odyssey Dawn, had commenced and with countless barrages of cruise missile attacks, precision air strikes by U.S., British, French, and Danish aircraft, the rebels were beginning to see some of the relief, especially in Brega, that would become standard throughout the ensuing seven months.

The coastal community of Bin Jawwad felt the first in an ongoing series of rolling attacks by rebel and loyalist forces alike, as this critical town lying along the major highway from Ajdabiya to Sirte would be occupied and attacked throughout the summer as each side fought to consolidate their gains and establish further footholds to their ultimate objectives; Benghazi for the loyalists and Tripoli for the rebels.

March also saw the beginnings of rebel use of larger-scale weapons as they began to train on main battle tanks and the antiaircraft machine guns. While the Libyan air threat was spotty and lasted but a month, these machine guns proved particularly deadly against ground targets, predominantly soft-skinned pickup trucks and lightly armored personnel carriers.

Muammar Gaddafi's most experienced warrior son, Khamis Gaddafi, and his expertly trained brigade of Libyan "Regulars" laid siege to Zawiyah and would continue to do so for the balance of the spring and summer.

April

Only Bin Jawwad could lay claim to being more or less in rebel control. The balance of the coastal cities, and the port city of Khums, either came under fresh attack from loyalist forces, or continued to be involved in back-and-forth occupation and extraction. Just like many of these cities had seen in early 1940–1941, the momentum shifts occurring with an infusion of men and materiel, on both sides, would be repeated until the cumulative balance of Coalition air power had sufficiently destroyed Gaddafi's means of making war on any large scale.

New to this month in fighting was initial action in Mizdah, a bit south of Tripoli, as rebel forces continued their spirited, if not disjointed, encircling attacks along border and transportation towns.

May

May would see the first of several increasingly heavy months for action as the Coalition air strikes targeted Muammar Gaddafi's many command-and-control sites (both for managing the ground war and directing any surface to air weapons if any were employed), weapons caches, military encampments, and training sites.

Misrata would, technically, fall into the hands of the rebels; however, given the strategic value, and almost dead-center split between Gaddafi's major enclaves of Tripoli and Sirte, this city would seem very heavy fighting throughout the remainder of the campaign.

New sites for the Coalition, as well as rebel interest, included Hun, Qaryat, and Sabha, as the rebel forces and Coalition strikes began to dig deeper into the supply networks and inland sites of loyalist resistance. Ajdabiya remained a very contentious site as both sides stubbornly refused to yield. This would be the case throughout the conflict. For the first time, Gaddafi's "compound" in the town of Az-Aziziyah came under attack. While the Coalition made no effort to surgically target Gaddafi, the fact that his headquarters was effectively his compound made distinguishing the two exceptionally difficult.

June

. June observed a striking increase in activity as the Coalition targeted the vast majority of identified Gaddafi loyalist sites. Added to the list from May were Bin Jawwad, Bir Al Ghanam, Gharyan, Jadu, Okba, Tarhunah, Waddan, Yafran, Zintan, and Zlitan. After the initial round of fighting in which Gaddafi's forces had used standard open-field warfare, their approach to fighting the rebels had resulted in no further captures of cities during June. Additionally, as the rebel alliance was beginning to mature, signs of factional disputes were occurring, as the residents from the western border region began to anticipate the opportunity to fight for their ethnically distinct region. Additionally, supporters of Gaddafi within communities, to include Tarhunah, much like the American colonists who sided with the British during the American Revolution, found themselves fighting the rebel loyal citizens of these same towns.

Much like any campaign in which there is a doldrums period where neither side can see an end, June was that month for the rebels, and also brought about concerns over how long the Coalition would remain in the fight.

July

July began to see a tightening of the noose around Gaddafi's last line of resistance in Tripoli. Bani Walid captured the attention of the Coalition as they went heavily after the command-and-control and weapons sites that existed in and around Tripoli.

New to this month's action were fresh air strikes on Badr, which also saw some limited fighting by both sides; Bin Ghashir, Durat Turkiyah, El Assah, Jawsh, and Jufra, all sites further inland where weapons caches, maintenance facilities, training camps, and fallback command bunkers existed. While various media reports indicated Brega had finally been captured by the rebels, there still remained very heavy violence on both sides for this strategic oil hub. Ras Lanuf held the same fate as it too could lay claim to some of the most heavily and oft-exchanged occupations of the war.

By July, there was no Libyan air power to contend with, but the Scud missile threat remained a viable fear. The Coalition air power had the opportunity to concentrate on ground targets as they had effectively wiped out the first line of defense in Libyan weaponry.

August

August began to turn the tide into the inevitable favor of the Coalition-supported rebel forces. The cumulative effect of first-world airpower stunting any potential gains by loyalist forces involved in any fight allowed the rebels to finally lay claim to control over Ras Lanuf. This had the second order effect of opening up yet another avenue for the transitional government to export what oil they had available, as a means of producing a revenue stream that would allow them to fund this war.

Bin Jawwad was also officially declared in rebel hands. While none of these victories could be considered permanent until the capitulation of Muammar Gaddafi, the rolling tide of rebel controlled towns began to take its toll on Gaddafi's propaganda machine, and much like wars past, the gains made by the rebels helped compel the Coalition to agree to an additional 90 days of air cover. This would prove critical in the hot days of September and just before Gaddafi finally met his match.

In brief, but deadly combat, Tawurgah was captured by the rebels and Zintan was considered to be occupied by the rebel movement. New targets added to this month's folder by the allies were sites at Tiji and Waha.

September

September introduced Buwayrat to the target listing as the ring around Gaddafi's inner circle tightened even further. Despite ongoing contact from pockets of loyalist forces, the rebels were comfortable in reporting that Gharyan, Hun, Jadu, Jufra, Sabha, and Waddan, were in their hands. The ring around Tripoli and Sirte had become even tighter.

October

Gaddafi's final stance, while heavily publicized and frequently debated, demonstrated a surprising lack of military awareness as he chose to make a scramble for any safe haven he could find, leaving anonymity in Sirte for a desperate dash across the open desert for any refuge that would have him. His death truly epitomized the analogy of decapitating the head of the snake in order to immobilize its fighting force.

Skirmishes between loyalist holdouts, emerging tribal militias, and remnants of mercenary clans from across the border would dot the landscape for months to come. But, Gaddafi was no more.

Sources:

Olivesi, Marine. "Families Returning to Libya's Rebel Held Zintan." PRI's *The World*. Accessed June 30, 2013. http://pri.org/stories/2011-07-14/families-returning-libyas-rebel-held-zintan.

"Gates Outlines U.S. Role as NATO Takes Libya Mission." American Forces Press Service.

Kenyon, Peter. "In Post-Gadhafi Libya, Enmities Continue to Smolder." NPR.org. Accessed June 30, 2013. http://www.npr.org/2011/11/09/142100954.

"Libya Conflict: Fighting for Tripoli Rages On." BBC News Africa, August 22, 2011. Accessed July 4, 2013. http://www.bbc.co.uk/news/world-africa-14611549.

"NATO Airstrikes Hit Gaddafi Compound." PressTV, August 23, 2011. Accessed July 4, 2013. http://presstv.com/detail/195262.html.

"NTC Fighters Biding Time before Final Assaults on Remaining Al Qathafi Bastions." *Tripoli Post*, September 22, 2011. Accessed July 4, 2013. http://www.tripolipost.com/articledetail.asp?c=1&i=6967.

The Final Talley

Operation Odyssey Dawn

Nations involved: 13
Missions flown: 336 (estimate)
Combat missions: 108
Aircraft lost: 1 (noncombat)

Operation Unified Protector

Nations involved: 18 (5 non-NATO)
Assets employed: 260 (exclusive of OOD aircraft)
Naval vessels: 21 (exclusive of OOD ships)
Missions flown: 26,500 (est.)
Combat missions 9,700 (dedicated to strike versus opportune)
Targets destroyed: 5,900 (ca. 400 artillery/rocket launchers; 600 armored vehicles)
Aircraft lost: 1 (non-combat in OOD; 0 in OUP)
Arms embargo: 3,100 vessels hailed; 300 boarded; 11 denied transit
Humanitarian aid: 2,500 movements into Libya coordinated/supported

Sources:

North Atlantic Treaty Organization (NATO) Public Diplomacy Division. Accessed
    June 2, 2013. http://www.nato.int/cps/en/natolive/news_71994.htm.
"Operation Harmattan." *The Aviationist.* Accessed June 2, 2013. http://
    theaviationist.com/tag/operation-harmattan/#.Uj2AwGWmrIU.
Parrish, Karen. "Pentagon Tallies Coalition Actions in Libya." Defense.gov,
    March 23, 2011. Accessed May 11, 2013. http://www.defense.gov/news/
    newsarticle.aspx?id=63269.

Bibliography

CHAPTER 1

African Union. "Constitutif Act of the African Union." Accessed September 29, 2013. http://www.au.int/en/sites/default/files/ConstitutiveAct_EN.pdf.

Buckingham, Maddie. "The Impact of the Moors in Spain." Accessed September 28, 2013. http://wuhstry.wordpress.com/2011/07/20/the-impact-of-the-moors-in-spain/.

Evans-Pritchard, Edward E. *The Sanusi of Cyrenaica*. Oxford: Clarendon Press, 1954.

Gailey, Harry A., Jr. *The History of Africa in Maps*. Chicago: Denoyer-Geppert, 1967.

Heritage-History. "Barbary Wars, 1500–1830: Barbary Pirates versus Christian Sea Powers." Accessed September 28, 2013. http://www.heritage-history.com/www/heritage.php?Dir=wars&FileName=wars_barbary.php.

Ibn Khaldun (1304–1369), *al-Muqaddimah* (Prologue).

Ibn Batuta (1332–1406), *Rehla* (Travels).

International Democracy Watch. "The Arab League." Accessed September 28, 2013. http://countrystudies.us/libya/27.htm

July, Robert W. *A History of the African People*. Long Grove, IL: Waveland Press, 1998.

Kwamena-Poh, M., J. Tosh, R. Waller, and M. Tidy. *African History in Maps*. Essex, England: Longman, 1995.

"Libya, What Happened and When?" Accessed September 28, 2013. http://www.libya-watanona.com/libya/libyans.htm.

Lobban, Richard A., Jr. *Historical Dictionary of Ancient and Medieval Nubia*. Lanham, MD: Scarecrow Press, 2004.

Murdock, George Peter, *Africa: Its Peoples and Their Culture History*. New York: McGraw-Hill, 1959.

"Pan-Arabism, African Union and the War in Chad." Accessed September 28, 2013. http://gaddafi.info/panarab.htm.

Paterson, Ian A. "Regiments That Served with the 7th Armoured Division." Accessed July 22, 2012. http://archive.is/Srqbv. (Original website: http://www.ian.a.paterson.btinternet.co.uk/battles1941.htm.)

Rusk, Donald C. "Libya: Petroleum Potential of the underexplored Basin Centers – Twenty-First-Century Challenge." Chapter 22. Accessed September 4, 2013. http://www.searchanddiscovery.com/documents/rusk/images/Rusk.pdf.

CHAPTER 2

Boddy-Evans, Alistair. "Tripolitan War of 1801–05. Accessed May 2, 2013. http://africanhistory.about.com/od/militaryhistory/ss/Tripolitan-War1.htm.

Buckingham, Maddie. "The Impact of the Moors in Spain." Accessed September 28, 2013. http://wuhstry.wordpress.com/2011/07/20/the-impact-of-the-moors-in-spain/.

Evans-Pritchard, E. E. *The Sanusi of Cyrenaica*. Oxford: Clarendon Press, 1949.

Heritage-History. "Barbary Wars, 1500–1830: Barbary Pirates versus Christian Sea Powers." Accessed September 28, 2013. http://www.heritage-history.com/www/heritage.php?Dir=wars&FileName=wars_barbary.php.

Hitti, Phillip K. *History of the Arabs*. 10th edition. New York: Palgrave/Macmillan, 2002.

Hourani, Albert. *A History of the Arab Peoples*. New York: Grand Central Publishing, Hachette Book Group, 1991.

Navy Department Library. "Battle of Derna, 27 April 1805: Selected Naval Documents." Accessed May 2, 2013. http://www.history.navy.mil/library/online/barbary_derna.htm.

New Cosmopolitan World Atlas. New York: Rand McNally, 1965.

Oakes, John. "Libya—the Recent Destruction in Tripoli of the Karamanli Tomb and with It Some of Libya's History." Accessed May 2, 2013. http://libyastories.com/tag/yusuf-karmanli/.

Rogan, Eugene. *The Arabs: A History*. New York: Basic Books, 2011.

Seitz, Barr. "Barbary Glory, Barbary Shame." Accessed May 2, 2013. http://military.com/NewContent/0,13190,041905_Barbary,00.html.

Singer, Jonathan. "The Pirate Coast: Thomas Jefferson, The First Marines, and the Secret Mission of 1805." Accessed May 2, 2013. http://contemporarylit.about.com/od/history/fr/pirateCoast.htm.

Spaulding, Jay, and Lidwien Kapteijns, 1994, *An Islamic Alliance: Ali Dinar and the Sanussiyya, 1906–1916*. Evanston, IL: Northwestern University Press, 1994.

Wheelan, Joseph. *Jefferson's War: America's First War on Terror 1801–1805*. Public Affairs. New York: First Carroll & Graf, 2003.

Wolf, John B. *The Barbary Coast: Algeria under the Turks*. New York: W. W. Norton, 1979.

CHAPTER 3

Brynen, Rex, Peter Moore, Bassel Salloukh, and Marie-Joëlle Zahar, *Beyond the Arab Spring: Authoritarianism and Democratization in the Arab World*. Boulder, CO: Lynne Rienner, 2012.

First, Ruth, 1970, *The Barrel of a Gun: Political Power in Africa and the Coup d'Etat.* London: Penguin Books, 1970.

Gaddafi, Muammar. *The Green Book.* Tripoli: The World Center for the Study and Research of the Green Book, 1980.

Gaddafi, Muammar, with Edmond Jouve. *My Vision.* London: John Blake Publishing, 2005.

Huntington, Samuel P. *The Clash of Civilizations and the Remaking of World Order.* New York: Simon and Schuster, 1996.

Ronen, Yehudit. *Qaddafi's Libya in World Politics.* Boulder, CO: Lynne Rienner, 2008.

Vandewalle, Dirk. *A History of Modern Libya.* New York: Cambridge University Press, 2006.

CHAPTER 4

AFP/Swedish Wire. "Sweden Sends Eight Fighter Jets to Libya." Accessed July 21, 2013. http://www.swedishwire.com/politics/9146-sweden-sends-eight-fighter-jets-to-Libya.

Al-Shaheibi, Rami. "Abdul Rahim El-Keeb, New Libya Prime Minister, Balances Demands of Rebels and West." *Huffington Post World.* November 1, 2011. Accessed July 21, 2013. http://www.huffingtonpost.com/2011/11/01/abdul-rahim-el-keeb-libya-_n_1069198.html.

BBC News Africa. "Libya Crisis: Profile of NTC Chair Mustafa Abdul Jalil." BBC News Africa, August 22, 2011. Accessed July 21, 2013. http://www.bbc.co.uk/news/world-africa-14613679.

Birnbaum, Michael. "France Sent Arms to Libyan Rebels." *Washington Post,* June 29, 2011. Accessed July 6, 2013. http://articles.washingtonpost.com/2011-06-29/world/35235276_1_nafusa-mountains-hans-hillen-libyan-rebels.

Blanchard, Christopher M. "Libya: Unrest and U.S. Policy." *Congressional Research Service.* Accessed June 6, 2013. http://fpc.state.gov/documents/organization/159788.pdf.

Clarke, Michael, Malcolm Chalmers, Jonathan Eyal, Shashank Joshi, Mark Phillips, Elizabeth Quintana, and Lee Willett. "Accidental Heroes: Britain, France and the Libya Operation." Saqeb Mueen and Grant Turnbull, eds. Accessed June 9, 2013. http://www.rusi.org/libya.

Cowell, Alan, and Steven Erlanger. "France Becomes First Country to Recognize Libyan Rebels." *New York Times,* March 10, 2011. Accessed July 6, 2011. http://www.nytimes.com/2011/03/11/world/europe/11france.html?_r=0.

Fisher, Max. "Ali Tarhouni." *The Atlantic,* October 3, 2011. Accessed July 21, 2011. http://www.theatlantic.com/magazine/archive/2011/11/ali-tarhouni/308670/.

Gritten, David. "Key Figures in Libya's Rebel Council." BBC News, August 25, 2011. Accessed July 21, 2013. http://www.bbc.co.uk/news/mobile/world-africa-12698562.

Harding, Thomas. "Libya: Royal Navy Warship HMS Liverpool Comes under Heavy Fire." *The Telegraph* (UK), August 4, 2011. Accessed June 21, 2013. http://www.telegraph.co.uk/news/worldnews/africaandindianocean/

libya/8682572/Libya-Royal-Navy-warship-HMS-Liverpool-comes-under
-heavy-fire.html.

Joint Forces Command, Naples. "Unified_Protector" Accessed October 27, 2012.
http://www.jfcnaples.nato.int/Unified_Protector.aspz?print=Y.

"Libya." *Combataircraft.com*. Accessed June 9, 2013. http://www.combataircraft
.com/en/Military-Aircraft/Libya/.

"Liverpool Conducts Historic Escort Mission in Libya." Navy News Reporting
Service (UK). Accessed June 21, 2013. https://navynews.co.uk/archive/
news/item/1031.

Marquand, Robert. "Germany Plays Catch-up after Being on Sidelines of NATO's
Libya Campaign." *Christian Science Monitor*. Accessed July 23, 2013. http://
www.csmonitor.com/World/Europe/2011/0825/Germany-plays-catch
-up-after-being-on-sidelines-of-NATO-s-Libya-campaign.

"Operation Unified Protector—Allied Assets Deployed to Libya." *International
Institute for Strategic Studies*. Accessed May 19, 2013. http://archive.is/cKiH.

"Operation Unified Protector Final Mission Stats." NATO Operational Media
Update, November 2, 2011. Accessed July 21, 2013. http://www.nato.int/
nato_static/assets/pdf/pdf_2011_11/20111108_111107-factsheet_up_facts
figures_en.pdf.

Quartararo, Joe, Sr., Michael Rovenolt, and Randy White. "Libya's Operation
Odyssey Dawn: Command and Control." *PRISM*, 3, no. 2 (March 2012).

Rogers, Simon. "NATO Operations in Libya: Data Journalism Breaks Down which
Country Does What." *The Guardian* (UK). Accessed July 23, 2013. http://
www.theguardian.com/news/datablog/2011/may/22/nato-libya-data
-journalism-operations-country.

Simon, Scott. "In Libya, the Fight for Ras Lanuf." NPR.org. Aired March 5, 2011.
Accessed November 23, 2013. http://www.npr.org/2011/03/05/134
288525/In-Libya-The-Fight-For-Ras-Lanuf.

Simpson, John. "Libya Crisis: Gaddafi Forces Adopt Rebel Tactics." BBC News
Africa, March 30, 2011. Accessed November 4, 2012. http://www.bbc.co
.uk/news/world-africa-12911904.

Vira, Varun, and Anthony H. Cordesman. "The Libyan Uprising: An Uncertain
Trajectory." Center for Strategic and International Studies, June 20, 2011.
Accessed July 21, 2013. http://csis.org/files/publication/110620_libya.pdf.

Wenande, Christian. "Air Force Makes Redaction Blunder in Libya Report."
Copenhagen Post, October 12, 2012. Accessed July 6, 2013. http://cphpost
.dk/news/international/air-force-makes-redaction-blunder-libya-report.

Younis, General Abdel Fatah, obituary, *The Telegraph* (UK), 29 July 2011. Accessed
July 6, 2013. http://www.telegraph.co.uk/news/obituaries/politics
-obituaries/8671455/General-Abdel-Fattah-Younes.html.

CHAPTER 5

"Abu Musa and the Tunbs: Sovereignty Dispute Between the UAE and the Islamic
Republic of Iran." MOFA.gov.ae. Accessed September 11, 2013. http://
www.mofa.gov.ae/mofa_english/Uploads/Banners/9_pdf.pdf.

Chompsky. "Gaddafi and the IRA." Broadsheet. Accessed June 29, 2013. http://
    www.broadsheet.ie/2011/08/23/gadaffi-and-the-ira/.
Dervan, Cathal. "Colonel Gaddafi Sent Millions of Dollars in Cash to Real IRA
    Last June." IrishCentral.com. Accessed September 11, 2013. http://www
    .irishcentral.com/news/Colonel-Gaddafi-sent-millions-of-dollars-in-cash
    -to-Real-IRA-last-June-130553498.html.
Fattouh, Bassam. "North African Oil and Foreign Investments in Changing Market
    Conditions." Oxford Institute for Energy Studies. Accessed September 4,
    2013. http://www.oxfordenergy.org/wpcms/wp-content/uploads/2010/
    11/WPM37-NorthAfricanOilandForeignInvestmentinChangingMarket
    Conditions-BassamFattouh-2008.pdf.
"Federal Minimum Wage Rates, 1955–2013." Infoplease.com. Accessed
    September 9, 2013. http://www.infoplease.com/ipa/A0774473.html.
Ganor, Boaz. "Libya and Terrorism." International Institute for Counter-Terrorism.
    Accessed August 25, 2013. http://www.ict.org.il/Articles/tabid/66/
    Articlsid/699/currentpage/40/Default.aspx.
"Historical Crude Oil Prices, 1861 to Present." ChartsBin.com. Accessed
    September 9, 2013.
"Historical Events for Year 1959." HistoryOrb.com. Accessed September 3, 2013.
    http://www.historyorb.com/events/date/1959.
"Libya—Mortality Rate: Mortality Rate, Under-5 (per 1,000 Live Births)." Index
    Mundi. Accessed September 8, 2013. http://www.indexmundi.com/facts/
    libya/mortality-rate.
"Libyan Economy Profile 2013." Index Mundi. Accessed September 23, 2013.
    http://www.indexmundi.com/libya/economy_profile.html.
"Libya Oil Almanac: An Open Oil Reference Guide." Accessed September 3, 2013.
    http://openoil.net/wp/wp-content/uploads/2012/08/Libya-PDF-v-2.0
    .pdf.
Ngab, Ali S. "Libya—The Construction Industry—An Overview." Enpub
    .fulton.asu.edu. Accessed September 4, 2013. http://enpub.fulton.asu
    .edu/cement/cbm_CI/CBMI_Separate_Articles/Article%2021.pdf.
Omojuwa, Japeth J. "African Union: A Stream Cannot Rise above Its Source."
    African Liberty.org. Accessed September 8, 2013. http://www.africanliberty
    .org/content/african-union-stream-cannot-rise-above-its-source.
"One Year Natural Gas Prices and Price Charts." Investment Mine. Accessed
    September 12, 2013. http://www.infomine.com/investment/metal-prices/
    natural-gas/1-year/.
Pace, Eric. "Armand Hammer Dies at 92; Industrialist and Philanthropist Forged
    Soviet Links." New York Times, December 11, 1990. Accessed September 7,
    2013. http://www.nytimes.com/1990/12/12/obituaries/armand-hammer
    -dies-at-92-industrialist-and-philanthropist-forged-soviet-links.html?page
    wanted=all&src=pm.
"Petrol Prices, 1896 to Present." The AA Motoring Trust. Accessed September 9,
    2013. http://www.theaa.com/public_affairs/reports/Petrol_Prices_1896
    _todate_gallons.pdf.
"Pump Price for Diesel Fuel (US$ per Litre)." The World Bank. Accessed Septem-
    ber 4, 2013. http://data.worldbank.org/indicator/EP.PMP.DESL.CD.

Rachovich, David. "World's Top 23 Proven Oil Reserves Holders, Jan. 1, 2012—OGJ." *Petroleum Insights*. Accessed September 3, 2013. http://petroleum insights.blogspot.jp/2012/01/worlds-top-23-proven-oil-reserves.html #.UkFnFWWmrIV.

Reynolds, Paul. "UTA 772: The Forgotten Flight." BBC News. Accessed June 29, 2013. http://news.bbc.co.uk/2/hi/uk_news/3163621.stm.

Rusk, Donald C. "Libya: Petroleum Potential of the Underexplored Basin Centers—Twenty-First-Century Challenge." GeoExPro, Chapter 22. Accessed September 4, 2013. http://www.searchanddiscovery.com/documents/rusk/images/Rusk.pdf.

Sampson, Anthony. "The Seven Sisters: The Great Oil Companies and the World They Made." Biofuel Library. Accessed September 4, 2013. http://www.journeytoforever.org/biofuel_library/sevensisters/7sisters10.html.

"Terrorism: Major Terrorist Groups." Towson University. Accessed September 11, 2013. http://www.towson.edu/polsci/ppp/sp97/terror/groups.html #PFLP-GC.

Vanderbruck, Tobias. "Gaddafi's Legacy of Libyan Oil Deals." Oil-Price.net. Accessed August 24, 2013. http://www.oil-price.net/en/articles/gaddafi -legacy-of-libya-oil-deals.php.

Vandewalle, Dirk. "Libya since 1969." Accessed September 4, 2013. http://www.commandposts.com/2011/03/libya-since-1969/.

Whaley, Jane. "Libya—The Next Chapter." *GeoExPro*. Accessed September 4, 2013. http://www.geoexpro.com/article/Libya_The_Next_Chapter/366a0f99 .aspx.

"The World War II Study: North Africa: Supplies." Topedge.com. Accessed July 2, 2012. http://www.topedge.com/panels/ww2/na/frame.html.

CHAPTER 6

Aftandilian, Gregory. *Egypt's New Regime and the Future of the US-Egyptian Strategic Relationship*. Carlisle, PA: Strategic Studies Institute, U.S. Army War College, 2013.

Boston Globe, August 18, 2009; October 6, 2009; May 5, 2011; July 2, 2011; July 3, 2011; July 8, 2011.

Boston Sunday Globe, October 11, 2009; November 7, 2010; May 1, 2011; May 8, 2011; June 26, 2011; August 7, 2011.

Brynen, Rex, Peter W. Moore, Bassel F. Salloukh, and Marie-Joëlle Zahar. *Beyond the Arab Spring: Authoritarianism and Democratization in the Arab World*. Boulder, CO: Lynne Reinner, 2012.

MCT (Media in Cooperation and Transition). *Reinventing the Public Sphere in Libya: Observations, Portraits and Commentary in a MCT Newly Emerging Media Landscape*. Berlin: German Federal Foreign Office, 2012.

New York Times, May 31, 2011; June 21, 2011; June 29, 2011; July 3, 2011; July 31, 2011; August 5, 2011; August 6, 2011; August 21, 2011; August 22, 2011; August 27, 2011; August 29, 2011; September 10, 2011; September 23, 2011; October 10, 2011.

New York Times Book Review, July 15, 2011.

Noueihed, Lin, and Alex Warren. *The Battle for the Arab Spring: Revolution, Counter-Revolution and the Making of a New Era*. New Haven, CT: Yale University Press, 2012.

Owen, Roger. *The Rise and Fall of Arab Presidents for Life*. Cambridge, MA: Harvard University Press, 2012.

Rogan, Eugene. *The Arabs: A History.* New York: Basic Books, 2011.

Sanger, David. *Confront and Conceal: Obama's Secret Wars and Surprising Use of American Power.* New York: Crown Publishers, 2012.

Wall Street Journal, February 3, 2011.

CHAPTER 7

Boston Globe, October 15, 2012; February 11, 2013.

Brynen, Rex, Peter W. Moore, Bassel F. Salloukh, and Marie-Joelle Zahar. *Beyond the Arab Spring: Authoritarianism and Democratization in the Arab World*. Boulder, CO: Lynne Rienner, 2012.

CBS News, October 24, 2012.

Chido, Diane E. *From Chaos to Cohesion: A Regional Approach to Security, Stability, and Development in Sub-Saharan Africa*. Carlisle, PA: Strategic Studies Institute, US Army War College, 2013.

D'Inka, Werner, et al. *Reinventing the Public Sphere in Libya: Observations, Portraits and Commentary on a Newly Emerging Media Landscape*. Berlin: Media in Cooperation and Transition (MICT), 2012.

The Economist, March 31, 2012; June 2, 2012; June 9, 2012; August 4, 2012; September 15, 2012; September 22, 2012; September 29, 2012; October 6, 2012; November 19, 2012; January 12, 2013; January 26, 2013; February 2, 2013; February 9, 2013; February 23, 2013; March 9, 2013; March 23, 2013; March 30, 2013; April 27, 2013; May 11, 2013; June 8, 2013; June 15, 2013; June 29, 2013; July 6, 2013.

Ghoneim, Wael. *Revolution 2.0: A Memoir.* New York: Houghton Miflin Harcourt, 2012.

Newsweek, October 10, 2012; October 15, 2012; October 22, 2012.

New York Times, March 15, 2012; May 14, 2012; May 21, 2012; June 5, 2012; June 6, 2012; June 10, 2012; June 11, 2012; June 15, 2012; June 24, 2012; June 25, 2012; June 26, 2012; July 2, 2012; July 3, 2012; July 7, 2012; July 9, 2012; July 10, 2012; August 10, 2012; August 20, 2012; August 22, 2012; August 29, 2012; September 16, 2012; September 17, 2012; September 21, 2012; September 23, 2012; September 24, 2012; September 28, 2012; September 29, 2012; October 3, 2012; October 6, 2012; October 7, 2012; October 8, 2012; October 16, 2012; October 22, 2012; November 2, 2012; November 17, 2012; November 19, 2012; January 21, 2013, January 22, 2013; January 23, 2013; January 25, 2013; February 8, 2013; February 12, 2013; March 12, 2013; March 14, 2013; March 25, 2013; April 14, 2013; May 6, 2013; May 9, 2013; May 10, 2013; May 11, 2013; May 14, 2013; May 29, 2013; June 1, 2013; June 4, 2013; June 10, 2013; June 11, 2013, Op-Ed, June 22, 2013; June 28, 2013; July 11, 2013; July 20, 2013; July 27, 2013; July 28, 2013; July 30, 2013; August 7, 2013; September 13, 2013; September 20, 2013; September 21, 2013; October 3, 2013; October 5, 2013; October 6, 2013; October 7, 2013.

New York Times Magazine, May 13, 2012.

Providence Journal, AP, July 9, 2012; November 23, 2012; November 27, 2012; February 18, 2013; June 6, 2013).

Siegle, Joseph, et al. *Africa and the Arab Spring: A New Era of Democratic Expectations.* Africa Center for Strategic Studies, National Defense University, 2011.

Siegle, Joseph. "Stabilizing Fragile States." *Global Dialogue,* 13, no. 1 (2011).

Wall Street Journal, September 6, 2012.

Index

About the Authors

RICHARD A. LOBBAN, JR. is the former Chair of Anthropology at Rhode Island College, where he taught for 36 years and was also the Director the Program of African and Afro-American Studies. He is now Professor Emeritus. He is the Executive Director of the Sudan Studies Association and has published scores of articles, reviews, chapters, edited works, and books on Sudan including his two-volume Sudan references: *Historical Dictionary of Sudan* and his *Historical Dictionary of Ancient and Medieval Nubia*; and *Global Security Watch—Sudan* (Praeger Security International). He has also translated the works on Sudan by the French traveler Pierre Tremaux. Dr. Lobban has researched extensively in Tunisia, Egypt, Cape Verde, and Guinea-Bissau, and was President of the Narragansett Society of the Archaeological Institute of America. He has a continuing excavation in the Sudan and leads archaeological tours to Egypt and Sudan. Since retiring, he is Adjunct Professor of African Studies at the Naval War College and Adjunct Professor at Carnegie Mellon University. In 2012–2013, Dr. Lobban sponsored the first Libyan naval officer at the Naval War College from Libya in 40 years, from whom he learned so much!

CHRISTOPHER H. DALTON is currently serving on active duty with the United States Marine Corps as a Deputy Director for Logistics with the 1st Marine Aircraft Wing in Okinawa, Japan. A former Social Sciences and English teacher, he has spent the past 20 years expanding his worldview, through two tours in Iraq, one of which was a combat tour. He spent three years as an observer/trainer with Joint Forces Command, in which he traveled the globe extensively, honing the logistics skills for deploying units preparing joint operations in Operations Iraqi and Enduring, Freedom. He spent significant amounts of time in Djibouti, Germany, and Korea. His previous publishing experiences have been as coauthor with Dr. Lobban on Opinion-Editorials related to a multitude of Africa-based issues. Independently, he has been the technical advisor, writer, or presenter for military logistics interactive media presentations. He received his undergraduate education degree from the University of Kansas and a master's degree from the Naval War College.